T0377891

Historical Archaeology and Indigenous Collaboration

UNIVERSITY PRESS OF FLORIDA

Florida A&M University, Tallahassee
Florida Atlantic University, Boca Raton
Florida Gulf Coast University, Ft. Myers
Florida International University, Miami
Florida State University, Tallahassee
New College of Florida, Sarasota
University of Central Florida, Orlando
University of Florida, Gainesville
University of North Florida, Jacksonville
University of South Florida, Tampa
University of West Florida, Pensacola

# Historical Archaeology and Indigenous Collaboration

## Discovering Histories That Have Futures

D. Rae Gould,
Holly Herbster,
Heather Law Pezzarossi,
and Stephen A. Mrozowski

FOREWORD BY CHERYLL TONEY HOLLEY

UNIVERSITY PRESS OF FLORIDA
Gainesville / Tallahassee / Tampa / Boca Raton
Pensacola / Orlando / Miami / Jacksonville / Ft. Myers / Sarasota

Published in the United States of America

25 24 23 22 21 20 6 5 4 3 2 1

The Library of Congress has cataloged the printed edition as follows
Names: Gould, D. Rae, author. | Herbster, Holly, author. | Law Pezzarossi, Heather, 1979– author. | Mrozowski, Stephen A., author.
Title: Historical archaeology and indigenous collaboration : discovering histories that have futures / D. Rae Gould, Holly Herbster, Heather Law Pezzarossi, and Stephen A. Mrozowski.
Description: Gainesville : University Press of Florida, 2020. | Includes bibliographical references and index. |
Identifiers: LCCN 2019015546 (print) | LCCN 2019019237 (ebook) | ISBN 9780813057330 (ePDF) | ISBN 9780813066219 (cloth : alk. paper)
Subjects: LCSH: Archaeology—Methodology. | Archaeology and history.
Classification: LCC CC73 (ebook) | LCC CC73 .G68 2019 (print) | DDC 930.1072—dc23
LC record available at https://lccn.loc.gov/2019015546

The University Press of Florida is the scholarly publishing agency for the State University System of Florida, comprising Florida A&M University, Florida Atlantic University, Florida Gulf Coast University, Florida International University, Florida State University, New College of Florida, University of Central Florida, University of Florida, University of North Florida, University of South Florida, and University of West Florida.

University Press of Florida
2046 NE Waldo Road
Suite 2100
Gainesville, FL 32609
http://upress.ufl.edu

## Contents

# Figures

# Tables

# Foreword

It seems that I was born with suspicion and doubt about the motives of others. So I had my doubts when I first heard about the pending archaeological investigations at Hassanamesit Woods, a tract of land held in trust by the town of Grafton and a known Nipmuc historic site. After all, archaeologists are famous for digging up not only the treasures of nearly extinguished cultures (or so they think) but the grave remains as well. I was not among those making the decision to "collaborate," so instead I watched and waited for the researchers to mess up. I downloaded every report that came out of their investigations and field schools, quizzed Rae Gould (the Nipmuc tribal historic preservation officer) about what they were really doing, and bided my time, knowing that all this digging would not turn out well for the tribe.

But then I started reading all those downloaded reports. And in those writings I discovered a wealth of information that I did not previously know. They shed new light upon my ancestors' everyday lives, things hidden in the past that no living Nipmuc remembered. I decided to visit the excavation and bring less suspicious tribal members to help assess the situation. Through Rae, we arranged a field trip to see the Sarah Boston site and hear in-person explanations from the researchers. Steve Mrozowski and his team were welcoming and took time to explain in detail what they were doing and how they interpreted what they found. Although it was a Saturday, Steve seemed excited and happy to see us. More than one of us asked whether any of our ancestors' remains had been found. The answer was always no, with details about what would happen if any graves were uncovered. My tribal members and I left feeling reassured that our history was in relatively good hands.

It was around this same time that Rae decided to pursue her Ph.D. in anthropology (concentrating in archaeology) with a focus on our tribe's reservation. All I could say to her was why? Why would you choose this? Her explanation was a good one, I'm sure, but my own disappointment would not allow me to hear it. From my perspective, Rae was joining the other side: no matter how genial our relationship with Steve and his team was, they were still the enemy because they were still digging. But she would soon prove me wrong.

As time went on, I continued to monitor activities at Sarah Boston. We brought a group of high school students not only to the excavation site but to Steve's lab at the University of Massachusetts, Boston. We looked at the place where recovered items were processed, and the kids got to practice a bit. All the artifacts recovered thus far were laid out in one room for us to see. While there were no Indiana Jones–worthy relics on display, the sight of the material culture of generations of Nipmuc women and their families brought the adults in our group to tears. The crying panicked the researchers, who thought that we were upset or angry. It wasn't that at all. Our tears flowed from the joy of seeing what remained, the grief that we had forgotten these women, and the knowledge that our decision to "collaborate" was the correct one.

But we were lucky. The archaeological team hired by the town to excavate our history *chose* a different path than most scientists who study indigenous peoples. Collaboration was not just a word to pacify the tribe; they meant it. Questions asked by skeptics such as me were always answered in an open manner, not in the defensive posture we were so used to. All items recovered did not belong to the town but to the tribe, a codicil suggested by Steve himself. Despite resistance, the University of Massachusetts team continued to view and pursue the tribe as active partners in their investigations. They embraced and studied our unique social history and current social constructs to inform their interpretations of our past.

Back to Rae. She proceeded with her archaeological investigations on our reservation. She armed herself with our ancestors' strength and knowledge before doing so. She asked for and received the blessings and guidance of our elders while conducting her tests. While that may seem unnecessary to some, as an indigenous researcher she understood that our history is a continuous flow that informs our present and guides our future. Our ancestors do matter. She did not need to be taught this or consult with others. She already knew the best way and followed that path. And that is the hope of indigenous-led archaeology and research. The beliefs, values, and experience of the indigenous community are key to any study of culture and history. Indigenous researchers and scientists can employ traditional knowledge and values not only to design the research process but to use that knowledge to shape the interpretation of uncovered history.

While this book describes the rich history of three historic Nipmuc sites, it also illustrates the process of collaborative archaeology so often talked about these days and demonstrates the need for indigenous-led research into the histories of our Peoples. As Sonksq of the Nipmuc People, I am grateful to this team for their work in uncovering and preserving so many of our stories.

*Cheryll Toney Holley*
*Sonksq*
*Nipmuc Nation*
*Hassanamisco Band of Nipmuc Indians*

# 1

# Introduction

## Histories That Have Futures

D. RAE GOULD AND STEPHEN A. MROZOWSKI

1715, Magunkaquog

On October 11, 1715, commissioner of Indians Samuel Sewall traveled from Boston to Magunkaquog (present-day Hopkinton, Massachusetts) with a parchment deed. In an elaborate ceremony, seven Nipmuc men including Isaac Nehemiah sold the Magunkaquog lands to Harvard College by signing with their marks. On October 11, 1715, an entry in the Harvard Donations book recorded the "great satisfaction" of the Native signatories.[1]

Just two weeks earlier several men from Magunkaquog had sent a letter to Sewall saying that they did not want to sell their land or even discuss the matter. These were their homelands, where Nipmuc families had lived for generations, but Harvard wanted to lease parcels to colonial farmers to generate income for the college.

On October 12, one day after the deed was signed, Isaac Nehemiah sat on the Magunkaquog hilltop. He could not imagine that these lands would no longer belong to his people; his children and grandchildren would know a very different world. He tied his belt around his neck and took one last look across the hillside, then darkness and silence. . . .

Isaac did not leave behind a letter, but his signature survives on the parchment deed archived at Harvard University. Samuel Sewall recorded his suicide in his handwritten diary. These two artifacts help to rebuild the documentary archaeology of Magunkaquog and are just two documents connected to the site studied and excavated by Stephen Mrozowski and Holly Herbster (see Chapters 3 and 4).

## 1798, Grafton

Sarah Burnee woke before light most mornings. But on this June day in 1798 she rose even earlier, wrapped herself in her shawl in the dark, and brought wood in from the stack outside. Until recently, she had happily left this chore to her husband, Boston, but his illness changed all that. The doctor could only make him comfortable. As her husband grew weaker, Sarah anxiously took on tasks that he could no longer do. When she shuffled back inside, her children—Sarah (called Sally), sixteen, and Ben, thirteen—were dressing for morning chores in the sleeping loft. Her husband coughed sharply. As she waited for the fire to grow, Sarah prepared thick slices of rye bread and bacon then collected tea and sugar from the larder. The elders were expected this morning, so she laid out extra plates and cups on the thick wooden table in the center of the room. Together, they would decide how to proceed with the summer's work and discuss prospects for the future.

Her brother Joseph stooped slightly as he limped into the house, removing his hat. The smoke from his pipe followed him across the room as he made the effort to greet his sister. He lowered himself gingerly into a chair, winded from his walk up the hill from his small house in the valley. Joseph placed his right foot on the chair beside him and gratefully accepted a cup of tea from Sarah. They sat and talked for a while before the others joined them: the rain was coming and Sarah's roof leaked; the oxen needed new shoes in about a month; they would need help to harvest rye from the fields. As the children came inside to eat their breakfast, Joseph admitted to his sister that he would soon need to write to the state for permission to sell more of the family land. She patted his hand and poured him another cup of tea. She would too.

Other Nipmuc elders arrived and thanked Sarah for her hospitality, inquiring about Boston's ailing health. As they began to discuss the future, Sarah's daughter Sally poured tea. With little Nipmuc land left to farm, they talked of other possibilities. Young Sally listened intently. She sat in the doorway weaving a handsome berry basket, which she had learned to make as a child from watching the women sit together and work . . .

Archaeology at the Sarah Burnee/Sarah Boston Homestead site in Grafton, Massachusetts, between 2006 and 2013 recovered a number of objects—pipes, cups, plates, a tea set, farming tools—that help us understand some activities of the homestead's occupants. Documents provide additional information about their lives: the death of Boston Philips in summer 1798; Sarah Burnee and Joseph Aaron's petition to the Massachusetts general court to sell land in the early 1800s to provide care as they grew older and to repair Sarah's home; and the rye that they grew on their farm. Research at this site by Heather Law Pezzarossi and Stephen Mrozowski provides insight into almost 100 years of occupation by one Nipmuc family (see Chapters 5 and 6).

### 1869, Grafton

On a warm day in 1869 the spring was flowing in the back yard, but Sarah Arnold Cisco was dealing with her contentious neighbor John Sweeney instead of enjoying a beautiful summer day. When he had first bought her uncle's piece of the family land next door over a decade ago, Sweeney did not seem as hostile. But over the years he became more determined to see Sarah and her sister lose their last few acres. He knew how much they struggled to make ends meet. Sarah felt vulnerable as she searched for answers.

Today she sat in the old rocker in the front yard, thinking about the land that she and her sister lived on and their small house, built by her grandmother in 1801, with additions by her father. Thinking about how much this place meant to everyone in her circle, including those beyond her immediate family, Sarah began to draft a letter in her head. She would write to the lawyer in town that she had talked to about their rights as Indians who had always lived in this place. It was now called Grafton but always known as Hassanamesit (place of small stones) to them . . .

This letter became one of the many documents preserved in the Nipmuc Nation tribal archive. As an artifact of the past in the form of a document, it provides a glimpse into the lives and actions of the people discussed in Chapter 7 by Rae Gould.

These vignettes are stories of real people who experienced different facets of English and American colonialism in the centuries following 1620 and the arrival of the pilgrims in the "New World." Although the stories vary according to gender and time, they provide pictures of individuals closely linked to their respective communities and with a common desire to maintain Nipmuc identity and land. In focusing on real people in this book—with names, sometimes faces, and a shared identity—our goal is to bring their histories into focus by connecting past to present and individual with community, in a space that was and continues to be dynamic. The past revealed through our combined work is not a static history bounded in any manner. Our goal is not, for example, to reconstitute the past on its own terms but rather as histories that had futures, some realized, others not, but continuing nevertheless up to the present. The spaces that we paint in this book are designed to be as real as possible through the lens of archaeology and historical research, because it is our common belief that history (as written by historians) does not always adequately create a picture embracing all the perspectives contributing to its composition. In this regard, this book seeks to accomplish something different, more connected to a present that involves long-standing conflict and struggle for a people whose lives are worth knowing, worth reflecting on, and worth retelling.

The stories that we tell are drawn from several sources: archaeology, documentary research, and oral history, a suite of approaches commonly captured under the heading "historical archaeology" in North America. This field has traditionally covered the period since Europeans began colonizing what is today called the Americas. This weaving together of sources produces portraits that emphasize the material lives of people living in the past. Although each of this book's contributors brings a unique set of experiences and approaches to the histories we seek to tell, each of us believes that it is through the study of daily life that the deepest contours of the past are revealed. Everyday life, as we envision it, is lived out through daily, weekly, monthly, and yearly routines that rely upon a rich assemblage of material objects, including documents. Having been left behind by their users and others, these items are discovered in most instances in spatial contexts that vary in scale from individual households and their surroundings to regions and landscapes full of meaning for their inhabitants. These are the spaces through which life was (and is) lived. They are like a canvas on which life is layered with color and experience. While these spaces were and are being altered, renewed and changed by human hands and nature over the past several hundreds (and thousands) of years, they retain traces of sustained commitment to places that remain vibrant parts of contemporary life. There is no break between past and present in these places, despite some histories lost through time that are waiting to be rediscovered through the lens of historical archaeology.

## Lines of Inquiry

The particular approach that this book takes to explore these spaces is a richly collaborative historical archaeology. The outstanding strength in a historical archaeologists' tool kit is the interdisciplinary approach brought to the study of the more recent past (since European contact). With a strong commitment to connecting past and present, historical archaeologists have access to a wealth of information by combining archaeology, documentary research, and oral testimony, for example. In the academic world each of these lines of inquiry has a particular label that sets it apart from other forms of evidence. This is particularly true for the various forms of written or oral testimony. Documentary evidence, for instance, involves a whole host of historical documents: wills; estate inventories; birth, marriage, and death records (vital records); town records; merchant account books; photographs; newspaper articles; and personal papers such as letters. These are called primary sources. Literature (historical accounts) was also written during the periods we examine and provides context for the research that historical archaeologists undertake. These would be secondary sources because they are drawn from primary sources and written by people who did not live during the period they wrote about.

The locations of the documentary record (privately held, part of a private institution such as a local historical society, or at courts, towns, cities, or churches) are often as important as the documents they house. For example, government archives often structure their holdings in a manner revealing biases that are part of deeper societal power dynamics. Keeping records by race is one example, which reveals how governments choose to classify their citizens, including those who do not share the same freedoms or privileges of others. This is part of the "othering" that is one of the most important topics that historical archaeologists examine. Institutionalized biases (such as those surrounding race) are just one example of how an archive serves both as a repository of records and at the same time as a reflection of how societies can be structured. These kinds of institutionalized divides exist in the academic world as well. Our work is one example of how those divisions are being disassembled.

One example of this practice involves the label "ethnohistory." Historians, archaeologists, and anthropologists have applied this term to the study of "non-Western" peoples (the "other") in keeping with anthropology's longstanding focus on non-Western societies.[2] In Europe, for example, the term "anthropology" is not as common among academics: "sociology" is used to reference any study of cultural or social behavior. Over the past thirty years the discipline of anthropology has undergone an important shift in two ways, especially in North America. First, anthropologists have expanded their focus to include Western and non-Western peoples alike. More importantly, the field is recognizing its strong connections to a colonial past that involved using science to support and reinforce various forms of inequality; racial, gender, ethnic, and cultural inequalities are all examples. Documents related to indigenous peoples, for example, have been classified differently in ethnohistory than those concerning "white folks."[3] It is important to acknowledge that documents describing or enumerating the lives of the "other," whether defined by race, gender, ethnicity, or class, are often produced by people who are not part of these groups (that is, by the dominant society). Despite this, historians, archaeologists, and anthropologists are making tremendous progress in understanding their own biases and the biases of those who produced the archives that exist today, to the point where research is more productive on many levels. Not the least of these is the emphasis placed on the structure of the archive itself, as noted above. In many cases, documentary evidence once thought too biased to be of empirical value is now being examined for important information concerning the lives of those living in the past.[4]

Oral testimony is one example of how nonwritten forms of knowledge can be considered less valid than others. Oral history (told from experience or personal knowledge) and oral tradition (information passed down from previous generations) can take many forms, from formal stories maintained as a record of the past to folklore in a variety of forms (such as myths or everyday stories) shared by members of a society. Oral testimony can be collected, transcribed, or recorded in several ways, including using digital technologies (such as sound or video recorders or even cell phones). Anthropologists, oral historians, and folklorists use oral testimony and uphold its veracity, especially as it relates to histories purposely maintained as a form of institutionalized memory. Despite this, legal systems often do not consider oral testimony as valid as written documentation.

One example of this was the 2004 decision to deny federal recognition to the Nipmuc Nation by the Bureau of Indian Affairs (BIA). The tribe's recognition was preliminarily approved in the final months of the Bill Clinton administration (January 2001) then reversed under the George W. Bush administration a few months later (October 2001), with a final determination against recognition in 2004. In rejecting the tribe's recognition the BIA said that the Nipmuc had not provided sufficient written documentation of social and political continuity over the past 200 years.[5] Despite strong oral testimony of tribal continuity (combined with other documentation), written evidence was considered more accurate than knowledge provided by tribal members through oral interviews, even when combined with other forms of evidence. In effect, the knowledge of Nipmuc culture and history that came from tribal members and the information passed down to them from earlier generations was negated in the BIA's assessment.

The Nipmuc federal recognition effort began in 1980 and was a continuation of the struggles of the Nipmuc people dating back to first contact with European colonists, followed by Christianization by missionaries, decimation of their population by disease and warfare, intense land loss, and imposed acculturation over the centuries. The most important thing connecting Nipmuc people today to their past is the land that they are connected to and have lived on extending back millennia, generations before the lives of those explored in this book. The landscapes or homelands of the Nipmuc are recognized as a cultural landscape connected to their cultural practices, language, history, and continued presence.

The concept of cultural landscapes, and indigenous cultural landscapes in particular, is central to understanding the individual sites discussed in this book as well as the connections among them. Landscapes are often defined as large-scale properties composed of multiple, linked features that form a cohesive area or place. They can be small-scale as well. One example is the three-and-a-half-acre Hassanamisco Reservation in Grafton, Massachusetts, discussed in Chapter 7, a smaller but important cultural landscape for the Nipmuc Tribe. The Nipmuc homelands extend from central Massachusetts into northeast Connecticut and northwest Rhode Island. This is an example of a larger-scale cultural landscape encompassing a web of locations like the reservation, the nearby Burnee/Boston Homestead (also in Grafton), and the Magunkaquog site in present-day Hopkinton (see Figure 1.1).

The definition of any cultural landscape is complex and can vary depending on the context and how it is used. For example, in addition to the physical, on-the-ground components, visual and audio aspects of cultural landscapes are often central to how they are defined. An indigenous landscape used for ceremonial practices could be affected by the presence of structures that impede a view or by noise interrupting an otherwise quiet area. An area historically

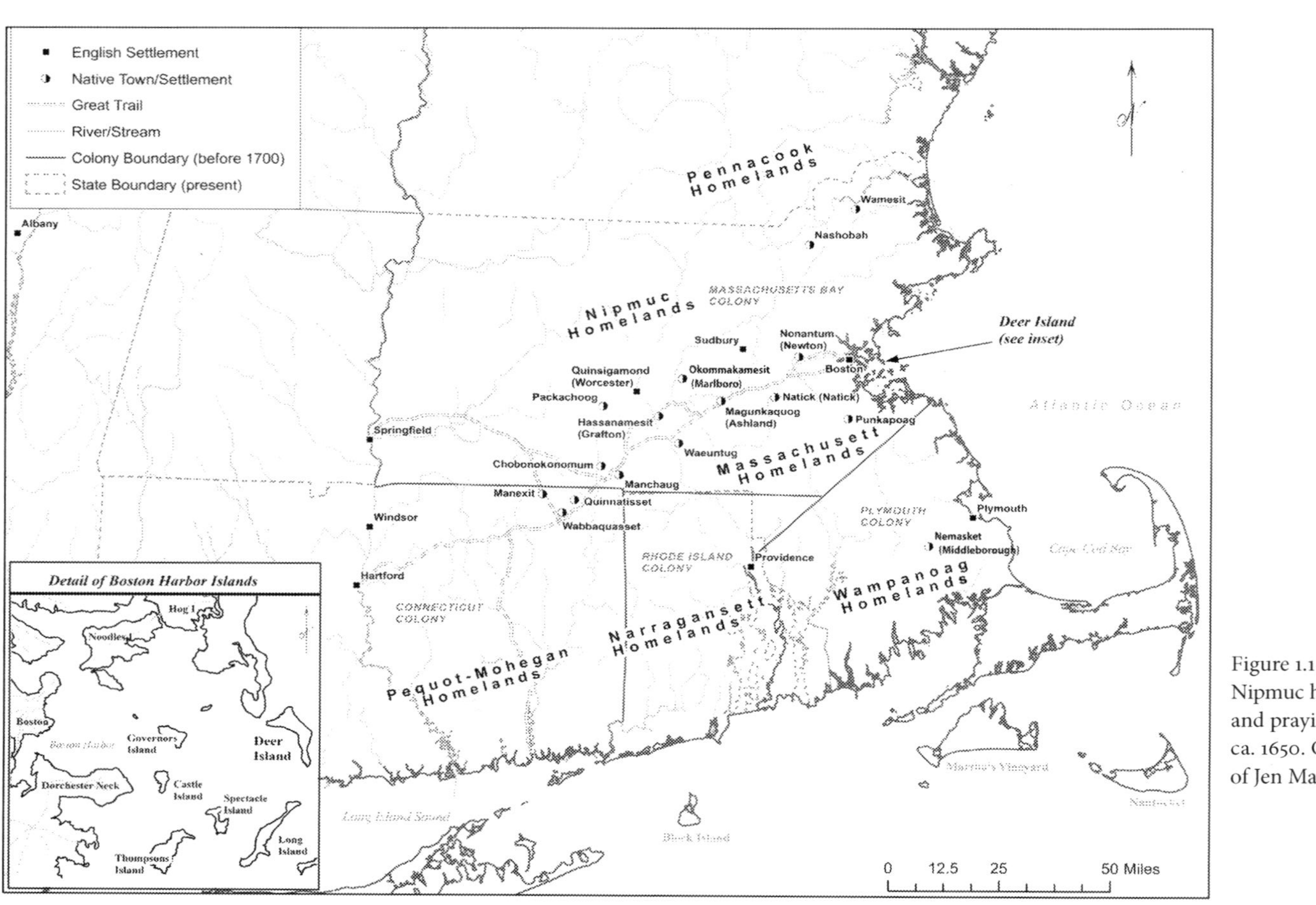


Figure 1.1. Map of Nipmuc homelands and praying towns, ca. 1650. Courtesy of Jen Macpherson.

used to gather plants and natural materials could be affected by construction of buildings or roadways. All of these considerations need to be taken into account by archaeologists when they explore an area or a site with an indigenous history. See Chapter 7 for further discussion of definitions of cultural landscapes and indigenous cultural landscapes in particular.

Perhaps the most critical approach or line of inquiry in this book is the braiding together of indigenous and Western thoughts and epistemologies by the contributors through their experiences, knowledge, and collaborations. This is a relatively new approach in the field of historical archaeology and perhaps one of the most important for defining future directions of the discipline.

## Historical Archaeology and Indigenous Collaboration

Historical archaeology is a rather young form of archaeological inquiry, coming into its own in the 1960s.[6] When the discipline developed, virtually all archaeology in North America until that point focused on the long history of the indigenous peoples of the continent ("precontact"). Strangely, very little of this research ever involved much collaboration with the indigenous peoples still living in the areas where archaeology was being carried out. It would be wrong to suggest that such communication never existed, because notable examples exist throughout North America.[7] Yet for the most part archaeologists interested in "rediscovering" the past of Native Americans had little interaction with the descendants of the very people whose histories they sought to recover and tell. With the growth of historical archaeology over the 1970s and 1980s, the focus of archaeology in the United States shifted from Native Americans to the history of Europeans who colonized their homelands and interactions with the indigenous peoples of North, Central, and South America. Historical archaeology has also focused on the lives of enslaved Africans, Afro-Caribbeans, and African Americans as well as the numerous later European and Asian peoples who immigrated to America over the centuries. Through the lens of material culture, historical archaeologists have produced an impressive corpus of new perspectives and understandings of the strong links among colonialism, urbanization, and industrialization that have contributed to shaping the modern world.[8]

As the field of historical archaeology has matured, its practitioners have become particularly adept at understanding the material dimensions of individual and group identities. Colonial encounters involved people with different backgrounds and cultural practices who found themselves in dynamic interactions. Sometimes these encounters were marked by violence, sometimes by cooperation, but in almost every instance new cultural forms, and the objects associated with them, emerged as a product of colonialism. The differences between peoples involved in colonial encounters have been complicated admixtures of several social variables. Newly formed identities emerged at the intersections of culture, ethnicity, language, gender, class, race, and age, especially for indigenous populations. New societal forms emerged through commerce, trade, conflicts, and other social interactions, initially shaped by a variety of relatively novel social relationships. Some were rather open and free; in these instances social relations formed in more organic ways. In other situations harsh power relations created structures that resulted in some being enslaved: Africans were forcibly transported to the New World, while some Native Americans were banished to slavery at home and abroad as the result of violent encounters with strengthening European powers.

Within Euroamerican populations issues of class, ethnicity, and gender often intersected to create social structures not unlike those in Europe that many colonists had sought to escape. Early motivating factors such as religion and the search for wealth to support European wars saw these conflicts extended to the Americas. New political economies such as the slave-based plantations of Brazil, the Caribbean, and the English colonies of North America brought yet another dimension to incipient societies that set the stage for later efforts to seek independence from parent governments. With the growth of urban coastal settlements (such as Boston) that traded throughout the Atlantic world—and later the Pacific—colonial America matured to become a critical player on a growing world stage. The eventual growth of industry in the newly independent United States (following the Revolutionary War) is perhaps the most noteworthy—but far from the only—example of America becoming a military and economic power that rivaled those of Europe.

The archaeology related to these early encounters and later social developments has pointed to the complex nature of the human/human, human/environment interactions that textured the daily lives of the actors who experienced these multifaceted histories. Again and again archaeology has unearthed intimate details of how people lived and died, some lives miserably short and difficult, others richer and longer, but clearly connected to larger historical processes that may not have been part of the consciousness of these actors. The individuals discussed throughout this book are just a few examples of this. Using archaeology to unearth evidence of worlds linked by far-flung economic connections is one of historical archaeology's most powerful attributes. Through examining social units varying in size from individual households to villages, farms, city neighborhoods, plantations, military installations, prisons, battlefields, religious institutions (such as missions), and a host of other settlement forms, historical archaeologists have linked intimate details of everyday life with global commerce and trade that spread European expansion across the earth.

Intimate objects of the everyday provide historical archaeologists with a glimpse of the often brutal character of interactions along racial, gender, or class lines.[9] In the process historical archaeologists have come to understand the dynamic quality of the vast economic expansion that has unfolded between the fifteenth century and the present through the material goods that fueled this expansion.[10] They have also been able to examine the biological dimensions of European expansion: the introduction of diseases, animals and plants, and large-scale processes such as colonialism, urbanization, and industrialization, and the inequalities that they often engendered. While the overriding power of capitalist expansion is a major theme within the field of historical archaeology, its practitioners have enriched and enlivened their understanding of the continuing impact that these deep historical processes continue to have on today's world and its immediate future.[11]

One of the more curious qualities of historical archaeology as a field of study in North America was the lack of interest in the rich histories of indigenous peoples and their cultural practices until relatively recently. In part this is due to the long-standing connection between anthropology and archaeology, the study of "prehistory," and the relegation of Native American history to a time before European colonization. There has been a real (yet at the same time false) divide between historical archaeology and the study of prehistory.[12] For some, North American prehistory ends with the arrival of Europeans, after which "real" Indians ceased to exist after they quickly disappeared through war or disease or assimilated. Yet in exploring Nipmuc history we cannot allow this artificial and false divide between history and prehistory to prevent linking what is obviously a continuous past connected to the present. Native American scholars have criticized the notion of prehistory as a product of colonialism itself. They point out that by classifying these societies as part of a prehistoric non-European past colonizers relegated them to a static and antiquated past, with an inferior place in an evolutionary scheme. This practice was embraced by archaeologists as the discipline emerged in the nineteenth century, when many indigenous peoples were viewed as fossilized (or static) versions of earlier societies. "Stone-age" populations in parts of North America, Australia, and Africa were used as comparisons for archaeologists interested in these "prehistoric societies."

One of the more negative facets of this tyranny has been a severing of the connection between indigenous pasts and presents by those who have studied them. As a result, a chasm developed between archaeologists and the very people whose history they sought to tell, as noted above. These relationships have differed across North America and across various individuals and groups, but collaboration has not been the norm. Change began in the United States with the passage of the Native American Graves Protection and Repatriation Act (NAGPRA) in 1990. This law requires that all museums and institutions with Native American human remains and other Native materials that receive federal funding must create inventories and summaries of their collections and consult with tribes, toward the goal of repatriation. Although this law has been met with resistance and has not been followed consistently,[13] one positive change has been a growing recognition by archaeologists that they must work collaboratively with Native American peoples if they want to continue researching their past.

A more significant development has been an ever-growing number of Native Americans who have trained as archaeologists, carrying out and directing research into their own histories as well as assuming positions overseeing NAGPRA compliance. This "indigenous archaeology" has continued to develop and is now an accepted part of the larger intellectual enterprise of working together at the intersection of archaeology, anthropology, and Native American and Indigenous Studies. It is the foundation of what we now understand as collaborative and community-based research, with a focus on research conducted with, by, and for communities, rather than *on* or *about* them.[14]

## Collaboration

The growing number of indigenous scholars has fostered the development of Native American and Indigenous Studies programs in universities across

North America, which extend beyond archaeology and are interdisciplinary. Similar developments have led to more indigenous scholars and programs in Australia, Africa, New Zealand, and Northern Europe, triggering a growing collaboration between these scholars and nonindigenous archaeologists.

This book is the culmination of one such collaboration and evolved in an organic fashion, like so many partnerships. It started when the Center for Cultural and Environmental History (now the Andrew Fiske Memorial Center for Archaeological Research) at the University of Massachusetts Boston (UMB) was asked by the Massachusetts State Archaeologist's office to investigate a site believed to be associated with the seventeenth-century "praying Indian" community of Magunkaquog. The site had been unearthed as part of a cultural resource management (CRM) survey for a new housing project on Magunco Hill in what is today Hopkinton, Massachusetts. The Public Archaeology Laboratory of Pawtucket (PAL), Rhode Island, had found what appeared to be a mid- to late seventeenth-century site on the eastern slope of the hill.[15] The developer of the housing project was less than thrilled that PAL had made a discovery considered significant enough to require further investigation. Instead of allowing the work to take place, he decided not to build on the lot immediately around the site. Eventually the developer did allow Stephen Mrozowski to conduct an archaeological field school on the site, carried out the summers of 1997 and 1998. Excavations confirmed PAL's original interpretation and unearthed the relatively intact foundation of what was the "meeting house" or "fair house" at Magunkaquog. Although the project was successful, this early look into life at this seventeenth-century Nipmuc settlement did not involve any direct collaboration with the Nipmuc Nation, which had a tribal office just two towns away.

Collaboration began several years later when the Fiske Center was asked to provide advice to the Nipmuc Nation tribal historic preservation officer (Rae Gould at that time) on Project Mishoon (a project focused on recovering several intact dugout canoes from Lake Quinsigamond in Worcester, Massachusetts).[16] Project Mishoon was itself a collaborative initiative involving the Nipmuc Nation, PAL, the Massachusetts Board of Underwater Archaeology, and UMB. UMB involvement included the use of ground-penetrating radar by then UMB professor Alan Gontz to map the lake bottom while Fiske Center archaeological conservator Dennis Piechota provided conservation advice. One of the unexpected outcomes of this collaboration was working with Rae Gould, who soon entered the Ph.D. program at the University of

Connecticut. As a Nipmuc woman knowledgeable about her tribe's history, Gould was the perfect person to serve as liaison for a collaboration that came to include archaeology, oral history, documentary research, and architectural history to reconnect with a Nipmuc past known only to a select group of tribal members.

Then in 2003 the Fiske Center was contracted by the Trust for Public Land to conduct an archaeological survey of a 202-acre parcel thought to contain a seventeenth-century "church" or meeting house, associated with the praying town period of the Hassanamesit settlement (modern-day Grafton, Massachusetts).[17] Although remains associated with the meeting house were not located, the survey did confirm the presence of a Nipmuc homestead owned by four generations of Nipmuc women (all named Sarah), home to the family between 1727 (when the land was divided between English settlers and Hassanamisco Indians) and 1840. Work on the foundation of the Burnee/Boston Homestead between 2003 and 2013 was done through a collaboration involving the Town of Grafton (which eventually purchased the land from the Trust for Public Lands) and the Nipmuc Nation. This meant working closely with the Nipmuc Nation Tribal Council and Rae Gould. As part of her own dissertation research Rae was combining archaeology, documentary research, architectural history, and oral history to reconstruct the history of the parcel of Moses Printer, another 1727 Nipmuc allotment in Grafton. This parcel became the last piece of Nipmuc land in continuous tribal stewardship and was recognized as the tribal reservation by the Commonwealth of Massachusetts in the early 1900s (as discussed in Chapter 7). Combined with the work carried out by the Fiske Center, the work that Rae has carried out over the past fifteen years constitutes what we envision as the larger Hassanamesit Woods Project.

## The Hassanamesit Woods Project

The Hassanamesit Woods Project grew out of efforts to preserve the 202-acre parcel noted above. An intensive survey of the parcel failed to discover any seventeenth-century materials, but a large concentration of material culture dating to between the mid-eighteenth and mid-nineteenth centuries was recovered. The original attribution of the foundation unearthed in 2005–2006 as "John Eliot's Indian Church" on an 1886 deed map produced by Royal Keith of "Keith Hill" fame in Grafton was a common practice in

New England. In a region well versed in its history it is not uncommon to see nineteenth-century buildings or undated cellar holes attributed to the earliest phase of European colonization (in this case, the presence of John Eliot and his missionizing work, discussed elsewhere in this book).[18] So it was not a surprise when the remains of a cellar hole filled after the 1938 hurricane (one of the major natural events in New England to punctuate the twentieth century) was labeled as a seventeenth-century "church" in the map of the Keith Hill properties. That archaeology would reveal a different reality was equally unsurprising.

When the Fiske Center agreed to conduct a survey of the Hassanamesit Woods parcel as long as the work was coordinated with the Nipmuc Nation, the Town of Grafton and the Hassanamesit Woods Management Committee readily agreed. In speaking with the Nipmuc Nation Tribal Council in 2003, Fiske Center archaeologists asked for help and support for the project, with the understanding that moving forward depended upon the tribe's approval. The tribe supported the project and decided that Rae would serve as liaison. An informal protocol was adopted, with close coordination between the Fiske Center and the tribal council, yearly or biannual visits to the council meetings, and collaboration on scholarly products such as conference papers and publications.

As this collaboration was being put into practice, Rae was completing excavations and historical research on the Moses Printer parcel across town in 2006 and 2007 (today known as the Hassanamisco Reservation). She carried out every phase of the work across town as a separate project, but the new collaboration surrounding the Hassanamesit Woods Project was informally extended to the Printer property. Rae was interested in what the archaeology of the Printer parcel revealed about landscape activities linked to the 1801 dwelling that still stands on the reservation. She was successful in obtaining several grants from the Grafton Community Preservation Committee to restore the building's exterior.[19] She also excavated around the building to date the landscape changes associated with the house's construction. During this phase, parallels between the projects suggested that comparing the foundation on the 1727 Peter Muckamaug/Sarah Robins lot (on Keith Hill at Hassanamesit Woods) with information from Moses Printer's parcel on Brigham Hill might prove fruitful.

Archaeological fieldwork was carried out between 2003 and 2013 at Hassanamesit Woods, focused mostly on the household of Sarah Burnee and her daughter Sarah Boston (descendants of Muckamaug and Robins). The site was home to Burnee and Boston between 1750 and 1840. Although it is part of the original 1727 lot of Muckamaug and Robins, only a few artifacts recovered date to their occupation. Through a combination of geophysical testing, large-scale excavation, archaeozoology, archaeobotany, micromorphological soils analysis, and material culture analysis, a rich picture of Nipmuc life at this site was reconstructed.[20] This analysis is discussed in Chapter 5. Combined with Rae's work at the Printer parcel, and with data from Magunkaquog, the information gleaned from more than two decades of research by this book's contributors provides a rare, detailed portrait of Nipmuc life between the mid-seventeenth and mid-twentieth centuries, with connections to the present.

Several events were watershed moments in the Nipmuc/English encounters in New England during these centuries. Although the Nipmuc were not directly involved in the Pequot War of 1636–1637,[21] the military tactics employed by the English (mostly from Massachusetts Bay Colony) were brutal enough to leave a strong impression on the indigenous communities of the region. King Philip's War, also known as Metacom's Rebellion, unfolded forty years later in the Massachusetts Bay Colony (1675–1676) and remains one of the most violent conflicts in North American history.[22] Both of these conflicts left long shadows over the landscapes and history of New England. The pain that they caused still resonates with indigenous peoples in the region today, although they are not considered foundational enough to America's history to be integral to school curricula.

A much less violent but no less significant event in the region's history surrounded the work of John Eliot, an English Puritan missionary who sought to Christianize the Native American peoples of Massachusetts Bay Colony.[23] In the mid-seventeenth century Eliot began meeting with local indigenous groups to proselytize them. Starting with Natick, fourteen Nipmuc "praying Indian towns" were recognized by the Massachusetts Bay General Court (Figure 1.1), including Hassanamesit, before the outbreak of King Philip's war. One of them was Magunkaquog (earmarked as a Christian settlement in 1660).[24] Chapter 2 discusses John Eliot and the praying towns in more detail and provides a brief background of King Philip's War.

As Christine DeLucia has noted, long before John Eliot and other colonists arrived in the early seventeenth century the landscape of southern New England "was already memorial terrain and had been for millennia . . . dotted with holes in the earth, continuously being cleared, refreshed, and narrated by those who walked by, powerfully linking together ancestors and their descendants."[25] The material objects that help us interpret the past are also connections between past and present. While they are artifacts of the past, they are very much interpreted by people in the present influenced by layers of academic, cultural, historical, and personal knowledge. As DeLucia notes, landscapes themselves are also historical artifacts, with places and their attached memories open to interpretation based on "culturally inflected ways of seeing" that are central to the epistemologies we use to interpret and understand the past. Even with clearly identified artifacts (cut glass and metal objects from the Burnee/Boston Homestead) and features (a stone foundation from Magunkaquog), their creations and our interpretations of their purposes are both "produced through historically, culturally specific actions of individuals and communities" from then and now.[26] These are part of the ingrained epistemologies that influence our work, as scholars and as archaeologists.

## Cross-Cultural Epistemologies: How We Study, See, and Understand the Past

Archaeological and historical records are just some of the resources used to understand the past; multiple ways of knowing and understanding any past exist, especially for indigenous histories. Different ways of knowing or understanding are called epistemologies, which are foundational for how cultures and individuals define themselves, remember and create the past and perceptions of time (through specific "lenses"), and justify or rationalize actions of the past and present. The creation of American Indian policy in America, for example, has been based on Euroamerican beliefs (or "knowledge") that Indians were (and are) subaltern or less developed peoples. Beginning with John Eliot and other colonists, through the nineteenth-century histories (discussed in Chapter 2), and up to present-day policies, Indians have been described as being idle, not productive, not civilized or orderly, and not following the correct religious or cultural practices. In reality these beliefs were justifications for war, genocide, land dispossession, and continued oppression of Native peoples across America. Without believing that Euroamerican culture was better (ethnocentricism), colonists could not have justified their actions. In many ways these ideologies persist in American culture in the twenty-first century.

Nomenclature (naming) has been central to Euroamerican epistemologies since the arrival of the first colonial settlers and even earlier. The naming of the indigenous homelands discussed in this book as "New England" provides an obvious example. Over the centuries different sources have used different nomenclatures for the topics and places discussed in this book, depending on the period, perspective, and rationale. For example, the praying towns, like other Native American settlements dating to before contact, were not nucleated when John Eliot arrived. Using terms like "town" and "village" imposed a Euroamerican concept and interpretation on what these places were or should have been. Eliot used this renaming of places like Magunkaquog and Hassanamesit to his benefit, to support his Christianizing efforts and garner support for his work. Praying towns were also called plantations and praying villages, but these were not indigenous words. These preexisting settlements were, however, remolded during Eliot's time into more nucleated and bounded locations focused on dislocating Native peoples from their lifeways and land and immersing them in Anglicized dress, Christianity, and sedentary agriculturally oriented labor.[27] For consistency with historical documents, this book uses the term "praying town" when referencing these settlements during their seventeenth-century occupations, although this is not necessarily what the Nipmuc people would have called them.

"King Philip's War" is another term that we have chosen to use for consistency, as most sources also refer to this conflict this way. How the Wampanoag, Massachusett, Nipmuc, and other Native peoples of the 1670s referred to this war was not well recorded, while Euroamerican records about the war and the Native leader Metacom (aka King Philip) became permanently etched into the historical record. Though the term "Metacom's Rebellion" reflects Native resistance against the invading colonial presence on the landscape, the seventeenth-century tribes may not have conceived of the war in that way. As Chapter 2 discusses, many Nipmuc people had to make difficult and conflictive decisions in the years surrounding the war. Except for the perceptions of Daniel Gookin (superintendent of Indians in the colony) regarding the struggles of Native people during the war,[28] a firsthand record of their thoughts, struggles, and memories of King Philip's War was not kept.

Other problematic terms used in this book include "New World," "contact," "historic," and, of course, "prehistoric." "New World" refers to the lands west of the Atlantic Ocean now known as North, Central, and South America, labeled as such because they were "discovered" by (or new to) European explorers. Use of this term suggests a vacant, undeveloped—even unoccupied—land open and available for colonial settlement. In reality, Native peoples had lived on this landscape for many thousands of years, with deeply developed connections to places, resources, and each other (as Chapter 2 discusses). The arrival of English and European settlers is referred to as contact, a period that was really colonization from the beginning. For the Native peoples of what is today New England, new and sustained engagement with colonial settlers was an event or punctuation in a long continuum of existence in their homelands. It was not a discrete event, however, that neatly divided time into two eras: one pre–European contact and one post–European contact. Rather, it has been a "continuous process of exchange, encounter, and strategic reckoning with how to best manage new relations" and remains so for the tribes of this region (and elsewhere across the Western Hemisphere).[29]

Using contact as the point to mark time from has led to the use of "precontact" and "postcontact" to reference time before and after colonial settlement of indigenous homelands west of the Atlantic. While these terms are used in this book and are preferred over "prehistoric" and "historic," they still reference time and activity centered around Euroamerican perspectives, actions, and agency. Chapter 2 further discusses use of these terms. How indigenous peoples discussed and thought about the arrival of English and European settlers was not central to the documentary record that we now have to work with. Isaac Nehemiah's death is just one example of a reaction only permanently recorded by non-Native Samuel Sewall. Likewise, "Indian," "American Indian," and "Native American" are labels for indigenous peoples assigned by nonindigenous explorers and colonial settlers. While specific tribal names (such as Nipmuc and Wampanaog) are used in this book, "Native" is also used because it is closest to and at times interchanged with "indigenous." The most appropriate terms are tribal names and places, which are used as much as possible. The same is true of older forms of English that appear in period documents that are cited in the text, which also retain the spellings and punctuation found in the individual documents.

In much the same way that precontact archaeologists have named periods before contact (see Chapter 2), historical archaeologists have divided the postcontact centuries into six periods for southern New England: the Contact and Plantation (1500–1675), Colonial (1675–1775), Federal (1775–1830), Early Industrial (1830–1870), Late Industrial (1870–1915), and Modern (1915–present) periods.[30] These divisions, like the artificial division between the precontact and postcontact periods for Native peoples,[31] are nomenclatures of convenience. They are created by scholars, often from Western-trained disciplines, for their study of, and epistemologies related to, the past.

Euroamerican places and spaces remembered and memorialized, such as Pulpit Rock discussed in Chapter 2, are more visible in the archaeological and historical records, while indigenous components have been more ephemeral. Once English material culture was incorporated into Native American daily life, the physical record increased. The sites discussed in this book are all examples of that; without the more visible record created by increased material culture, we might have never found these sites. The adoption of English-style structures, in particular, often provides a much stronger archaeological presence, as it did at Magunkaquog, the homestead at Hassanamesit Woods, and the Cisco Homestead.[32] The same is true of the historical documentation used to augment the archaeological record: once Native people engaged in English systems and processes (petitions, guardianship systems, and land sales), whether willingly or not, their presence on the landscape is also perceived to be more visible. In reality, as Chapter 2 discusses, Native peoples' presence extends back to at least the end of the last ice age in this region (10,000–12,000 years ago).

This book asks us to think about our engagements with, and knowledge about, places and spaces with long histories but also with connections to present-day peoples. Stephen Silliman has noted the uncritical use of culture contact terminology for what needs to be recognized as situations of a colonial nature, as suggested above.[33] By the time John Eliot began his missionary efforts in the 1630s, interactions with and between the tribes of the region were clearly defined by a colonial condition. Even settlements that engaged in contact and sustained settlement decades later than Natick did were existing in colonial conditions by the early decades of the 1600s. For example, intertribal relationships that existed generations before contact were immediately and permanently altered by Euroamerican influences even during the protocontact period; these influences continue to affect these relationships today.

The ways in which Native people think about and understand the past and their connections to each other are influenced by their continued colonial condition. Some tribes are federally recognized, while others (such as the Nipmuc) are not, creating political and economic imbalances that reverberate through many components of our relationships.[34] Another example is how the research on the Wabbaquasset area (discussed in Chapter 2) was heavily focused on maps, documents, and archaeology. In a casual conversation with her father one day Rae Gould mentioned an area on an old map called Hatchet Pond (named after the story of an Indian who threw his hatchet into this body of water). Her father knew of this place, where he and others used to hunt and fish, going back decades (and generations). What was common knowledge to him became a "discovery" to Gould during her academic search for knowledge about her tribe's history in this area of Nipmuc homelands. Generations of her family were born in this area and have maintained connections to the people and places that remain. This story demonstrates that, while archaeology and documentary research provide one way of knowing about the past, it is not always the most complete way. The incorporation of indigenous knowledge, passed down from one generation to the next (often as oral testimony), is critical to the study of any place connected to indigenous people.

This became clear to the authors of this book, who all began their knowledge of the places explored in these chapters as academically focused projects. Stephen Mrozowski and Holly Herbster began their relationships with Nipmuc tribal members following excavation and research at Magunkaquog. For Herbster, the relationship expanded through her career in cultural resource management and consultation with the Nipmuc Tribe on projects in its homelands. Mrozowski then expanded his teaching practices of the next generations of archaeologists to include consultation and collaboration with tribes whose past was of interest to his students. Pezzarossi's work on the Burnee/Boston site was one result of this.

Three hundred years after his death, John Eliot was again central to connections in Nipmuc homelands, just as he was when he traveled through settlements, renamed them "praying towns," and worked to spread Christianity. He was a central figure in the Magunkaquog site's history and the reason that an English-style stone foundation became the most visible component of Herbster and Mrozowski's excavations in the 1990s. And Eliot was central to Gould's early research as an academic trying to find the Wabbaquasset settlement (see Chapter 2) and as part of Hassanamesit's long history. But he is only one part of a larger, deeper history of Nipmuc people in their homelands in present-day central Massachusetts, northeast Connecticut, and northern Rhode Island. While this book focuses on three sites in that homeland, we should think of them as nodes in the network that Eliot traveled during his lifetime, as did the Nipmuc people who lived throughout that network for thousands of years before his arrival, and as the places that connected the authors of this book over the past few decades.

## Nipmuc Spaces in New England

This book continues the story of Nipmuc people, their resiliency, and their documented presence across the landscape of their homelands (today called southern New England) in the post–King Philip's War, postmissionary period. This study provides a context for thinking about Native Americans in New England over time and space through case studies that explore three Nipmuc archaeological sites. The stories of these places pick up in the decades when Native people of the region began to resettle and reclaim their homelands following King Philip's War of 1675–1676. The authors share their interpretations of places long known to Nipmuc people and connected in a landscape by people whose lives sometimes intersected and sometimes did not. Like the people whose lives we retell in Chapters 2 through 7, our lives intersected because we chose to explore Nipmuc places and the lives associated with them. In the limited space of this book, narratives of a handful of tribal members, past and present, are illuminated through the sites that we have explored. Together we have worked on developing deeper understandings of the Nipmuc past through sites in Massachusetts for a combined total of seventy years.

Topics explored here include past and present loss and survival, renewal and revival, colonialism and racism, and political and legal struggles. Our goal is to use the people and places as touchstones for these difficult topics to make them more accessible and more well known. By retelling the life histories of everyday people (a focus of historical archaeology), we hope to bring you into their worlds and add historical context to your understanding of contemporary Native American issues and the history of New England in particular. Their stories provide a better understanding of how these histories are clearly connected to the present and future of the Native peoples of this region; they are histories that have futures.

Just as important, the approaches used in this book, from the archaeological and documentary research to the collaborative writing process, provide a model for a decolonized method of archaeology. Our work counters the colonial dominance that began in the early 1600s, continued through the missionizing of Nipmuc people and then King Philip's War, and was maintained through the development of an archaeology in America shaped by Western knowledge and belief systems. As noted earlier in this chapter, the interpretations, project planning, and research results were completed in collaboration with the Nipmuc Tribe, braiding together knowledge from multiple sources and perspectives. Our work over the years, independently and collaboratively, has provided new insights into New England's past, the region's tribal history, ourselves, and, perhaps most importantly, how archaeology is practiced.

We asked several primary questions as we approached this book. Have we sufficiently included indigenous knowledge, past and present, in our work? What ethical practices must be considered when working with tribal peoples? How do Native peoples in the twenty-first century think about identity and memory differently than Euroamerican descendants? And how can our work impact politics? Knowing that the BIA placed a higher value on knowledge from outside "experts" to determine federal acknowledgment of the Nipmuc Nation, for example, was an important precedent for us. We do not want our work to be seen as outside "experts" telling Nipmuc history.

This book provides a model for doing archaeology and working with Native peoples and communities (Native and non-Native) in general. Historical archaeologists who work with indigenous communities understand that their work is one component of a continuum of time reaching back thousands of years, with the division between precontact and postcontact being an artificial one created by Western notions of time and history. In addition to being an example of indigenous, community-based, and collaborative archaeology (with one author who is a member of the tribe explored),[35] this book is the first complete text devoted entirely to Nipmuc archaeological sites.

All of us have learned from each other, gaining critical perspectives about our work and careers through our collaborations and sharing our experiences of the learning processes. Through investigation of the Mugunkaquog site discussed in Chapters 3 and 4, Stephen Mrozowski first connected with members of the Nipmuc Tribe and with Rae Gould in particular (author of Chapter 7). Mrozowski's work on Nipmuc sites continued at the Burnee/Boston Homestead site in Grafton, a focus of Heather Law Pezzarossi's work (Chapters 5 and 6). While other work initially connected Holly Herbster and Gould, their common explorations of Nipmuc sites, and Herbster's focus on the Magunkaquog site for her master's thesis, strengthened their personal and professional relationships. This book is a culmination of several decades of individual research projects, combined with a collective learning about this tribe's past and about each other through our collaborations. We entered new spaces both physically (through archaeology) and epistemologically (through new ways of understanding) that can sometimes be uncomfortable yet were able to create a shared understanding of what our work means.

In schools across America, New England Native American history is often discussed during the month of November, when this country celebrates the story of a peaceful gathering of pilgrims and Indians for the first Thanksgiving. Grade-school children make paper turkeys and wear black paper pilgrim hats for afternoon parades, and maybe a real Indian visits their school to retell the romantic hunting and gathering lives of their ancestors. What is often forgotten in this public remembering of Native American history is that the present is directly connected to the past through a string of events and people who have lived on the landscape in places with specific stories to tell. Through historical archaeology we can share some of these stories; the words and actions of the Nipmuc people we engage with are heard and remembered.

## Notes

1. Historical Records Survey (HRS) 1942, 14.

2. Rather than presenting a broad overview of archaeology in New England or the history of a tribe, in this book you will meet little-known individuals of the past whose lives and actions are revived in our chapters, sometimes changing the course of history for individuals or for a tribe. Detailed stories of their everyday lives, and how their decisions influenced future lives, unfold in the following chapters. Memories of them may have passed into the depths of time, except for one important commonality: they were all Nipmuc Indians who navigated a landscape of change, along with complex social, political, and personal challenges, that came with being Indian in New England over the centuries.

3. For example, the focus of the American Society for Ethnohistory is "creat[ing] a more inclusive picture of the histories of native groups in the Americas" (n.d.), http://ethnohistory.org/index.php/about/, accessed May 24, 2019.

4. See Law Pezzarossi 2014a and 2014b, for example.

5. See the BIA's Final Determination for the Nipmuc Nation petition (2004) at https://www.bia.gov/sites/bia.gov/files/assets/as-ia/ofa/petition/069A_npmcna_MA/069a_fd.pdf. Also see Gould 2013.

6. See, for example, Deetz 1977; Hume 1969; and South 1977.

7. For a discussion of earlier collaborations in North America as well as Africa, see Kehoe and Schmidt 2017.

8. Examples include Delle et al. 2000; McGuire and Paynter 1991; and Mrozowski et. al. 1996.

9. See Delle et al. 2000; Fairbanks 1971 and 1984;, Ferguson 2004; Fogel and Engerman 1974; McGuire and Paynter 1991; Mrozowski et al. 1996; and Orser 2007.

10. See, for example, Leone and Knauf 2015; and Orser 1996.

11. See Leone and Knauf 2015, for example.

12. The reasons for this division are multiple and complex. For a detailed discussion, see Schmidt and Mrozowski 2013.

13. See Gould 2017.

14. See Atalay 2012.

15. Garman and Herbster 1996.

16. Project Mishoon involves the identification and potential recovery of several intact dugout canoes (*mishoonash*) from Lake Quinsigamond in Worcester, Massachusetts. See Project Mishoon (2014), http://projectmishoon.homestead.com/.

17. The Trust for Public Land is the oldest land preservation organization of its kind in the world.

18. See Yentsch 1988.

19. She received an additional grant through the Massachusetts Historical Commission.

20. Soil micromorphology is the study of soil development and change through the microscopic study of small, plasticized thin sections that reveal fine-grained details of soil properties.

21. For more information about this important early colonial war, see Battlefields of the Pequot War (2019), https://pequotwar.org/about/.

22. For more on the history, impact, and legacies of the Pequot War and King Philip's War, see Brooks 2018; Calloway 1997; Cave 1996; DeLucia 2018; Drake 2000; Lepore 1998; Mandell 2010; and Schultz and Tougias 2000.

23. Massachusetts Bay Colony existed from 1628 to 1691 along the eastern shore of present-day Massachusetts, westward toward the Dutch settlement in New Netherlands (which became New York), and north into parts of present-day New Hampshire and Maine. It was created by the Massachusetts Bay Company. The southeastern portion of present-day Massachusetts was a separate colony (Plymouth Colony, 1620–1691) until a merger created the Province of Massachusetts Bay in 1691.

24. The "original" seven praying towns recognized by Eliot were Natick, Punkapoag, Hassanamesit, Okommakamesit, Wamesit, Nashobah, and Magunkaquog (see Carlson 1986). Another seven were added to his list prior to King Philip's War (by the early 1670s).

25. DeLucia 2018, 15–16.

26. DeLucia 2018, 17.

27. Delucia 2018, 39.

28. Gookin 1836 [1677].

29. DeLucia 2018, 127.

30. Steinitz et al. 1985.

31. See Schmidt and Mrozowski 2013.

32. Similar patterns have been documented at the Mohegan, Mashantucket, and Eastern Pequot reservations in southern New England.

33. Silliman 2005.

34. Federally recognized tribes have what is called "standing" under federal laws like NAGPRA and Section 106, which require consultation with federally recognized tribes but not with non–federally recognized "Indian groups."

35. Several definitions of community-based, collaborative, and indigenous archaeology exist. See Atalay 2006, 2012; Colwell-Chanthaphonh and Ferguson 2008; and Silliman 2008 for examples.

# 2

# Threads of Continuity

## Cultural and Temporal Intersections across Nipmuc Homelands

D. RAE GOULD, HOLLY HERBSTER,
AND STEPHEN A. MROZOWSKI

In the picturesque New England town of Woodstock, Connecticut, Pulpit Rock Road is connected to the center of town, locally referred to as "Woodstock Hill." In this area of northeast Connecticut, historic Roseland Cottage (a National Historic Landmark) recalls the grand Victorian era.[1] The town's high school (Woodstock Academy) across the green has educated youths since 1802. Part of the town's history as a tranquil agricultural settlement (in what was rebranded a few decades ago as "The Quiet Corner") includes the location of historic Pulpit Rock, for which Pulpit Rock Road is named.[2] The event that this spot commemorates is Protestant missionary John Eliot preaching to the local Indians during his efforts to convert them to Christianity in the 1670s, a few years before the outbreak of King Philip's War.

Although Nipmuc people have been connected to the landscape of northeast Connecticut for thousands of years, the presence of John Eliot on a few brief occasions in the late 1600s is what makes this place worthy of commemoration in the minds of local residents.[3] A 1917 postcard recently for sale on the internet was labeled as "Pulpit Rock, Where John Elliot [*sic*] Preached to the Indians—Woodstock, Connecticut Original Vintage Postcard." While Eliot is the focus of the postcard's photograph, "the Indians" remain nameless and, we assume, passive recipients of his actions. The rock in the 1917 photo is inscribed "1686 Pulpit Rock Sacred Forevermore 1886,"[4] indicating that it remained an important place in the town's history 200 years after being earmarked as the location where Eliot stood, worthy of receiving a per-

Figure 2.1. Pulpit Rock, Woodstock, Connecticut: a place that memorializes John Eliot but erases the Nipmuc people he preached to. Photograph by D. Rae Gould.

manent memorial (Figure 2.1). In reality, it is almost impossible to know the exact location(s) of Eliot's visits to the Wabbaquasset Indians in present-day Woodstock. Most of what we know about his travels to this area comes from the records of Daniel Gookin, who served as superintendent of Indians in Massachusetts Bay Colony during the 1600s.

In 2004 Rae Gould embarked on a research project to locate the Wabbaquasset settlement that Eliot visited 350 years ago. Her ancestors are from this area and she grew up nearby, residing in Woodstock several times. While her family has generations of links to northeast Connecticut, it is not clear whether these go directly back to the early seventeenth-century Nipmuc inhabitants. Like others, Gould envisioned a "praying town" where Native Americans would have lived out their daily lives and welcomed Eliot as he passed through their settlement. Conventional thought was that Wabbaquasset may have looked something like the Magunkaquog or Hassanamesit settlements discussed in this book, perhaps with a meeting house or at least a central gathering space where Eliot would have held court during his brief visits to the area.

Like many others, Gould's vision of the landscape that her ancestors lived on was based more on the historical record created by Eliot and others than on knowledge from people in her tribe. The pursuit of an academic project to locate the settlement, ironically, led to a more in-depth understanding of tribal knowledge as she began to share her findings and discuss the project with other tribal members, including her own family. This coming together of different knowledge sources and forms of memory represents a departure in epistemology that rests at the heart of this book, as discussed in Chapter 1.

John Eliot's presence at places like Wabbaquasset is just one part of the larger story of Nipmuc presence and a comparatively small piece in a longer history of Native American occupation of the southern New England landscape. Wabbaquasset was occupied long before Eliot's arrival, and the form of what he labeled a praying town would not have differed much from other Native settlements encountered by Eliot and others as they explored interior Nipmuc homelands. A more English-style town, with a meeting house, for example, did not exist at Wabbaquasset. In places where meeting houses did exist (as at Magunkaquog and probably Hassanamesit), they were constructed as part of long-standing occupations and land use patterns of Native people reaching back thousands of years and as an accommodation and integration of English cultural practices.

At Wabbaquasset Eliot encountered a preexisting Native settlement that he attempted to convert to Christianity in a short two- or three-year period in the early 1670s. Gookin stated that he and Eliot visited "some of these towns" in interior Nipmuc country beginning in July 1673. They began to "encourage and exhort them to proceed in the ways of God," again suggesting that an organized settlement was already in place. Gookin noted that a recognized sagamore existed.[5] Gookin and Eliot may not have had a word in their English vocabulary for a non-nucleated, unbounded Native settlement, given their worldview and experience growing up in crowded England. They used the nomenclature most familiar to them, even if it was not appropriate or accurate from a Nipmuc perspective. While we use some of these terms in this book, we acknowledge their origins and in some cases inappropriateness (see Chapter 1).

Almost all (if not all) of the original seven praying towns identified by Eliot were in settlements already inhabited by Indians.[6] Determining the boundaries of these settlements is difficult due to their non-nucleated and more dispersed nature: clear-cut boundaries may not have existed. Wabbaquasset would have been a more dispersed settlement, much like the other settlements that Eliot visited. He in fact complained that it was sometimes difficult to get the Native inhabitants to come together for sermons during his visits.[7]

Eliot's renaming of these places as praying towns suggested that their history began with his arrival and contributed to the notion that they were "established" with the arrival of English settlers. In addition to the documentary record confirming the presence of Native American inhabitants at the places Eliot visited and preached, archaeology has provided evidence of a long Native presence in southern New England dating back at least 11,000 years, following the retreat of the last glaciers (see below).[8] Given that English settlement had not occurred in the Wabbaquasset area during Eliot's encounters, the Nipmuc people living here would have continued to use a broader, rather than limited, area for their settlement and subsistence because they had no competition for the land. When English settlement began a few years after King Philip's War, Nipmuc people had not abandoned the area. They returned to Wabbaquasset following the war, while the English were establishing their first homesteads.[9]

Historian Ellen Larned, in classic late nineteenth-century prose, related how the new inhabitants felt about the continued presence of Wabbaquasset Indians in 1692: "Now that Woodstock had secured minister, mills, pound, ways and bridges, she began to be seriously annoyed by Indians. Many Wabbaquasset had returned to their ancient homes and hunting fields, little improved by their sojourn in Mohegan, or inclined to be friendly with Massachusetts settlers in possession. Their chief, Tokekamowootchaug, and his followers, were idle, drunken and disorderly."[10]

Dealing with the "Indian problem" was a common theme in late nineteenth-century America, and New England was no different. Captain John Sabin was remembered in the Wabbaquasset area as a hero who resolved this problem for the town's pioneer settlers, much the way John Eliot's heroics are (literally) etched into local history. In 1691 Sabin took possession of 100 acres "near Roxbury, alias Woodstock, supposed to be in Connecticut." By 1696 he had constructed a house with fortifications, had "gained much influence and authority over the Indians," and was placed "in authority" over the Wabbaquasset, at least as recalled in the late nineteenth century.[11] This version of history, with white settlers conquering both the land and the idle and disorderly Indian inhabitants, is a common thread in American history-making practices, especially for New England. Belief in this myth enabled Euroamerican settlers to justify the land dispossession and genocidal practices central to their heritage.

Although the Nipmuc people had taken refuge with their Mohegan kin to the south for a few years during and after King Philip's War,[12] the critical part of the story is that they maintained connections to this land, their homelands. The continued use of the term "Wabbaquasset" as late as the 1930s for Native people residing in northeast Connecticut also confirms the connection between those who returned in the late 1600s and their descendants, who were still distinguished from the Euroamerican residents of the town.[13]

The continued presence of Nipmuc people in Woodstock during the eighteenth and nineteenth centuries, despite displacement to the Hatchet Pond area of town, is also well documented. Foundations of the Hatchet Pond settlement still exist in a large, undeveloped parcel in the north part of town.[14] The continued presence of Nipmuc families (including Rae Gould's) in Woodstock into the twenty-first century provides additional proof of their long-standing connections to Wabbaquasset and has been documented through vital, probate, and historical records.[15] Gould's grandmother, for example, was born in this area in 1919 to a large family that was part of an even larger extended family still in the region.

## John Eliot, "Apostle to the Indians"

Eliot's presence at Wabbaquasset was part of the continuing Nipmuc presence at this place, as it was at other Nipmuc places he passed through. Wabbaquasset represents just one example of interactions occurring throughout Nipmuc homelands in the decades following English colonization of what is today northeast Connecticut when Christianity was introduced. Pulpit Rock commemorates a small part of a larger past yet, like so many places remembered by non-Natives in New England who recorded the region's history, it focuses on one man; much of American history has been taught this way. It is important to understand the role that colonialism has played in that history-making process. Eliot's role in the history of southern New England is an important part, but only one part, of a deeper and richer history. Much of this book is devoted to revealing that deeper history, but understanding it requires a brief recounting of Eliot's legacy, beginning with his earliest days of preaching at what he called Indian praying towns. The historical record of his work was created, saved, and valued by colonial settlers and their descendants, so it is not surprising that Eliot was remembered as providing a sympathetic voice for Native people during and following King Philip's War in addition to his decades of Christianizing Indians in Massachusetts. For these efforts he was referred to as the "Apostle to the Indians."

John Eliot first arrived in Boston in 1631 as an English emigrant shortly after Massachusetts Bay Colony was established in 1628. He first took a temporary position at a Boston church and a year later assumed the position of teacher in a nearby Roxbury church, which he held for more than fifty-seven years.[16] When Eliot was first settling in the colony, the Nipmuc were having their earliest encounters with colonial settlers. The earliest written reference to the Nipmuc dates to 1629 and the first eyewitness account to 1632.[17]

Turbulence between Native peoples in southern New England and colonists already existed by the 1630s. Eliot's interest in the local tribes may have been sparked during the Pequot War of 1636–1637. In 1643 he began to learn the Algonkian language and within three years was able to preach basic sermons in the local dialect.[18] Over the next twenty years he translated a large number of educational and religious texts into the language, an effort that culminated with the 1663 publication of the complete Bible: *Mamusee Wunneetapanatamwe Up-Biblum God*.[19]

Although Eliot is considered to be a founder of the missionary movement in New England, no personal writings or other records describe how his work began. Most scholars agree that Eliot simply felt a duty to carry out the Bay Colony's charter mission to "wynn and incite the Natives . . . to the Christian Fayth."[20] Sometime around 1646 Eliot met with other ministers in the area to discuss how they could spread Christianity beyond their own congregations,[21] resulting in the 1647 London publication of the pamphlet *The Day Breaking, If Not the Sun-Rising of the Gospell with the Indians in New-England*. This became the first in a series of ten similar pamphlets known as the "Eliot tracts," detailing progress of the missionary work in New England and used to solicit funds from England for Eliot and others.

*The Day Breaking* laid out some reasons why Eliot and others responded to the call, not the least of which was to answer criticism from England that Massachusetts Bay Colony was failing in its charter obligations. The pamphlet responded by explaining that the effort was extremely difficult and that "wee have not learnt as yet that art of coyning Christians, or putting Christ's name and Image upon copper mettle."[22] For a time, Eliot and some colleagues also adhered to the theology of millennialism, believing that the tribes they encountered were one of the ten "Lost Tribes of Israel." Out of this movement Eliot's early ideas about spreading the mission were formed. Whatever his motivations, he was clearly committed to the religious and civil education of the Nipmuc, despite nearly constant financial and administrative difficulties. He best described his views regarding his place in the New England mission by borrowing a biblical phrase: "I am but a shrub in the wilderness,"[23] as he wrote to New England Company governor Robert Boyle in 1664.[24]

Eliot's first documented trips preaching to Native people outside of Boston date to the fall of 1646 and were, by his own admission, not well received. He was accompanied by Thomas Shepard and several other colleagues. Throughout the seventeenth century Eliot was one of only a few colonial ministers and laymen with interest in the missionary movement. Very few Puritan ministers worked with Eliot or volunteered to assist with his mission work. The exceptions were Eliot's son (John Jr.), the Mayhews on Martha's Vineyard, John Cotton in Plymouth, and Richard Bourne on Cape Cod. Only his son actually assisted with the instruction and operation of the original seven praying towns in Massachusetts Bay Colony. Daniel Gookin was actively involved with Eliot and the Indians he worked with, but his assignments were more closely associated with civil order than with religion in his role as superintendent of Indians for the colony.

As a result, almost all teachers and other religious leaders in the praying towns were Native Americans who were trained by Eliot himself or had been instructed by other (usually) bilingual Native residents.[25] While Eliot maintained his position at the First Church in Roxbury, the praying towns were left for long periods without Euroamerican oversight or interactions. Eliot was aware, early in his ministry, of the need to rely on Native teachers for the mission to be successful and sought out "the sachems of greatest note" to support his efforts, noting in 1651 that "the most effectual and general way of spreading the Gospel . . . will be by themselves."[26]

Eliot's earliest Native assistants were men who spoke English and could translate sermons and help answer questions. These assistants in turn instructed other Native teachers, creating a network of individuals who performed most of the missionary work around the colony under Eliot and his few colleagues. Eliot encouraged the Massachusetts General Court to appoint "some of the most prudent and pious Indians, in every Indian village that had received the gospel" to assume leadership roles and teach the gospel to their kin.[27] Although the decision to appoint these leaders came from the colonial government, choices regarding who assumed these roles were made by the Native communities. This is just one example of how the praying towns remained largely self-sufficient. In effect these instructors acted as "culture brokers,"[28] who dealt with the colonial strangers and acted as intermediaries between these separate cultural, ethnic, and political groups.

Eliot's initial sermon to Indians was recorded as being in 1646 at Nonantum (present-day Newton), just west of Boston. As Eliot's visits continued at Nonantum, Nipmuc Indians from interior sections began attending. In 1650 Punkapoag (present-day Canton) was the second settlement that Eliot labeled as a praying town. Material culture from this site dates through the 1680s, although it continued as a Native settlement well into the nineteenth century.[29] Natick was recognized as a praying town in 1651 and continued to have Native landholders well into the eighteenth-century. English settlement in Nipmuc homelands did not occur until the 1650s, with the first land grant recorded in 1654 (for the present-day east central Worcester County area).[30] Hassanamesit was labeled as a praying town in 1654 and Magunkaquog in 1660. More interior Nipmuc groups may have developed an interest in Eliot's work after the colony's western border became unstable during this turbulent time and seen Eliot as a possible advocate for aiding them.[31] Settlements like Wabbaquasset were on the westernmost front of colonial settlement during this time.

Eliot's missionary efforts followed an "affective model," which suggested converts should exemplify Puritan virtues of piety, industry, frugality, constancy, sobriety, honesty, and austerity. In this view, Christian Natives would emulate the behavior of colonists as the necessary first step to being accepted into the full Christian communion. Religious instruction was certainly an important part of the process, but until converts were properly prepared they could not expect to receive the gospel.[32]

The four-stage process envisioned by the Puritan missionaries began with "civilizing" Nipmuc people, who were considered to lack the order, industry, and manners that were essential qualities of life. Central to the Natives' "disorder" were their settlement and subsistence practices. Seasonal residential movements within large kin-based territories and the lack of bounded fields or personal real estate—combined with too much free time and their clothing, grooming, and personal behavior—were considered inappropriate by Puritan standards. The second stage involved teaching Protestant Christianity to replace Native belief systems. In accepting Christianity, the Nipmuc were supposed to abandon their traditional worldview. The third step, often referred to as "conversion," required Native communicants to have personal relationships with God. The final step was admission as a church member. Native converts were expected to follow the last two stages in the same ways colonists did: through a public examination in Christian doctrine and presentation of a "conversion narrative" delivered to the congregation, who decided if the applicant had experienced a divine intervention and hence become a "visible saint" eligible for full church membership.[33]

To support the mission efforts, in 1649 the Society for the Propagation of the Gospel in New England (SPG) was created to promote the "preaching and propagating of the Gospel of Jesus Christ amongst the natives, and . . . [the] maintaining of schools and nurseries of learning, for the better educating of the children of the natives."[34] The society created a direct conduit for funds from England to support missionary work in New England. Eliot's goal was to use these funds to transform Native political, social, religious, and subsistence systems by "gather[ing] them together from their scattered course of life, to cohabitation and civill order and Government."[35] This was the vision of the nucleated "praying town" that persisted in historical renderings of that period. In this statement Eliot reveals his assumption that Nipmuc people did not have social or political order unless (or until) they were Christianized. While intratribal and intertribal relations were certainly affected by the introduction of new religious and cultural practices in the decades between first contact and King Philip's War, the long presence of tribal entities in this region, going back thousands of years, supported a continued autonomy still present today. Engagement with John Eliot and other colonial settlers began a 400-year history of interaction and acculturation that is now one part of the long continuum of the tribal cultures of this region.

The Christian Nipmuc found themselves in a difficult situation as King

Philip's War approached in the mid-1670s; many had conflicted allegiances or did not want to be embroiled in the hostilities. As a result the praying towns experienced a host of challenges, from political fracturing, with residents imprisoned on Deer Island (see below), to seeing their postwar communities depleted by the loss of men sent into slavery or other forms of servitude in places as distant as Bermuda and the Caribbean more generally. The intersection of King Philip's War and the Nipmuc people is foundational to the histories of the sites and families discussed throughout this book.

## King Philip's War, 1675–1676

Growing tensions within Plymouth Colony (the first Massachusetts colony, founded in 1620 and located south of Massachusetts Bay Colony, see Figure 1.1) came to a head in 1675 with the devastating conflict that has been called King Philip's War. In June 1675 three Wampanoag men associated with Wampanoag sachem Metacom (called King Philip by colonists) were hanged in Plymouth, convicted of killing John Sassamon, a Native teacher from the Nemasket praying town (near present-day Middleborough). Sassamon was a student at Harvard College and one of John Eliot's proselytes who had moved from Natick to Nemasket. Several weeks before, Sassamon had reportedly warned Plymouth officials that Metacom was gathering Native support for war with Euroamerican settlers. His murder was considered proof that attacks were imminent.

Several Euroamerican observers connected Metacom's hostility with the fact that Sassamon was a "Christian Indian" preaching not far from Metacom's residence at Mount Hope (present-day Bristol, Rhode Island).[36] In June 1675 John Easton, Rhode Island's deputy governor, met with Metacom and some of his men in an attempt to ward off possible attacks. One of Metacom's complaints was that the missionary movement threatened to engulf the Wampanoag, who had resisted conversion to Christianity. He described "praying Indians" as "in everi thing more mischievous."[37] Several attempts to reconcile Metacom and Plymouth Colony officials failed, and suspicions between them grew. That same month, soldiers were sent to capture Metacom but were unsuccessful. The Wampanoag responded with a series of raids that left many towns in Plymouth Colony destroyed.

In July the conflict spread to Nipmuc territory when a group of Nipmuc attacked the town of Mendon. Massachusetts Bay Colony authorities sent a small group to negotiate with the Nipmuc, but the party was ambushed and most killed. Subsequent raids by hostile Native groups in Brookfield, Hadley, Springfield, and Deerfield convinced colonial leaders that the Nipmuc were generally not to be trusted. In the same month, the colony's General Court ordered Daniel Gookin to gather men from the Boston area and send them to Mount Hope to defend against Metacom.[38]

As the fighting threatened Boston, authorities became increasingly uneasy with the communities congregated in praying towns. Rumors and fear led many to see a distinction between "friendly" and "enemy" Nipmuc. The conflict signaled a shift in the recorded descriptions of New England's Native peoples. Prior to the war, many written accounts (especially Eliot's) discussed Native peoples as "children" who could be saved or redeemed through Christian conversion. Afterward, most descriptions focused on instances of Native brutality or blasphemy, with little suggestion that they could ever achieve civility. Gookin noted the inherent bias in Euroamerican accounts of the war and decided to write his own description of events. His manuscript "An Historical Account of the Doings and Sufferings of the Christian Indians," which focused on Christian Indians and their role in the war, was submitted to the New England Company for publication in 1677, but the group decided not to do anything with the text for almost a century. In contrast, the 1682 King Philip's War captivity narrative by colonist Mary Rowlandson published in London was a best seller.[39] This demonstrates how even the primary documents that archaeologists rely on to understand the past can be biased from their inceptions.

In August 1675 Massachusetts Bay Colony authorities ordered all praying Indians to consolidate in Natick, Punkapoag, Nashobah, Wamesit, or Hassanamesit. Gookin noted that "the poor Christian Indians were reduced to great sufferings" by the decision, as they were restricted from hunting, gathering corn, or traveling beyond one mile of town centers unless accompanied by a colonist. Perhaps most importantly, the order stated that *any* Indians found to be in violation of the restrictions were to be captured or killed if they refused to surrender.[40]

Throughout the fall of 1675 Nipmuc people moved eastward and were joined by their kin in the five praying towns. In October a group at Natick was accused of burning a house in Dedham; the court responded by imprisoning them on Deer Island in Boston Harbor.[41] Eliot traveled to Natick to offer support to the group, who were allowed to take only a few possessions on carts. Deer Island was a privately owned pasture: the Indians were told they could not cut any wood or take any sheep kept there. By all accounts, conditions on the exposed island were horrible as winter approached. Anyone who attempted to leave could be shot and many were illegally captured and sold into slavery by colonists. When Eliot and Gookin visited in December, people from Punkapoag and Nashobah had also been imprisoned on Deer Island, with nearly 500 starving men, women, and children in all. Gookin wrote about "their wigwams poor and mean, their clothes few and thin," and their subsistence based on the few shellfish they could harvest at low tide supplemented by a meager supply of corn that they brought.[42] Many praying town occupants decided to leave their homes entirely rather than face confinement, which is understandable given the horrid conditions suffered by their kin. The displacement that had begun fifty years earlier with the arrival of English colonists was compounded by King Philip's War.

In November 1675 about 300 "enemy" Nipmuc arrived at Hassanamesit, where around 200 people (including approximately 50 men) were living. Nearly all 500 left Hassanamesit and joined other Nipmuc who, three months later, captured Mary Rowlandson. While many labeled these Nipmuc as deserters, Gookin described them as unwilling participants, persuaded—-rightfully so—that the colony would take them prisoner if they stayed behind.[43] Regardless of the facts, most colonists at the time saw the Hassanamesit "deserters" as proof that the Christianized Nipmuc could not be trusted. Some suggested killing all of those interned on Deer Island; others wanted them to be sent to "some place farther more from us."[44]

Gookin, like Eliot, was seen as a sympathizer with the Natives during the war. Neither held the same standing in colonial society afterward. After speaking out on behalf of the Deer Island prisoners, Gookin received death threats, was called a traitor, and was not reelected as a general court assistant in 1676 (a position that he had held since 1651). During the period of confinement, some Deer Island men that Eliot and Gookin knew personally were forced to serve as spies and scouts for the colony. Among these was Job Kattenanit, a teacher at Magunkaquog, who had come to Gookin after avoiding a Nipmuc raid on Hassanamesit. While few colonists were willing to trust them completely, English-speaking Nipmuc who had worked with Eliot and Gookin were asked to assist when it suited the needs of the colony.

By the spring of 1676 colonial soldiers had gained ground by buttressing existing Euroamerican towns and deflecting more attacks by Metacom's groups.

Attacks decreased as more Native people were captured, killed, or deserted Metacom to retreat from the fighting. In May surviving Deer Island prisoners were allowed to leave, although the colony made clear that any expenses incurred were the responsibility of Eliot and Gookin. The decision to evacuate Deer Island was due partly to the deplorable conditions and the overall poor health of the survivors, who were unable to plant or harvest corn while captive. More than half of those interned on Deer Island died that winter.[45] Survivors were sent to Cambridge, where they stayed on the land of Thomas Oliver, who offered his farm along the Charles River as a temporary residence. Gookin noted that most stayed in Cambridge through the summer, although some scattered to nearby places. In August 1676 Metacom was captured and killed. Although some fighting occurred afterward, his death is considered to be the end of the war.

Later in 1676 most of those remaining in Cambridge returned westward to their old settlements in the interior of Nipmuc territory. Gookin documented one group living in Nonantum and another at Brush Hill in Milton. When spring of 1677 arrived, he wrote that "most of them repaired to their plantations at Natick, Magunkog, and some planted at Hassanamesit," although the latter was deserted after Mohawk threats.[46] One of the worst postwar raids occurred in 1678 at Magunkaquog, where twenty-two Indians were captured and taken to New York (see Chapter 4). Mohawk parties continued to plague the resettled Nipmuc towns, raiding corn and the few belongings not plundered during the war and carrying off captives.

Eliot and Gookin continued their involvement with the religious and civil oversight of the postwar praying towns, although both were aging and unable to travel much. This era of missionary activity ended with the deaths of Gookin at seventy-five (in 1687) and Eliot at eighty-six (in 1690). Eliot's friend Cotton Mather recorded his final words at his deathbed, as a new century approached: "There is a Cloud . . . a dark Cloud upon the Work of the Gospel among the poor Indians. The Lord revive and prosper that Work, and grant it may live when I am Dead."[47] As noted above, men like John Eliot and Daniel Gookin, who recorded their experiences and thoughts, became the focus of historical research for centuries. Books and places memorialized their lives and activities for future generations, while Native people, places, and perspectives became invisible and nameless. This book is one of several that provides a deeper look at indigenous peoples, places, and knowledge of the landscape that came to be called New England.[48]

## The Aftermath of King Philip's War

The period following this volatile war marked a new era in relations between colonial and Native inhabitants of southern New England. Many colonists and their descendants created and continued a myth of extinction, claiming that after the war the remaining Native populations lost their cultural identities and merged with the surrounding white, African American, or mixed populations of the region or (as at Wabbaquasset) were idle and disorderly and not contributing to local society in meaningful ways. Important places on the landscape—such as Natick, Magunkaquog, Hassanamesit, and Wabbaquasset—that had been central to Native lifeways long before the war were no longer solely occupied by Nipmuc populations by the early eighteenth century. For example, by 1735 most of Hassanamesit had been acquired by English settlers and was renamed Grafton. Similarly, in the 1680s Wabbaquasset was renamed New Roxbury and then Woodstock by 1690. The division and selling of Nipmuc lands, combined with English renaming of settlements, contributed to the attempted erasure of Native peoples, Christian and non-Christian, from the landscape.[49]

A continuation of Native cultural practices based on the mobility that existed before and during the praying town period became even more critical following land loss and dispossession from English settlement in Nipmuc homelands. Land loss began with the earliest colonial settlers, continued through King Philip's War, then accelerated in the early decades of the eighteenth century. By 1746 Massachusetts law assigned three guardians to the Native settlements that remained, who had the authority to "manage, allot, lease, and sell Indian lands as they saw fit."[50] Thus began the guardianship system of Massachusetts Indians responsible for the loss of their remaining lands, including all but three and a half acres of the Nipmuc reservation in Grafton still held by the tribe today.

This book is very much about the continuation of the people, places, and stories connected with Nipmuc homelands where mobility, transition, and connections were maintained as part of Native lifeways over centuries, despite not being part of the historical record. In addition to the three sites discussed in this book, several other archaeological sites in southern New England document that long-established indigenous cultural practices (subsistence strategies and use of stone and animal bone for tools, for example) continued well into the colonial period, when they were then combined with English material culture and new cultural practices.[51]

Magunkaquog, the Burnee/Boston Homestead, and the Cisco Homestead are just three examples of important places across the New England landscape that Nipmuc people have remained connected to over time. These connections extend from the present back into a deeper past (which is not the primary focus of this book). Reconnections to these places today and to the history that they hold is possible, in part, through archaeology. While archaeology has been a discipline of the colonizer, more and more Native people are embracing it as one way to understand and connect to the past.

## Deeper History

There is more than a touch of irony in the fact that Rae Gould, as a Nipmuc person, found a connection to her own past embodied in a glacial erratic linked to John Eliot (Pulpit Rock). The southern New England landscape is strewn with such large rocks deposited by retreating glaciers over 12,000 years ago. Like sentinels of the past, these large remnants of glacial history have remained silent for thousands of years while human history has unfolded around them. Often these permanent landscape features were incorporated into the activities of past peoples, connected to histories captured in oral traditions, or unearthed through archaeology. All human societies maintain close connections to the places they call home, whether through religious cosmologies, oral traditions, or commemorations of events and individuals long since passed. The cultural intersections at Wabbaquasset/Woodstock provide one example.

For much of its own history archaeology has struggled with how to conceptualize time. Starting with the work of Danish antiquarian Christian Jurgensen Thomsen,[52] archaeologists conceptualized time according to material culture, leading to the famous tripartite division into the Stone, Bronze, and Iron Ages. Archaeologists in many parts of the world have developed complex chronologies based on regional artifact types.[53] In New England this has resulted in classification of Native American precontact history into three periods: Paleoindian (12,000 to 9,000 years ago), Archaic (9,000 to 3,000 years ago), and Woodland (3,000 years ago to contact).[54] Data on the settlement and subsistence patterns of precontact southern New England indicate that a degree of territoriality and regionalism was in place well before Europeans appeared off the coast, with year-round occupation of the uplands area of present-day northern Connecticut and Rhode Island and Massachusetts.[55] Archaeologists often use the term "contact" to refer to the arrival of Europeans in the "New

World" (as noted in Chapter 1), but this label tends to overstate the finality of colonialism as a historical process. Colonialization of indigenous peoples in this hemisphere brought genocide, with catastrophic results. But, as argued in this book, Native American societies and identities have endured culturally and politically.

The empirically based notions of time and temporality (the duration of time experienced by people) that archaeologists have employed in North America rest on the division between history and prehistory.[56] For a host of reasons we reject the notion of prehistory.[57] First, it places an artificial barrier between the recent and deeper pasts. Second, it places greater significance on colonial and postcolonial history, suggesting that they represent a complete break or rupture with a much longer Native American history. Third, we reject prehistory as a concept because its origins can be traced to colonial practices that sought to portray Native American societies as essentially dead, with their cultural and political history ended as a result of European domination and acculturation.[58] Until recently archaeologists have chosen to limit their inquiries to either history or prehistory, with few attempts to transcend this artificial divide. Although there are many reasons for this,[59] this book focuses instead on a way of conceptualizing Nipmuc history as a continuum.

Much of the book is centered on a small group of people who lived between 100 and 400 years ago in a rather circumscribed area. There are very clear links, however, between these lives and a deeper cultural past that had been communicated to them through memory and oral tradition as well as everyday practices. One way to conceptualize the broader contours of this deeper past is to focus on the strong links that exist between any group of people and the landscape or space that they live in. In the case of the Hassanamisco Nipmuc that is a small area of upland associated with the Blackstone River Valley (which connects modern-day Worcester, Massachusetts, and Providence, Rhode Island).[60] They were part of a larger population of Nipmuc also occupying the uplands of southern New England (away from the coastal areas). Archaeologists have done a good job of finding evidence concerning the economic and cultural practices of the ancestral populations of today's Nipmuc.[61] This book, however, focuses primarily on the area surrounding Hassanamesit as well as Magunkaquog.

The people of Hassanamesit had strong links to an economy and social relations rooted in a landscape dominated by the Blackstone River and its various tributaries to the southeast into Narragansett Bay. Over hundreds, if not thousands, of years the Nipmuc maintained relations with the surrounding coastal groups, including the Massachusett and Wampanoag to the east and the Narragansett and Mohegan-Pequot to the south. The rich forests that covered the uplands of present-day Massachusetts were home to a variety of animals that Nipmuc families relied on for food, clothing, and other resources. Like many large river valleys, the Blackstone River was home to several species of anadromous fish (such as salmon, shad, and herring) that returned to their spawning grounds each year.[62] Waterfalls along the Blackstone are ideal locations to catch these fish, which could be eaten or used as fertilizer for the maize, beans, and squash that were part of Nipmuc foodways.[63] These same falls later provided energy for a very different kind of economy: rural industries (see Chapter 6).[64] The lakes, swamps, and streams that dotted and crossed Nipmuc homelands provided a variety of fish for eating and were sources of woods such as cedar used for tools and building. The surrounding forests provided hard and soft woods for making baskets and other tools as well as firewood.

In the period identified as the Woodland by archaeologists, a shift occurred from an economy based on hunting, fishing, and gathering wild and early domesticated plants to one in which maize, beans, and squash were more important to the daily diets of the ancestral Nipmuc. The broader contours of these changes remain poorly understood except in the most general terms. Maize became a dietary staple by at least 700 years ago, if not earlier. Based on ethnographic and historical information, women played a primary role in horticulture, resulting in political leadership as well.[65] These kinds of changes were taking place over hundreds of years throughout eastern North America. And to gain a full understanding of these broader historical currents it is important to examine a longer history and wider geography than what is provided in this book. There is one way of linking the Nipmuc to this deeper history, however: by literally following the material culture where it takes us. The changes, continuities, and complexities of these larger histories are perhaps best understood by focusing on a smaller piece of this broader picture: a single class of material culture—lithic (stone) tools—over the landscape.

Lithic materials were an abundant resource provided by the uplands. Interior Nipmuc traded with groups along the coast for a variety of resources, such as shellfish, but a lively exchange of lithic materials also existed throughout the interior region for thousands of years. This exchange involved trade and tool production from quartz, quartzite, rhyolite, argillite, chert, slate, hornfels, and steatite.[66] In his analysis of lithic materials from Nipmuc homesteads dating to the eighteenth and nineteenth centuries (including the Burnee/Boston and Deb Newman sites), Bagley notes that local materials such as quartz and quartzite were collected from large veins for at least the last 7,000 years. Following colonial settlement, despite the availability of metal knives and other tools, long-used lithic materials were still a ready source for "instant tools," such as small blades for cutting and working bone and wood.[67]

Bagley also identified ground stone tools (such as a pestle) from the Burnee/Boston Homestead as well as fragments of a small steatite (soapstone) bowl (see Chapter 5). Several sources of steatite exist in southern New England, all close to or within what is today considered the Nipmuc homeland. And strong evidence supports the assertion that these materials were in high demand throughout much of eastern North America, particularly between 4,000 and 3,200 years ago.[68] Exchange networks covered much of this region, including trading soapstone over much of the area. The network appears to have collapsed sometime around 3,200 years ago.[69] Although questions concerning the use of soapstone after the development of ceramic technologies (sometime around 3,600 years ago) remain, its intensified appearance in religious contexts such as burials for another thousand years argues for the religious importance attached to this material.[70]

The use and exchange of lithic materials across large expanses of North America for thousands of years is just one example of a deeper history that allows us to imagine the links that exist between earlier cultural practices and individual artifacts such as the small steatite bowl from the Burnee/Boston Homestead. This example is not presented as evidence of a direct link between the Nipmuc women of the eighteenth and nineteenth centuries and the 3,000-year-old use of steatite across eastern North America. It can be argued, however, that Sarah Burnee and Sarah Boston knew the history of the use of steatite by their ancestors and those with whom they traded. Precisely how these Nipmuc women conceptualized their relationships with materials or specific artifacts remains unclear, but it is not uncommon for tribal elders to ask pointedly where the "Native" material is when they are shown English or European materials recovered from known Nipmuc sites. These elders may see their own connections to their ancestors in these materials, whether they were manufactured by European or Native hands; if they were part of a Nipmuc household, they are part of Nipmuc history.

Within 500 meters of the Burnee/Boston Homestead is a quartzite quarry that has been in use for close to 4,000 years (based on the style of the lithic tools recovered from the site). Other quarries in the area of Keith Hill in Grafton were also used by Native Americans and Europeans alike to gather foundation stones for structures. The long history of lithic use in southern New England is not part of a dead past; it is part of a living history that still echoes today in the same way that most world religions have roots spanning thousands of years. These are not static histories of unchanging practices but rather long histories punctuated by periods of change and continuity. Colonial settlement and engagement with new peoples, like John Eliot, was one of the many punctuations over that long history.

Threads of the past ran through the lives of Nipmuc people of this region in the eighteenth and nineteenth centuries, as they do today in everyone's life. For this reason, this book reflects forward more than looks back: to see the experiences of the Nipmuc and the spaces in which they lived out their lives as part of a continuum in which past, present, and future are examined simultaneously. Rather than thinking of these pasts as being ruptured by colonialism, the historical processes of the past 400 years are still very much unfolding and are informed by the histories outlined in this book. The individuals who take center stage in these histories reveal experiences that were shared by millions, yet our focus is on the intimate details of individual daily lives. Whether the source of the information is material culture, historical documents, oral histories, or the detailed analysis of soil particles or plant materials such as seeds, the goal remains the same: to produce a history that reflects everyday life against a backdrop of momentous change.

## Notes

1.“Roseland Cottage (1846),” https://www.historicnewengland.org/property/roseland-cottage/ (accessed May 28, 2019).

2. “Welcome to the Quiet Corner,” http://www.visitnect.com/ (accessed May 28, 2019).

3. See DeLucia 2018 for an expanded discussion of memorialization of places in New England.

4. Royal Keith produced his deed map of Keith Hill that includes his name in 1886, etching his name permanently in the history of Grafton.

5. Gookin 1970 [1792], 49, 51.

6. Cogley 1999, 140–146; Herbster 2005, 129.

7. Gould 2005; Herbster 2005. Daniel Gookin's accounts provide rich details about the settlements he and John Eliot visited, including information about the people, buildings, and daily life of the inhabitants, all part of what he depicted as cohesive, established settlements.

8. What has traditionally been referred to as the “prehistory” (or precontact) period of

southern New England—dating back to post–ice age occupation 10,000 to 12,000 years ago—is well documented by archaeologists. See, for example, Dincauze 1968, 1976; Jones 1997, 1999, 2004; Jones and Forrest 2003; Lavin 2013; Leveillee 1999; McBride 1984, 1989, 1992; and Snow 1980. Some of this research, though, was based on excavation and analysis of Native American human remains, which is not an acceptable practice today.

9. Larned 1976 [1874], 185.

10. Larned 1976 [1874], 33–34.

11. Larned 1976 [1874], 185–186.

12. Trumbull's research (1852, 450, 474–475) noted that Wabbaquasset Indians sought refuge with the Mohegan during King Philip's War. Other connections between the Wabbaquasset and Mohegan are documented by a trip to Boston during King Philip's War by Oneko (eldest son of Mohegan sachem Uncas) and a delegation of "about 28 Indians. . . . They desired the confirmation and assurance of their ancient inheritance of land at Mohegan and Wabaquisit" (Gookin 1836 [1677], 465).

13. The 1931 *Putnam Patriot* obituary of Woodstock resident Lovan Tiffany Dixon noted that she was a Wabbaquasset Indian (Nipmuc Nation Tribal Archive; McBride and Soulsby 1986).

14. Nicholas Bellantoni and Robert Gradie, personal communications, 2005.

15. Hatchet Pond remained a popular fishing spot for Nipmuc people of the area throughout the twentieth century (Donald Gould, Nipmuc Nation Tribal Council, personal communication, 2005); Nipmuc Nation Tribal Archive.

16. Winslow 1968.

17. Correspondence by Thomas Dudley of Plymouth in 1629 and a 1632 entry in Governor John Winthrop's journal (Hoffman 1990, 237).

18. Bowden and Ronda 1980.

19. Eliot's Bible again became central to tribal cultural practices when it was used as a source to revive the Wampanoag language by linguist Jessie Little Doe Baird beginning in the 1990s. See the Wôpanâak Language Reclamation Project (2018), http://www.wlrp.org/.

20. Shurtleff, 1853–1854, 1:17. In addition, the original seal of the Massachusetts Bay Colony depicted a Native American holding a bow and arrow, uttering the phrase "COME OVER AND HELP US."

21. Copplestone 1998, 47–49.

22. Shepard 1834b, 15.

23. Boyle 1772, cited in Winslow 1968, 188.

24. In 1649 the Society for the Propagation of the Gospel in New England (also known as the SPG) was created by an act of the English Parliament to formalize and fund the Christian missionary movement in the colonies and remove the burden from the Massachusetts Bay and Plymouth colony leaders, who lacked the money or desire to take up the task. In 1660 the organization was rechartered as the Company for the Propagation of the Gospel and thereafter became known generally as the New England Company. Most historians use either "SPG" or "New England Company" to refer to the organization that funded the work of Eliot and the other seventeenth- and eighteenth-century New England missionaries; both names appear in subsequent sections of this book.

25. Copplestone 1998, 225.

26. Whitfield 1834a, 83 (first quotation), and 1834b, 170 (second quotation).
27. Gookin 1970 [1792], 37.
28. Wolf 1959.
29. Carlson 1986, 42; Mrozowski 2009.
30. Hoffman 1990, 238.
31. Cogley 1999, 61–65.
32. Cogley 1999, 5–6.
33. Cogley 1999, 6–9.
34. Stock 1924, 209.
35. Oberg 1999, 124, citing Eliot's "Strength Out of Weaknesse."
36. Lepore 1998, 24–25.
37. John Easton (1675), cited in Copplestone 1998, 249. Thomas and Matthew Mayhew led a missionary movement on the islands of Martha's Vineyard and Nantucket, but by most accounts the physical separation of the islands meant that the Wampanoag did not become involved in the later conflicts.
38. Gookin 1836 [1677], 442.
39. Lepore 1998, 45; Rowlandson 2007 [1682].
40. Gookin 1836 [1677], 450–451.
41. Indians were also interned on several other nearby islands during the war.
42. Gookin 1836 [1677], 485–486.
43. Cogley 1999, 161.
44. Lepore 1998, 140.
45. Lepore 1998, 141.
46. Gookin 1836 [1677], 518–519.
47. Mather 1967 [1702], *Magnalia Christi Americana*, 207, cited in Kellaway 1961, 121.
48. Lisa Brooks's *Our Beloved Kin* (2018) and Christine DeLucia's *Memory Lands* (2018) also contribute to more current literature focused on indigenous knowledge of the places, people, and events across New England. DeLucia also details how Eliot (and other Euroamerican men) have been memorialized over the centuries.
49. Jean O'Brien (2010) provides a comprehensive discussion of the practice of eliminating Native peoples from historical records and local memories.
50. Calloway 1994, 104–105.
51. Such as Fort Shantok in Connecticut, Fort Corchaug in New York, and Bark Wigwams, Natick, Punkapoag, and Okommakamesit in Massachusetts. See Brenner 1984; Johnson and Bradley 1987; Kelley 1999; MacCulloch 1965; Simon 1990a, 1990b; Van Lonkhuyzen 1990; and Williams 1972.
52. See Trigger 2006, 121–165.
53. See Trigger 2006, 211–313.
54. Dincauze 1968, 1976; Jones 1997, 1999, 2004; Jones and Forrest 2003; Lavin 2013; Leveillee 1999; McBride 1984, 1989; and Snow 1980.
55. Bendremer 1993; Bragdon 1996; Fitzhugh 1985; McBride 1992.
56. On temporality, see Bergson 1999 [1922].
57. See Schmidt and Mrozowski 2013.
58. Acculturation theory has been debunked and rejected for its obvious connections to a

particular European historical narrative whose legitimacy is dependent upon a narrative of indigenous extinction (see Schmidt and Mrozowski 2013).

59. See Schmidt and Mrozowski 2013.

60. For more information on the Blackstone River Valley, see John H. Chafee Blackstone River Valley: History & Culture (2019), https://www.nps.gov/blac/learn/historyculture/index.htm.

61. Summarized in Bragdon 1996.

62. Buckley and Nixon 2001.

63. Bragdon 1996; Buckley and Nixon 2001.

64. Prude 1999.

65. Bragdon 1996.

66. Bagley et al. 2015.

67. Bagley 2013; Bagley et al. 2015.

68. Sassaman 2006, 2010, 2016; Sassaman and Brookes 2017.

69. Sassaman 2016; Sassman and Brookes 2017.

70. See Sassaman 2010, 199–206.

# 3

## The Archaeology of Magunkaquog

STEPHEN A. MROZOWSKI

Magunkaquog was the seventh of what would eventually be fourteen Nipmuc praying towns recognized by the Massachusetts General Court at the request of John Eliot (see Figure 1.1). The descriptions of these communities provided by Eliot and Daniel Gookin published in 1674 provide some detail of the individual settlements before their daily lives were violently upended by King Philip's War. Magunkaquog is described as a community of between fifty and sixty "souls" led by Pomhaman, whom Gookin described as being "a sober and active man and pious." The Native American teacher for the community was named Job.[1] Eliot and Gookin's descriptions often depict the praying towns as small communities of several families who lived in English-style dwellings, walked English-style streets, and gathered in English-style meeting houses that served both as schools and places of religious worship.[2] As Herbster outlines in more detail in Chapter 4, the residents of Magunkaquog were removed to Deer Island in Boston Harbor at the height of King Philip's War in 1675 and remained there until the conclusion of the conflict in 1676. Two years later, Magunkaquog reappears in the documentary record in a report resulting from a Mohawk raid there in 1678 that involved the forced removal of twenty-two women and children (see Chapter 4). In its complaint to New York colonial authorities, the Massachusetts General Court requested that all captives be returned and the Mohawk raiders be punished. In their own defense the Mohawk noted that the residents of Magunkaquog had "a Castell so well fortiyed with Stockadoes," which they interpreted as evidence of the settlement's warlike posture.[3]

These documented references to the history of Magunkaquog and other praying towns provided virtually no clues concerning the actual location of the settlements; for more than a generation archaeologists of New England searched in vain for them. On three occasions over the past fifty years Native American graves had been disturbed by construction in Natick, Punkapoag (today Canton, Massachusetts) and Okommakamesit (now Marlboro, Massachusetts). During that same period no archaeological evidence of the actual settlements was ever encountered. Using historical references, descriptions by Eliot and Gookin, and the latest techniques designed to locate archaeological sites, a group of well-educated, highly competent scholars found absolutely no evidence of any of the communities they were looking for, including Magunkaquog.[4] One of the heavily investigated areas was Magunco Hill in Ashland, Massachusetts. Despite the seemingly obvious connection to the seventeenth-century Magunakaquog settlement, no archaeological findings were made there.

After more than a decade of continuously looking for these praying towns, archaeologists began to ask how it was possible that they could not be found. They focused on two hypotheses. The first was that the descriptions provided by Eliot and Gookin were completely false or at least heavily embellished. The second was that the lifestyle of Native inhabitants of communities such as Natick, Hassanamisco, and Magunkaquog resulted in them living in these settlements only on a seasonal basis. Each of these ideas had some merit, but the main reason archaeologists failed to find these settlements was because they were being overly influenced by depictions provided by Eliot and Gookin.

Some degree of change ultimately resulted in the first archaeological evidence of one of the sites. In the late 1990s, during the construction of a housing development on Magunco Hill in Ashland, Massachusetts (known as Apple Ridge), state approval required an archaeological survey to be conducted. During that work in 1996 members of the Public Archaeology Laboratory (PAL) in Pawtucket, Rhode Island, discovered what they thought might be part of the seventeenth-century town of Magunkaquog.[5] After systematically surveying the entire area of the development, PAL archaeologists recovered a small concentration of English material culture dated to roughly the third quarter of the seventeenth century, precisely the period when Magunkaquog would have been a praying town. After being asked to look at the artifacts PAL archaeologists had recovered, I was fairly confident that the assemblage, while small, did indeed date to that period. In addition to the artifacts, PAL identified two nearby wells that were still visible on the landscape. Eventually the developer and PAL could not agree on a way to protect the archaeological remains or provide for their proper excavation, so he chose instead not to develop the area immediately surrounding the location where the artifacts had been recovered. Fortunately for the developer, the area that PAL had identified was fairly circumscribed (about one acre) so he could move forward with the rest of the construction without destroying what proved to be an amazingly important archaeological site.

Although PAL archaeologists could not prove that they had found part of the Magunkaquog settlement, the discovery of mid-seventeenth-century material culture on the eastern slope of Magunco Hill suggested that they were correct. In 1996 the Massachusetts state archaeologist, Brona Simon, asked me whether I would be interested in excavating the site that PAL had uncovered as part of an archaeological field school. Although doing so involved a much slower excavation process than is normally the case when professional archaeology firms such as PAL carry out the work, it provided the developer with a no-cost alternative to have the research completed. After meeting with the developer, who was amenable to this arrangement, it was decided that I would carry out excavations during the summers of 1997 and 1998. Additional excavations were carried out in fall of 1998. The Magunkaquog Project became one of the first projects carried out by the newly established (1996) Center for Cultural and Environmental History at the University of Massachusetts Boston. In 1999 the center was renamed the Andrew Fiske Memorial Center for Archaeological Research, which has continued the kind of heritage-based archaeology that involved UMass in the Magunkaquog project in the first place.

During the two summers of excavation on Magunco Hill much of the work involved uncovering the remains of a dry-laid stone foundation along with a rich array of artifacts, substantiating the claim that the building remains represented the "meeting house" of the seventeenth-century Magunkaquog settlement (Figure 3.1). At first our excavations focused on the area where PAL had recovered the seventeenth-century materials and two wells. This quickly established that the wells were constructed during the nineteenth century and therefore not related to the site's earlier occupation. However, the area where PAL recovered seventeenth-century material proved to be a foundation set without mortar and not large by modern-day standards, approximately 12 by 9 feet (4.3 × 3 meters). It was not symmetrical in form and included an apparent footing for a round or crescent-shaped structure that was an extension of the foundation's western wall, which raised the question of whether this could have supported a small tower of some kind that would have been viewed as a defensive work by the Mohawk.

Two musket balls recovered from the site suggest that some sort of engage-

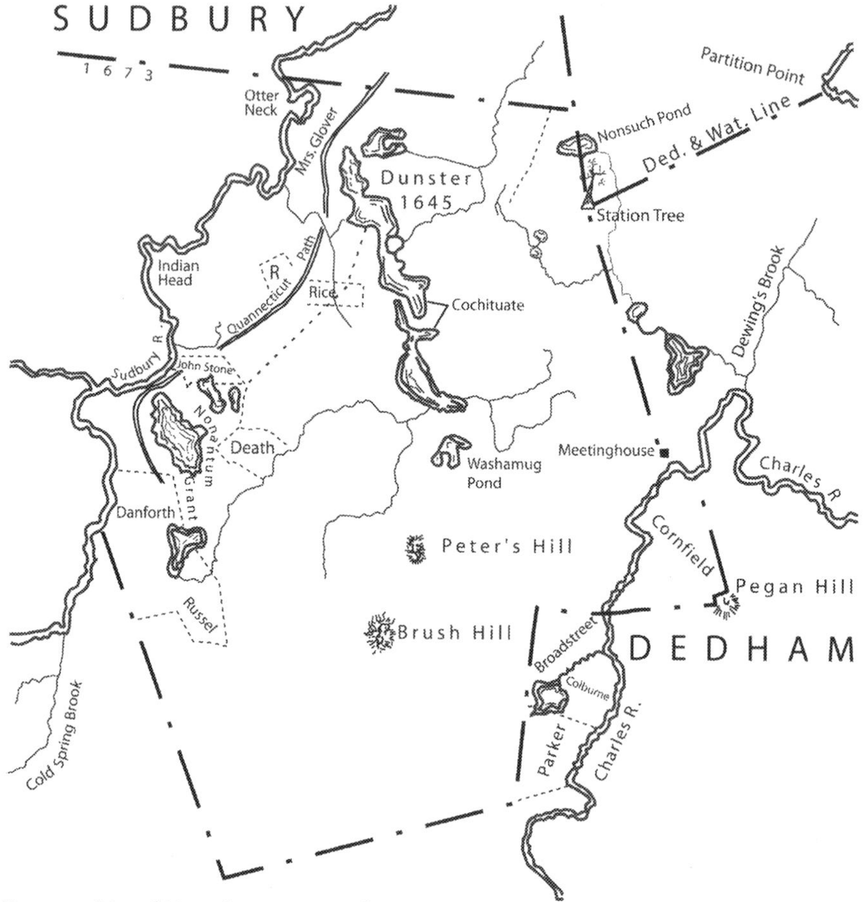

Figure 3.1. Map of Magunkaquog, Massachusetts, area.

ment may have taken place here. Both of the balls were cut in half. Archaeologists who specialize in weapons analysis suggest that the purposeful alteration of balls was so they might inflict the greatest human damage.[6] While we may never know for sure whether these artifacts are linked directly to the conflict described in the 1678 documents, it seems highly probable given the site's location on the slope of Magunco Hill and the preponderance of artifacts dating to the very period of the Mohawk raid. This last point is important for two reasons. First, it confirms that Magunkaquog residents returned to the settlement after King Philip's War and that the structure found on Magunco Hill is very likely the meeting or "fair house" for the Magunkaquog settlement the Mohawks raided in 1678.

## The Foundation and Building

It took two full seasons to uncover the complete remains of the foundation. When completed, excavations revealed the entire foundation of the building and portions of its yard (Figure 3.2a). It appears that the foundation was purposely built into the eastern slope of Magunco Hill so that its western wall could serve as a windbreak, while the eastern wall probably held an entry/exit point from the building's cellar. A very similar construction method was used at the Burnee/Boston site as well (see Chapter 5). The Magunco Hill foundation was a mixture of fairly large boulders that formed much of the lowest course of stones. Most of those uncovered during excavations were rather rounded and in some instances appear to have been purposely placed on their sides. These bottom stones were most likely augmented by smaller, flatter stones (often referred to as shims) used to form flat surfaces for the wooden sills that were the bottom-most frame of the building.

Despite the presence of numerous iron kettle fragments and an iron spit hook for cooking meats, no evidence of an interior hearth existed. Although traces of ash and charcoal were seen in the soil fill of the foundation and embedded in the floor, no evidence of either a brick or stone chimney base like those common in English dwellings of the period was found. Based on the orientation of the foundation and its placement on the down slope of Magunco Hill, the building that it supported may have been a single story with a cellar that emptied into a lower yard. Given the size of the foundation and some of the larger boulders used in its construction, it may have consisted of a cellar, first floor, and loft (similar to the original Cisco Homestead discussed in Chapter 7). Much of the material culture associated with the foundation was recovered from inside the structure or immediately down the eastern slope area.

John Eliot described the "fair house" at Natick as a gathering place for community worship and the main residence of the Native teacher, as well as a place where Eliot or Gookin might spend the night when they visited. He also mentioned that each community was given a common stock of tools and other items for its use, which were stored in the fair house. The spatially tight distribution of material items across the landscape at Magunkaquog suggests a building consistent with this description, but it is difficult to know precisely what the building looked like.

Iron artifacts recovered from the foundation included some 1,200 nails as well as pieces of building hardware that provide a hint of the building's appearance.

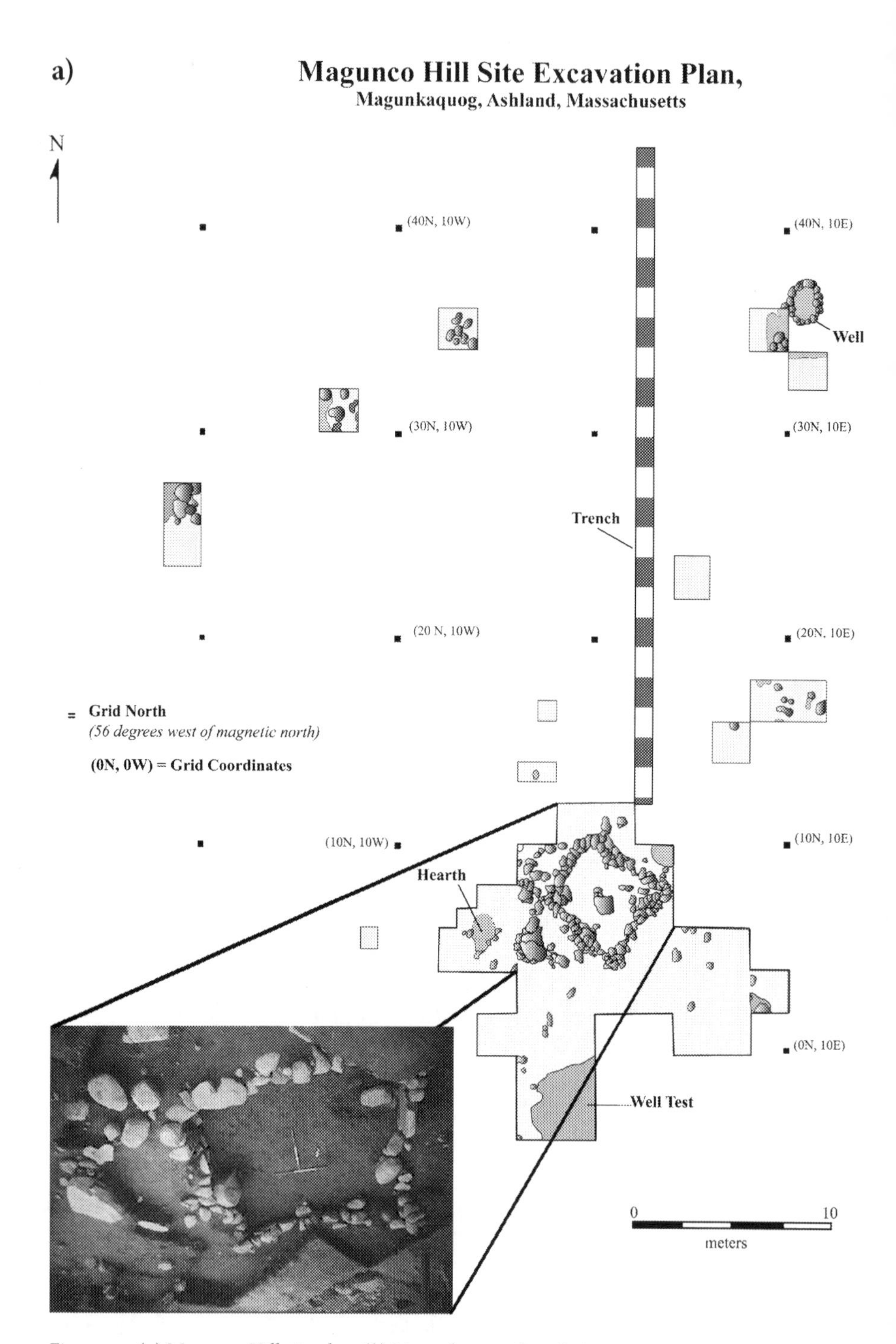


Figure 3.2. (*a*) Magunco Hill site plan; (*b*) Magunkaquog foundation map.

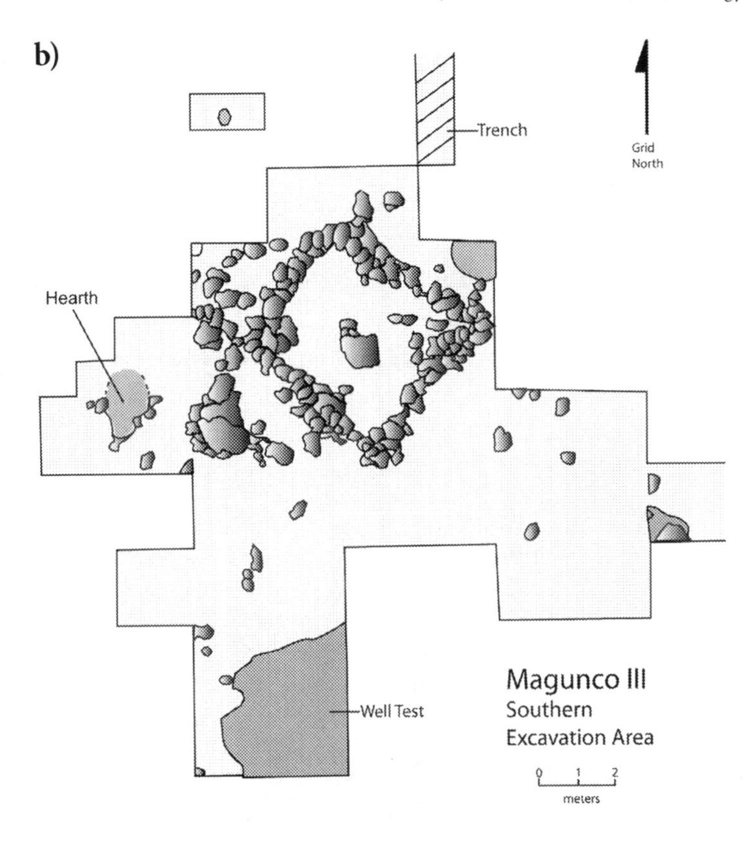


Virtually all of the nails were recovered from excavation units within the foundation and were hand-wrought, commonly used during both the seventeenth and eighteenth centuries. In addition to the nails, building hardware included three strap hinges that would have been part of the door(s) for the structure. An iron building staple used to bolster either a door or a window frame was also recovered from inside the foundation. Although no lock parts were found at the site, a key was recovered, consistent in size with a door key. An iron latch hook used to keep the door open was also found.

More than a thousand fragments of window glass were recovered from excavations of foundation. Although many of these were rather small, their thickness and distinctive bluish color are consistent with the type used in seventeenth-century buildings. Window glass was found in virtually all of the excavation units placed in and around the foundation, with 90 percent of the material from units along the northeastern wall or the yard area immediately downslope of where the building would have stood. This not only confirms that the building had windows but also suggests that the structure fell or was pulled to the east and downslope of the foundation when it collapsed or was torn down.

Beyond the foundation, no notable features (such as pits or postholes from other structures) were found in this area. The rounded extension along the southwestern wall of the foundation may well have supported a towerlike structure, as noted earlier, but no evidence of the stockade mentioned by the Mohawks who raided the site was found.

The only true archaeological feature outside the foundation was a fairly large hearth that contained animal bone, charcoal, and several large quartz cobbles that appear to have been purposely heated to aid with the extraction of crystals. Sixteen such crystals (Figure 3.3) were recovered from the foundation area, including three that were probably purposely buried in the structure's corners.[7] The same practice has more recently been discovered in an eighteenth-century Mohegan foundation in Connecticut by Craig Cipolla and James Quinn, archaeologists for the Mohegan Tribe.[8] According to John Murphy (2002), who

Figure 3.3. Stone crystals from the Magunkaquog foundation.

examined the quartz collection from Magunkaquog for his master's thesis, there is strong archaeological evidence of the spiritual importance of quartz crystals among the indigenous populations of southern New England for at least 4,000 years. In fact, evidence suggests that quartz crystals hold religious importance for indigenous populations throughout the Americas. Therefore the discovery of the crystals in the foundation at Magunkaquog suggests that their presence was part of religious practices widely known throughout North, Central, and South America for thousands of years.[9]

## Phosphate Analysis

In addition to the excavation results, soil samples were collected and analyzed to determine the levels of phosphates captured in the dirt. Most soils contain phosphates: a set of chemical tests reveals whether the percentage of phosphates is higher than normal. Higher phosphates can be attributed to a variety of factors, but archaeologists have found correlations between the presence of more phosphates and the density of organic materials associated with human occupation, such as food remains and human or animal waste. The phosphate analysis for Magunkaquog was completed by Paul Mohler (another UMass Boston graduate student), who compared his results from Magunkaquog with those of three other known colonial-era domestic sites. He found that most of the soils surrounding the foundation on Magunco Hill did not contain unusually high phosphate concentrations.[10] In fact, most of the samples from in and around the foundation were similar to the surrounding yard area and beyond.

In two areas, however, higher phosphates were recorded; the highest phosphate levels were within the foundation, with the second highest from the area of a hearth immediately outside the foundation (Figure 3.2a and b). The locations with high phosphates also had the highest concentrations of animal bone at the site. The combined results of the phosphate analysis indicate that food remains were one source of the higher phosphate levels and that the exterior hearth appears to have served as a cooking and possibly eating area.

## Material Culture

While the foundation on Magunco Hill was itself both interesting and informative, the large collection of associated material culture was particularly illuminating. Several classes of material culture were recovered from the site.

In pure numbers, the ceramics were easily the most numerous: more than 6,600 sherds that represent close to 50 percent of all artifacts from the site. Despite these numbers, fewer actual vessels were represented than might have been anticipated. The ceramics included interior-glazed, red earthenwares used for both cooking and food preparation. Other earthenwares included a North Devon Plain milk pan, the earliest English-manufactured artifact recovered from the site (dating to 1625–1660). Fragments of a seventeenth-century tin-glazed, buff-bodied plate were also recovered as well as later buff-bodied midlands slipwares from Staffordshire sometimes referred to as "combed slipwares" (the name stems from the manufacturing process of using a comb to facilitate the mixing of still liquid red-bodied paste with the white kaolin slip layered over the body) (Figure 3.4). Drinking vessels of the same ware type

Figure 3.4. Staffordshire ceramic artifacts recovered from the Magunkaquog site.

Figure 3.5. Fulham stoneware jar from the Magunkaquog site.

were also recovered, as well as a small collection of English and German stoneware vessels used for food storage. These included the remains of an almost intact Fulham stoneware jar (Figure 3.5) and a German stoneware bottle. Both of these vessels would have served well for storing liquids or milk products. The ceramic assemblage also included the remains of two white-saltglazed stoneware vessels, which are clearly later and date from 1720 to 1775. The remaining ceramics included a single Chinese porcelain plate that dates to the period 1685–1730.

As a group, these ceramics look remarkably similar to those recovered several decades ago from cemeteries associated with the "praying town" period of Natick, Punkapoag, and Okommakamesit. Although excavating Native American cemeteries is not an acceptable practice today unless conducted under the guidance of tribes, excavations conducted decades ago do provide information about earlier lifeways. The actual interments found in Okommakamesit contained no accompanying material culture. The Natick and Punkapoag cemeteries did contain objects purposely buried with the individuals. When they are compared with the material recovered from Magunco Hill, the similarities are startling. Virtually identical combed-slipware vessels were found in the Magunkaquog, Natick, and Punkapoag assemblages, suggesting that they came from a common source (John Eliot) who received support from English benefactors in the form of such goods.[11] This assertion is also supported by documentary evidence that Eliot was requesting and receiving shipments of English goods for the Native communities he worked with. These are assumed to be part of the "common stock to lend one as well as another, that no man my sit idle, or loose a days wrk for want of a tool," as Eliot noted in his descriptions of the praying towns.[12]

Beyond the ceramics, other rich classes of material culture were recovered at Magunkaquog. Before discussing them I want to point out something about the ceramics that was highly important to the overall interpretation of the site. It is difficult to determine precisely how the various ceramic vessels were actually used for preparing food around the meeting house. Little physical evidence exists on the ceramics themselves to provide clues regarding how they may have functioned. One approach would be to assume that the English and the Nipmuc naturally shared an understanding of their uses, but evidence suggests otherwise. It is here that examples of Nipmuc identity and cultural practice surface in this collection.

One example is red-paste earthenwares with intense charring. The vessel in Figure 3.6 was known as a butter pot and could have served as such, but it could have also served as an all-purpose food preparation vessel. The exterior of the vessel from Magunkaquog was blackened in a way that indicates it was placed directly on a fire, a practice common among Native Americans but not among the English. Postcolonial theorists refer to such practices as examples of "cultural inversion," when an item introduced by colonizers is used differently by colonized populations. In this instance a ceramic not designed to be placed directly on a fire was used in a way consistent with Native American practices at Magunkaquog.

Despite the overall richness of the archaeological assemblage from Magunkaquog, the evidence suggests a sparsely furnished interior. Many of the metal artifacts, for example, appear to have been stored in the building. Some of these are related to activities that could have been carried out within the building or its surrounding yard while others hint at the presence of both horses and oxen that probably grazed freely in the surrounding area. Of particular note are elements of a bridle and harness ornament consistent with

Figure 3.6. Charred redware from the Magunkaquog site.

horse furniture (Figure 3.7). A small fragment of what could be a curry comb also suggests the care of horses.

In his description of Magunkaquog in 1674 Daniel Gookin noted the presence of cattle and pigs. Ample evidence of horse and oxen shoes was recovered there. Oxen have a cleft hoof, so their shoes were worn in pairs: each animal needs eight shoes. Horses only need single shoes for each hoof. In her analysis of the iron materials from Magunkaquog, Nadia Waski has found that many of the oxen shoes show evidence of wear.[13] Given that Eliot and Gookin visited the settlement and traveled by horseback, the presence of horse-related items may suggest activities related to the care of horses and oxen, consistent with the kinds of work that Eliot encouraged among the praying town Natives.

In addition to the animal-related items, evidence of individual pieces of

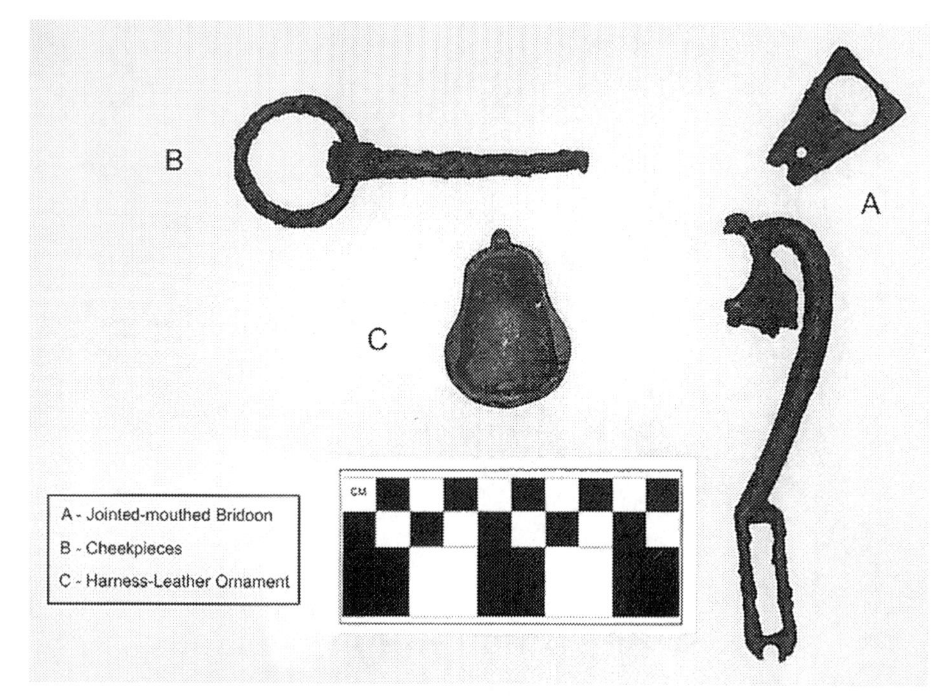


Figure 3.7. Horse hardware from the Magunkaquog site.

furniture that may have been used in the building exists at Magunkaquog. These include a set of curtain rings, a set of drawer pulls, and daisy-decorated escutcheon plates as well as a set of chair tacks also decorated with flowers (Figure 3.8). The curtain rings are most likely from a bed, whether it was free-standing or built into the structure of the building. In any case, the presence of curtain rings clearly communicates a concern for privacy. It is not clear whether this reflects the building's use by Pomhaman or Job, both of whom may have visited other communities, or whether the furniture was primarily for use by English visitors. Descriptions of the fair house at Natick suggest that it served as a gathering and teaching place where much of the English material culture provided for the community was stored. Eliot emphasized the need for the Native residents of Natick to learn to share a common stock of tools and most likely animals, such as oxen. This suggests that a combination of household furnishings and tools used in a variety of activities might be found within a structure such as the building on Magunco Hill.[14]

The collection of furniture-related items evokes a picture of a rather Spar-

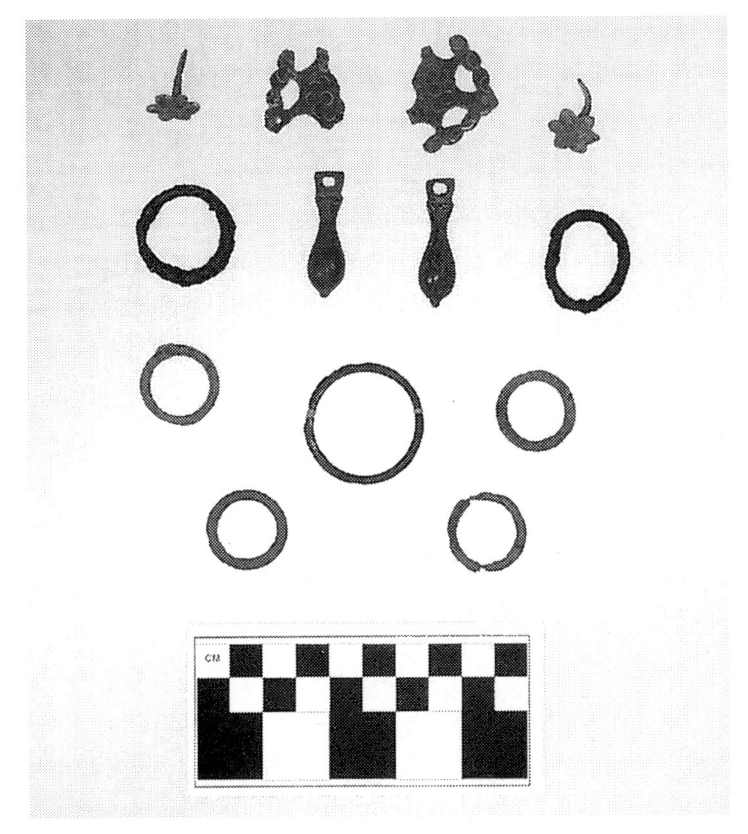


Figure 3.8. Furniture hardware from the Magunkaquog site.

tan interior. In addition to the bed curtain rings, the remaining objects may indicate the presence of individual furniture pieces. The tear-dropped shaped drawer pulls may have been paired with the daisy-decorated escutcheon plates as parts of a small chest.

The similarly decorated chair tacks would have been used as part of a leather or fabric-covered chair, creating a picture of a single, modestly outfitted room available to Eliot or Gookin during their visits. The historical record is relatively silent on just how often Eliot and Gookin visited the praying towns, but given the number of communities (a total of fourteen by 1675), it is quite possible that they maintained a fairly regular schedule of visits to a number of towns. This is important to keep in mind. One way of interpreting the building and its uses is to imagine it as a place where daily activities were conducted by the community and its leaders. During Eliot's visits, however, the building would have served as a good illustration of the Native community's desire to present a picture of the "English ways" they were learning as part of their larger training in Christian practice.

The artifacts recovered from inside and around the foundation indicate that some of the activities that may have been part of this education in English ways. In addition to the possible evidence of horse and oxen care already mentioned, a small but noteworthy collection of thimbles and buttons was also found (Figure 3.9). Sewing, including the making and mending of clothing, was women's work in English society, just as in Native society. Perhaps the most obvious examples of artifacts related to clothing are the numerous buttons recovered from the site. Buttons were sometimes made of bone or wood in the seventeenth and eighteenth centuries, but more often than not they were metal. Such was the case at Magunkaquog, where buttons made of iron, copper, lead, and pewter were recovered. Most of the buttons were round, flat disks that would have been covered by fabric. No fabric remains were recovered, but the variety of materials (four types of metal) suggests at least four different articles of clothing and possibly more.

One of the challenges of interpreting buttons is that it is not clear whether they were associated with particular articles of clothing or whether their pres-

Figure 3.9. Thimble, scissors, and button artifacts from the Magunkaquog site.

ence is linked to sewing activities at the meeting house. Obviously these interpretations are not mutually exclusive, but a closer examination of the buttons suggests the first of these two interpretations. Many of the buttons recovered from Magunkaquog appear to be from clothing associated with men, including coat, waistcoat, and breeches buttons. Most of the buttons are round with eyes attached and vary in size, suggesting that they were used both for breast and sleeve buttons. A small number of rectangular buttons, probably from men's coats, were also found.

In addition to the buttons, a few iron, brass, and copper buckles appear to be knee buckles for men's breeches (because of their size). No shoe buckles were recovered from the site, but this is not unusual: they only became popular during the eighteenth century. Seven of the eight identified buckles recovered from the site are clearly knee buckles. Three of these are made of iron, three of copper, and one of brass. All of the buckles are either square or rectangular in shape except for one oval iron example that had the remnants of two tines. A complete square iron buckle could be either a harness or belt buckle. Given the presence of other animal-related items, it is likely that this artifact was associated with a horse or oxen harness.

In addition to the buttons and buckles recovered from the site, along with the small assemblage of thimbles is a fragment of iron scissors. Three of the ten thimble artifacts show obvious traces of use wear. The others show no evidence of use, suggesting that they could be part of the "common stock" given to the praying towns. Based on their characteristics the thimbles appear to be seventeenth-century examples, possibly linked to education of Native American women. Some sewing would have been done alone, but it was also a group activity, so it is very possible that women from Magunkaquog gathered at the meeting house to work.

## Metal Artifacts

Several metal artifacts were recovered during the excavations on Magunco Hill. Some of these have already been described, including building and furniture hardware, animal-related items, and the clothing items. In addition, a number of interesting iron tools were identified. Two barrel hoop fragments suggest the presence of wooden vessels such as barrels, but it is difficult to know precisely how large these might have been. Several examples of knife blades were also recovered from the site, including part of a folding knife similar to a modern-day jackknife. Another small blade resembling those seen on penknives could have been used for a whole host of activities, from cutting up fruits and vegetables to working with wood. Also recovered was a blade from a draw knife, used by English settlers to shape wooden shingles and by Native basket makers. Part of an axe head with a rounded (rather than square) back was found, suggesting that it most likely dates to the seventeenth century. This artifact could have been used for any number of purposes.

The other major category of iron artifacts consists of numerous iron kettle fragments found over the widest area of the site. Based on the fragments recovered, the kettle forms were most likely those commonly found in most English colonial homes. The fragments also suggest the presence of at least one large and one small kettle at the site. A spit hook and an iron cooking pot handle (likely from a Dutch oven) suggest that cooking occurred there as well. The lack of an interior hearth implies that most cooking occurred outside the structure, which might explain the wide distribution of kettle fragments.

Bone recovered from the site provides additional evidence of both food preparation and consumption. Most of the 334 bone fragments were difficult to identify down to the species level because the bone was shattered and split, suggestive of Native cooking practices. Based on the combined evidence, it seems safe to say that the community and its visitors dined on beef, pork, sheep/goat, deer, and turtle and may have had at least one cow for milking. Deer and turtle were commonly eaten by the indigenous peoples of New England, and by the mid- to late seventeenth century European domestic animals were also being consumed. The exterior hearth and kettle fragments could indicate communal or seasonal eating, but it is difficult to say for sure.

In her analysis of Magunkaquog metals Nadia Waski concluded that none of the items were altered or repurposed for something other than their culturally subscribed use in English society.[15] In fact, as a whole the assemblage seems to conform to the kinds of tools and domestic items that John Eliot provided as "common stock" to the various praying towns. He wanted these items kept in a central location so that they would not be lost or traded away. The assemblage also reinforces the notion that the meeting or fair house was both a repository for these items and an area where they could be used by indigenous men and women to learn the English domestic arts that Eliot wanted them to emulate. When compared with other classes of material culture from the site, the metal items tend to mask the presence of Native actors, while others provide strong testimony of their continuing cultural practices.

## Glass

Although the assemblage of glass is small, it is informative on several levels. The remains of only three spirit/wine bottles were recovered from the site, which may well reflect the sobriety alluded to by Eliot in his description of Pomhaman, the Magunkaquog community leader. The bottles themselves date to the 1720s to 1730s, in the postwar era and after the death of Eliot in 1690. The praying towns that survived King Philip's War remained active after Eliot died, but Magunkaquog seems to have ceased to be active by the time much of the land was purchased by Henry Frankland in 1749 (see Chapter 4). One of the noteworthy facets of the bottle glass recovered from the site is that it was used to make tools. Figure 3.10 provides a close-up of three bottle glass flakes fashioned into what some archaeologists call instant tools (quickly made or resharpened blades that could be used for virtually anything). Like the butter pot used directly on the fire and the quartz crystals, these glass tools represent a continuity of practice: in this instance, Native lithic tool production and use with a new material (also discussed in Chapter 5). This joining of tradition and novelty reflects both the strength and vibrancy of

Figure 3.10. Flaked bottle glass pieces from the Magunkaquog site.

Magunkaquog cultural practices, indicating a community in which long-standing cultural practices mixed with new religious ideas and economic activities.

## Pipes

In English society smoking tobacco and drinking alcohol were commonly shared activities, especially in the taverns that served as gathering places where food, drink, and tobacco facilitated political dialogue. Smoking tobacco is, of course, a long-standing Native American practice, yet it differed from English and European practices that incorporated the rapid and widespread use of tobacco as a recreational stimulation. In Native societies smoking had more spiritual and ritual significance. Although it seems that English and Dutch pipes were popular with Native smokers, it is likely that smoking and drinking did not necessarily go together in indigenous society, at least not in the same way as in English or European society. A recent analysis of the pipes and bottle and drinking vessel glass from the Burnee/Boston Homestead site (see Chapter 5) indicates that smoking and drinking were not taking place in the same parts of the home lot and that smoking did not necessarily occur during daily activities. This same analysis suggests that a similar pattern of pipe use occurred at Magunkaquog.

A total of 675 white kaolin pipe stem and bowl fragments was recovered from the site. Most of these came from within the foundation itself, but pipe remains were found over the site as a whole, unlike evidence of other classes of material culture. Several examples of complete pipe bowls with partially broken stems were recovered. Historical archaeologists often use pipes for dating purposes. Based on a combination of bore-stem sizes and datable bowl types, the pipe artifacts suggest a long period of use from the mid-seventeenth century to the late eighteenth century. The latter examples most likely postdate the Magunkaquog settlement, but it is difficult to say for sure. Some artifacts also postdate the assumed end of the settlement, circa 1749, with others clearly dated to the seventeenth century. Given these factors, the large collection of pipe stems and bowls probably indicates Native American tobacco use consistent with indigenous cultural practices, but it is also possible that the site was visited by Euroamericans between the mid-eighteenth and mid-nineteenth centuries when two wells were constructed and Native occupation had dwindled.

## Gunflints and Other Lithic Artifacts

One of the most informative classes of artifacts recovered from the site included gunflints and other lithic materials. Gunflints are common finds at colonial-period archaeological sites. Most were made from either English or European flint (which were both recovered from the site). A small collection of quartz gunflints was also recovered, which the late Barbara Luedtke analyzed (focusing on the lithic technologies and production processes). In most instances European gunflints show very little evidence of reuse. They are often skillfully and consistently made, but with virtually no evidence of additional primary or secondary flaking (such as reworking the edge). Magunco Hill lithics were clearly reworked and have evidence of intensive reuse (Figure 3.11).

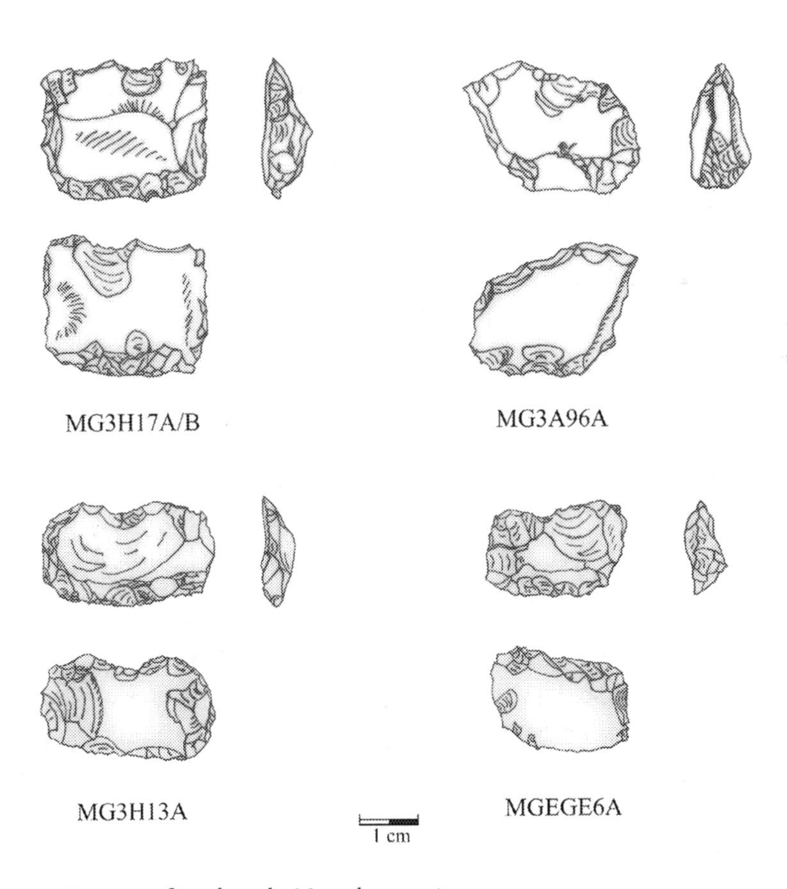


Figure 3.11. Quartz gunflints from the Magunkaquog site.

Luedtke interpreted these characteristics as consistent with the production and use practices of Native American New Englanders.[16] She also felt that the Native users appreciated the qualities of English and European flints, evidenced by the reworking of items. Repeated episodes of retouching and resharpening illustrate the value placed on these materials.[17]

The quartz gunflints were an unusual find in that they illustrated production practices consistent with the scrapers made by indigenous peoples of New England for thousands of years. Here again, the melding of cultural practices was an earmark of life for Magunkaquog residents. A collection of lithic debitage also suggests that stone working could have been taking place around the meeting house. The remains of quartz cobbles that were being heated and recovered from the hearth near the foundation provide further evidence of such practices on the site. Some of the debitage may date to an earlier Native occupation, as also found at Hassanamesit (see Chapter 5), and a connection between the location of the foundation and access to these materials may have existed. In fact, the presence of quartz crystals and quartz more generally may be linked to what are perhaps best conceived as religious practices linked to the establishment of settlements. Finally, evidence of indigenous practices provides further support for the underlying interpretation of the structure as being associated with the praying-era Magunkaquog settlement.

## Discussion

The rich artifact assemblage and foundation remains at this site evoke a number of images. It is difficult to avoid seeing the events surrounding King Philip's War and its aftermath as something of a disjuncture in the otherwise daily lives of the Native residents of Magunkaquog. The material culture recovered indicates that the building and its surrounding yard were most heavily in use between 1669 (during the period of the praying towns and adoption of English material culture) and approximately 1730. The few later materials recovered—from later stages of the eighteenth century and then again around the mid-nineteenth century—do not suggest reuse of the site, except possibly as a landscape feature in a pasture that made use of the well. The discussion of the 1678 Mohawk raid and references to a structure like a "castle" in combination with evidence of the foundation and material culture strongly suggest that the community had been resettled after the war and

Deer Island imprisonment. Despite the documentary evidence that Harvard College purchased the greater Magunco lands around 1719 (see Chapter 4), the evidence of worked early eighteenth-century bottle glass, along with other Native cultural practices, points to a continuation of Native use possibly as late as 1749.

Combined evidence suggests that the building on Magunco Hill was the meeting or fair house for the Magunkaquog settlement. Given the large concentration of material culture that is virtually identical to the artifact assemblages from known "praying Indian" cemeteries, it seems that the building served as a storage point for "common stock" given to praying towns by John Eliot. The large collection of domestic material culture, including both furniture elements and food-related artifacts (such as ceramics, iron kettles, glassware, and faunal material), is consistent with a domestic structure. Furniture pieces (a small chest and bed curtain rings) indicate the building served as a living space for community leaders and/or visitors such as John Eliot and Daniel Gookin or other colonial officials. Visitors would have come on horseback, so the presence of horse furniture makes additional sense.

We will probably never know precisely how events unfolded at Magunkaquog, but the artifacts and building remains evoke an image of a community and space involved in a coming together of English material culture and religious practices with Native cultural practices that were themselves a mix of old and new ways. I think that the building did indeed serve as the meeting place for the community to gather for any number of activities. These probably ranged from regular or sporadic Sunday worship that could have included meals to gatherings to hear from Eliot or other religious teachers from other Native communities to daily work groups focused on tasks like sewing. The journey to Magunkaquog from Cambridge or Boston would have necessitated that visitors spend at least one evening in the community, but possibly more. Care for horses would have been part of this arrangement. The high levels of soil phosphate from within the foundation suggest that animals could have been housed in the cellar of the building. Soil phosphate analysis indicates that the foundation was one of the few areas of the site where higher than normal phosphate levels were recovered. High phosphates also found in the animal bone concentration indicate possible cooking and eating outside the meeting house.

Such cooking and eating was just one example of Native cultural practices continuing past the era of King Philip's War. The use of butter pots for cooking directly on the fire, the use of spent bottle glass for making tools, and the presence of quartz crystals in and around the foundation all indicate that Native identity remained strong and flexible enough to accept new technologies into daily cultural practices. This strong Native identity also seems to have allowed Christian religious teachings to be adopted not as a break with older practices but as a continuation. The results of our investigations suggest that everything the Nipmuc did during these years of transformation involved accepting new ideas and technologies in lives that were expressed and interpreted along familiar lines of practice. Through its life as a place for gathering, teaching, and sharing, the meeting house on Magunco Hill was a dynamic space at a dynamic moment in history.

King Philip's War was a devastating conflict. Despite the stated desire of many "praying Indian" leaders to remain neutral in the conflict, many Nipmuc joined with Philip. The conflict had a long shadow, straining relations between English and Native peoples of southern New England beyond reconciliation. Yet it seems that the residents of Magunkaquog returned to their home after the war and continued to live in the area as more and more English colonists migrated to New England. The archaeology of the building on Magunco Hill is a testament to a continuing indigenous presence and cultural practices. Although the evidence indicates that use of the site by Native Americans probably ended sometime between 1730 and 1750, the history of the praying Indian communities did not end when the remains of the building fell back into the earth. We are well aware that our work disrupts a quiet peace, but it also brings histories back into the consciousness of today's world. That is the paramount goal of any archaeology.

## Notes

1. Gookin (1970) [1792], 78–79.
2. Eliot 1671, 1834, 1846, 1865, 1882a, 1882b; Eliot and Mayhew 1834; Gookin 1970 [1792], 1836 [1677].
3. Fernow 1881, 528; Shurtleff 1853–1854, 199–200.
4. Brenner 1980, 1984, 1986; Carlson 1986.
5. Garman and Herbster 1996; Mrozowski et al. 2009.
6. Valosin 2016, 215.
7. Murphy 2002; Mrozowski et al. 2009.
8. Cipolla and Quinn 2016.
9. Mrozowski 2013.

10. Mohler 2000.
11. See Mrozowski 2009.
12. Eliot 1882b, 294.
13. Nadia Waski, personal communication, 2017.
14. See Eliot 1882b; Gookin 1970 [1792].
15. Nadia Waski, personal communication, 2017.
16. Luedtke 1999a and 1999b.
17. See Mrozowski et al. 2009.

# 4

# The Documentary Archaeology of Magunkaquog

HOLLY HERBSTER

In October 1669 John Eliot petitioned the Massachusetts General Court to grant land "to a company of new praying Indians . . . set down in the western corner of Natick bounds called Magwonkkomok." This group, composed of "some Nipmuck Indians who [had] left their own places,"[1] formed the seventh praying town in Massachusetts.

Throughout the remainder of the seventeenth and into the early eighteenth century Magunkaquog was mentioned occasionally in legal records, published broadsides, private letters, and religious treatises. Located midway between the first and largest praying town at Natick and a large Native settlement at Hassanamesit, Magunkaquog likely existed as a largely self-sufficient gathering of approximately fifty-five Native Americans associated with the neighboring Natick community (see Figure 1.1).

In 1715 the Trustees of Harvard University entered into an agreement with the Indian proprietors at Natick to purchase the Magunkaquog lands. After securing permission from the General Court, the deed was signed by seven Native men. Harvard trustee and Indian commissioner Samuel Sewall recorded the transaction, writing that he "went to Natick and finished the purchase of Maguncoog and Donations were distributed to the Indians to their great satisfaction."[2] Sewall's description suggests that the Magunkaquog sale was acceptable to both groups and proceeded like many other standard land transactions of the period.

The documentary record is not limited to this description, however, and suggests that the sale was much more controversial. One month prior to the October deed signing, fifteen Native men had written to Sewall saying, "we are boor indias we are nto will to sal our landes or to debate with it any ways."[3] This document, held in the Harvard University Archives, clearly indicates that at least some at Magunkaquog were not in agreement and did not approve of Harvard's takeover. One day after the parchment deed was signed, Samuel Sewall was informed that Isaac Nehemiah, one of the Native signatories, had hanged himself with his own belt. Sewall recorded the sale and the suicide in his diary, without noting any connection between the two.

The dramatic events recorded around the October 1715 sale of the Magunkaquog lands mark the official "end" of the praying town established less than fifty years earlier and document two very different perspectives. These dates, however, merely serve as two points along a continuum of Native occupation in the area long before the arrival of John Eliot and up to the present day. The incidents described above have been preserved as solitary moments in the documentary record. Strung together, they provide a chronological sequence of people and activities within a small Native community that appears to have existed on the fringes of more organized colonial and Native settlements. The records hint at the complex relationships that existed between Euroamericans and Native people at this dynamic point in New England's history. On their own, the written records do not tell a complete story. They are part of the "documentary archaeology" of Magunkaquog: the written history of people and events over time that must be uncovered and interpreted from different perspectives, just like the archaeological site discussed in Chapter 3.

The interpretation of Magunkaquog's historical record is framed by a number of questions. Why was it established in the first place? What was its relationship to the parent plantation at Natick? To what degree did the residents come into contact with missionaries and other Euroamerican colonists? Did residents return after their forced removal during King Philip's War in 1675–1676? Why did Harvard pursue purchase of the Magunkaquog lands and what caused some members of the Native community to oppose the sale so vehemently? Primary documents and historical records hint at answers to some of these questions, but attempts to answer them cannot be guided by these records alone. Archaeological research (see Chapter 3), comparisons with documentary research at other praying towns (see Chapters 6 and 7), and, most importantly, collaborative dialogue are helping to interpret places like Magunkaquog in more layered ways.

Magunkaquog's recorded history spans a period well beyond the half century of the community's "official" existence. It begins prior to the arrival of missionaries in New England, spans the turn of the eighteenth century, continues through the texts of nineteenth-century historians, passes through the critical analysis of twentieth-century academics, and stops (temporarily) with the development of a subdivision and the identification of structural remains and artifacts on Magunco Hill.

The effort to uncover Magunkaquog's documentary archaeology includes attempts to locate any and all written records, letters, legal documents, and eyewitness accounts of the settlement and the individuals associated with it over time. The gathered documents have been and continue to be reviewed, compared, critiqued, and shared with archaeologists, historians, and tribal members to weave a new narrative history.

## Source Materials

In general, the primary seventeenth and eighteenth century sources that provide information about Magunkaquog can be grouped into legislative and missionary records, published broadsides, and private correspondence.

The Massachusetts Historical Society and Massachusetts State Archives hold original seventeenth-century materials, but the majority of their collections have been reproduced and/or transcribed for research. Personal letters and records relating to the Society for the Propagation of the Gospel in New England (known as the SPG or New England Company; see Chapter 2 for additional background) and John Eliot are located in a number of repositories in the United States and Great Britain. Many have also been compiled and published.[4]

*The Records of the Governor and Company of the Massachusetts Bay in New England* (*RMB*) are the earliest legislative documents relating to the founding and early history of the Bay Colony.[5] The volumes include virtually every official record related to the Massachusetts Bay Colony, ranging from laws and proclamations that affected Indians and colonists to petitions filed by individuals seeking remedies for unlawful actions. Similar types of records appear in the *Acts and Resolves, Public and Private, of the Province of Massachusetts Bay* (Acts and Resolves 1869–1922).[6] They also contain additional legislative orders and votes of the court that do not appear in the *RMB*. The Massachusetts Archives also contains a set of microfilmed records relating to Native New Englanders in the colonial period. Volumes 29–34 deal exclusively with "Indian Affairs," with an accompanying index that allows researchers to search for individuals, places, subjects, or dates.

The Morse Institute Library in Natick, Massachusetts, contains a microfiche copy of the Original Indian Record Book (OIRB), a register of proprietors' meeting notes and vital records that served as Natick's earliest town records.[7] The paper records, written in the Algonquin language and in English, are in very poor condition, and many of the original texts are difficult to read. The available OIRB records are dated to the first few decades of the eighteenth century and generally list the Native officers elected for each year.

Seventeenth-century pamphlets published by the SPG are collectively referred to as the "Eliot tracts" even though several other authors contributed text.[8] The tracts, often written in letter format, provide some of the earliest detailed descriptions of New England's Native population after the first wave of Euroamerican settlement in the early 1600s and are considered to be one of the main primary sources for information on the organization of the original praying towns. While these documents served as propaganda to solicit financial support for the SPG in New England, they provide important details about the development of each of the early praying towns and the Native peoples associated with them.

Daniel Gookin was not trained as a minister but became actively involved in the Indian mission around 1646 soon after Eliot's first sermon to a group of Native people at Nonantum (present-day Newton). He served as the first official superintendent of Indian affairs in the Massachusetts Bay Colony and as such appears frequently in official documents relating to Native peoples. Gookin accompanied Eliot on his annual trips to the praying towns and compiled a written description of missionary activities in the years between 1674 and 1677. Gookin's two published volumes, *The Historical Collections of the Indians in New England* (Gookin 1970 [1792]) and *An Historical Account of the Doings and Sufferings of the Christian Indians of New England, in the Years 1675, 1676, 1677* (Gookin 1836 [1677]) are standard reference works for anyone studying the mission period.[9] Gookin provided a chronological sequence of events involving the Indians in Massachusetts and elsewhere, with detailed descriptions of each praying town, its location and land allotment, number of individuals, and names of leaders.

The SPG's transatlantic operation required a great deal of correspondence between the directors and the commissioners in London and New England. As a result, the organizational records present a rich source of information on its workings, the relationships between its members, and the goods and materials used to support the Indians in Massachusetts.

The formal act of letter writing served a vital role in seventeenth-century New England. In many cases, original letters and diaries serve as the only documentation of important events and transactions not recorded elsewhere. They provide a wide range of information that helps to connect both Euroamerican and Native individuals to specific events in Magunkaquog's history.

One of Magunkaquog's most dramatic records is the original letter sent to Samuel Sewall and preserved in the Harvard University Archives. Relatively few surviving texts from the colonial period written by New England Indians truly represent their own voices, and the Magunkaquog letter explicitly states the Indians' position on this matter (or more accurately the position of the group of Native men who signed it).

Samuel Sewall became actively involved in events at Magunkaquog toward the end of the seventeenth century. He served in a variety of legislative and judicial positions in the Bay Colony and was a United Colony commissioner, Indian superintendent, and Harvard trustee in addition to serving as the first secretary of the trust used to purchase the Magunkaquog lands. His dealings with the praying towns occurred in many different contexts. Sewall's published and archived letters, and especially his diary,[10] contain details about the relationships he maintained in each of these different roles. Sewall's dual role as the primary colonial representative in meetings surrounding the Magunkaquog purchase can be seen as at odds with his role as Indian commissioner, as reflected in the documentary record.

The bulk of the original written documents that deal exclusively with Magunkaquog are maintained by the Harvard University Archives. The archives hold a collection of original documents relating to the Charity of Edward Hopkins, the fund used to purchase the Magunkaquog lands from the Indians in 1715.[11] In addition to the Native letter described earlier, the Charity collection includes the original parchment deed to Magunkaquog, several handwritten letters later transcribed into the college's records, receipts for services (such as surveying) related to the land purchase, and early rental deeds to colonists who leased the Magunkaquog lands in the eighteenth century.

Secondary sources include town and county histories, biographies, and topic-specific historical studies and narratives. Many of these were compiled in the nineteenth or early twentieth centuries by authors who had access to earlier documents either no longer available or difficult to locate. Some of the works written in the early part of the nineteenth century included information passed on by elderly informants, who themselves were little more than a generation removed from the period when Magunkaquog was occupied. In this regard, secondary sources provide a critical link between the primary documents and modern-day histories and academic studies. These sources become, in essence, snapshots of the periods in which they were written and help modern researchers understand how historical events were remembered (and sometimes altered) over time, as discussed in Chapter 2.

Researchers must be careful to view these sources as products of their time, often written by people who had a very different perspective on the region's history than today's reader (as discussed below). Understanding the origin of these documents, and viewing them through the lens of history, is an important and critical part of the documentary archaeology.

## The Magunkaquog Praying Town: 1669–1715

The written archive of Magunkaquog fits within a fairly short span of time. Land records from 1657 and 1663 provide the earliest documentation of the Magunkaquog place-name in the Massachusetts Bay Colony records and clearly indicate that the hill and surrounding territory (where the archaeological evidence of Magunkaquog was found) were identified as part of the local Native geography. Early twentieth-century ethnographer J. Hammond Trumbull recorded the name as a Nipmuc word, spelled alternately as "*Magunkahquog, Makunkokoag,* or *Magunkook.*" Although Daniel Gookin described Magunkaquog as signifying "a place of great trees," Trumbull concluded:

> This would be decisive were it not that Eliot, who could not be mistaken as to the meaning of the name of a town that he had a chief hand in planting, wrote, in 1669, *†Mag∞onkkomuk*, which means "the place (or town) of the gift"—*i.e.*, "granted place," from *Mag∞onk*, "gift," and *komuk*, "place." Possibly this, the original name, had, when Gookin wrote, been changed by the Indians themselves to the more familiar and more easily pronounced *Magunkook*, "place of the great tree," or the plural *Magunkakook* (= *Mogkunkakauke*), "place of great trees." [12]

It is unclear whether Eliot's interpretation of the name "granted place" refers to the organization of the praying town at the site. It is obvious that Native people referred to this place before Eliot's initial attempts to create a designated praying town there, so Native people may have consciously reinterpreted the place-name as a way to identify the physical location of the meeting house (see Chapter 3). The various interpretations of the name were, at least partially, Euroamerican constructs and may or may not reflect the actual Nipmuc understanding of Magunkaquog as a place on the physical and cultural landscape (as discussed in Chapter 1).

Magunkaquog was officially recognized in October 1669 after a thirteen-year hiatus in new praying towns, during which time Eliot appears to have focused on the promotion of the six existing towns as part of his fund-raising efforts.

The first mention of Magunkaquog in the context of the missionary system comes in a 1669 petition presented by Eliot to the General Court "in the behalf of the poor Indians of Natik & Magwonkkommuk." Eliot wrote that "whereas a company of new praying Indians are set downe in the westernmost corner of Natik bounds called Magwonkkommuk who have called one to rule, & another to teach $y^{m}$, of wm the latter is of the Church, the former ready to be joyned & there is not fit land for planting, toward Natik, but westward there is though very rocky. these are humbly to request yt fit accommodations may be allowed $y^{m}$ westward."[13] John Grout and Thomas Eames were appointed by the court to review the land request and report back.

An October 1670 court entry indicates that a year later the Magunkaquog land had not yet been surveyed or formally set off, which was "greivous to the poore natives, thereby being disapointed of their hopes." A survey of not more than 1,000 acres was ordered, excluding any previous colonial land grants.[14]

A little more than five years after its official recognition as a praying town, Magunkaquog had approximately fifty inhabitants.[15] This relatively small group may have included a single extended family or kin group, possibly one that had lived within the vicinity of Magunco Hill before Eliot became active in the area. The presence of Native American archaeological deposits on and around Magunco Hill that appear to predate the colonial period supports this interpretation (see Chapter 3). Taken as a whole, the documentary records suggest that there was no colonial occupation in the vicinity of Magunkaquog prior to 1669, despite earlier grants that used Magunco Hill as a landmark.

Eliot provided a 1669 account of the newly designated Magunkaquog praying town in a progress letter to the SPG in London. He described eight praying towns, of which "Maqwongkommuk" was listed fifth. His description reads only "they call it a new Towne. the Church appointed & sent Wohwohquoshadt to teach $y^{m}$ & Pomham is theire ruler."[16] The mention of "the Church" probably refers to Natick, where the first admitted Christian Native members had been able to gather in 1660. The Magunkaquog description is the shortest in this letter; Eliot described the other towns in much more detail, including information about some of the residents and their progress toward Christian communion. Eliot's brief account also suggests that he was perhaps not as personally familiar with Magunkaquog as he was with the other towns.

Eliot included a more detailed description of Magunkaquog a year later in *A Brief Narrative*, the last of the missionary's tracts:

> Magunkukquok is another of our Praying-Towns at the remotest Westerly borders of Natick; these are gathering together as some Nipmuk Indians who left their own places, and sit together in this place, and have given up themselves to pray unto God. They have called Pomham to be their Ruler, and Simon to be their Teacher. This latter is accounted a good and lively Christian. . . . The Ruler hath made his Preparatory Confession of Christ, and is approved of, and at the next opportunity is to be received and baptized.[17]

This account of Magunkaquog is the first explicitly stating that the people gathered in this location were Nipmuc. The reference is important because it supports the idea that Magunkaquog was populated by people who had remained within their homelands. By 1669 Natick was composed of individuals from several distinct Native groups, including the Massachusett, Nipmuc, and Pawtucket. Eliot wrote that Magunkaquog's residents had "left their own places," but it is possible that he interpreted the gathering of these individuals within a "town" as an abandonment of their traditional settlement practices in favor of a Euroamerican lifestyle. If Magunkaquog's first residents were in fact a diverse group gathered from elsewhere in Nipmuc homelands, they still may have had a connection to the area around Magunco Hill as part of the traditional landscape.

The most-cited primary source on Magunkaquog comes from Daniel Gookin, who visited all of the praying towns in 1673 and 1674. Gookin's *Historical Collections* includes a section describing each of the settlements based on his observations. After a lengthy discussion of Natick as the "model town," Gookin wrote:

> Magunkaquog is the seventh town where praying Indians inhabit. The signification of the place's name is a place of great trees. It is situated partly within the bounds of Natick, and partly upon land granted by the coun-

> try. It lieth west southerly from Boston, about twenty four miles, near the midway between Natick and Hassanamesit. The number of its inhabitants are about eleven families, and about fifty five souls. There are, men and women, eight members of the church at Natick, and about fifteen baptized persons. The quantity of land belonging to it is about three thousand acres. The Indians plant upon a great hill, which is very fertile. These people worship God, and keep the sabbath, and observe civil order, as do the other towns. They have a constable and other officers. Their ruler's name is Pomhaman; a sober and active man, and pious. Their teacher is named Job; a person well accepted for piety and ability among them. This town was the last setting of the old towns. They have plenty of corn, and keep some cattle, horses and swine, for which the place is well accommodated.[18]

Gookin repeated some of the information provided earlier by Eliot, but he also added details about Magunkaquog not in other contemporary sources. If Gookin's statements are accurate, the residents appear to have been primarily kin groups and/or families rather than individuals from different Native groups. The reference to fifteen baptized adults and eight church members strongly suggests that these individuals had previously been associated with Natick, either as residents or as weekly attendees at lectures.

Gookin's description also indicates that the land at and around Magunco Hill was utilized for subsistence if not also for settlement. The "great hill" where the Indians had their cornfields is presumably Magunco Hill and possibly some of the gentler slopes around it (see Figure 3.1). Gookin also described the presence of livestock, including horses, in 1673/1674, suggesting that animal pens, wells, and/or barns were located in the vicinity. This description is supported by the recovery of horse bridle and harness hardware at the Magunkaquog archaeological site (see Chapter 3). No mention was made of public buildings, homes, roadways, or other colonial-style developments at Magunkaquog, but these features are not included in Gookin's descriptions of the other towns around Natick.

The documents described above are the available primary sources for information about Magunkaquog prior to King Philip's War and the oldest layer of the documentary archaeology of this place. Nineteenth- and twentieth-century historians added information to construct more detailed narratives about the settlement, recorded in secondary sources such as town histories. For example, J. H. Temple's 1887 *History of Framingham* expanded upon seventeenth-century documents:

> Each family had its own wigwam, granary, and cattle, and caught and cured its own fish. All united—after the then prevalent fashion of the whites—in fencing in a common planting-field, though each squaw had her separate lot in the field. The wigwams stood on what is known as the Aaron Eames place, now owned by William Enslin. The fort was built on the knoll where Mr. E.'s barn now stands, handy to the spring at the foot of the knoll, a few rods to the south. . . . The burial-ground was on a sandy knoll sixty rods to the southwest. The spot was crossed by the Central turnpike, and then and afterwards many skeletons were brought to light, being buried not more than three feet below the surface.[19]

Temple went on to write, "At first the Indians selected a planting-field on the rolling land near their wigwams, and built a fence around it; but it did not prove fertile." If true, this lack of arable land was likely what led to a 1669 Eliot petition resulting in the 1,000-acre grant "including the whole of what is now known as Magunka hill. Their new planting-field was on the top of the hill directly west of their fort. Their barns were set in the slope of the hill, a little north of east of the field. Some of them may still be seen in an old orchard now owned by Russell Eames."[20]

The information presented in this history was probably collected, at least in part, from Ashland residents living near Magunco Hill in the late nineteenth century who were aware of the seventeenth-century Native settlement in this area. Landscape features on and around the hill, possibly remnants of the Magunkaquog settlement and meeting house, may have still been visible at this time or knowledge of them may have passed through families living on the land for generations. The Eames surname is associated with an event at Magunkaquog that occurred shortly after King Philip's War (described below). It is certainly possible that descendants of the original family were living in the Magunco Hill area two hundred years later. Temple's description also links the 1,000 acres (for which no original survey plan has been located) to specific landowners and roads that can be located in late nineteenth-century property records and maps. These geographic data helped guide testing during the initial archaeological survey and helped interpret the deposits during the subsequent UMass excavations (see Chapter 3). Much like Wabbaquasset (discussed in Chapter 2), the Native American presence was discussed in the past tense—as if Native inhabitants no longer occupied their homelands of the region—and in relation to Euroamericans (mainly men).

A 1942 history of Ashland compiled as part of the Works Progress Administration (WPA) program borrowed heavily from earlier town histories, repeating much of the information about Magunkaquog verbatim. The introductory chapter noted that "the Indian town of Magunco was an artificial development. Prior to 1659/60, there was no Indian village at this place." The text went on to explain that, "as time went on, the little settlement took on more and more the appearance of the ordinary frontier villages of the white pioneers. Wigwams were replaced by houses, paths were widened and made into streets and roadways. . . . For some years the place flourished, until at last it reached a point where some form of recognition by the General Court was both desirable and necessary."[21] This romanticized description of Indians, and especially references to them abandoning their "wild" or "uncivilized" ways in favor of a civil and orderly "white pioneer" lifestyle, is typical of many accounts from the nineteenth and early to mid-twentieth century, and far from the realities of seventeenth-century Native life.

## Magunkaquog during King Philip's War: 1675–1676

As Native-colonial tensions escalated with the start of King Philip's War, Magunkaquog and the other praying towns were subject to intense scrutiny. Magunkaquog documents from this period focus on the conflict and highlight some of the Native-colonial interactions. By July 1675 about forty men and additional women and children left Hassanamesit, Magunkaquog, Manchaug (Oxford), and Chobonokonomum (Dudley) for the relative safety of Marlborough, the colonial town next to the praying town of Okommakamesit (see Figure 1.1).[22] Gookin explained that the Native inhabitants felt unsafe in unprotected settlements and decided to move closer to an established English town. Nothing in the existing records indicates that any Indian raids or colonial assaults occurred at Magunkaquog during this period. Gookin's description suggests that the move was voluntary rather than coerced.

Less than a month later, Massachusetts Bay Colony restricted all praying Indians to Natick, Punkapoag (present-day Canton), Nashobah, Wamesit, or Hassanamesit. The regulation made it illegal for any Native person to travel more than one mile from these towns and effectively barred residents of Magunkaquog, Okommakamesit, or any of the newer praying towns still occupied to tend their fields as harvest time approached or to protect their land.

Conditions worsened through the fall: colonial authorities were increasingly pressured to "remove these Indians from their plantations to some other places, for the security of the English and Indians also." A proposal was circulated to send Natick residents to Cambridge; the Wamesit to Noddle's Island in Boston Harbor; Nashobah Indians to Concord; Punkapoag to Dorchester; and the "Hassanamesit, Magunkog, and Marlborough Indians to Mendon."[23] The proposal languished because none of the Euroamerican towns were willing to accept the Natives.

In October 1675 colonists' growing suspicions won out: the Natick residents were ordered to Deer Island in Boston Harbor. Gookin noted that many from Natick chose to "run away" rather than face internment. Those remaining in praying towns were also subjected to risks at the hands of hostile Native groups. In early November Magunkaquog's teacher Job Kattenanit and Natick resident James Speen were able to evade a raiding party that had reportedly attacked Hassanamesit. Kattenanit's children were among the group that left Hassanamesit for Deer Island, and he appealed to Gookin to be allowed to search for them. On November 13, 1675, Gookin was able to secure a pass that read, "These may certify that the bearer hereof, Job, of Magunkog, is a trusty Indian" and requested his safe passage to gain much needed intelligence for the colony regarding the location of any hostile Native groups. The pass also stated that if any colonist was to meet up with Job outside one of the designated praying towns, "they will not misuse him, but secure him, and convey him to the Governor or myself, and they shall be satisfied for their pains."[24] Despite this authorization, Gookin noted that Job was captured shortly after he left for Hassanamesit and sent to Deer Island after spending three weeks in jail.

In December 1675 the colony asked Gookin to select "two or three of the principal men" at Deer Island to gather information after a major battle with a group of Narragansetts and allied Indians.[25] Job Kattenanit and James Quannapohit were offered five pounds in exchange for their service and left for Nipmuc Country on December 30. The men were instructed to pretend they had been released from Deer Island and were trying to locate lost relatives. James returned in January but Job apparently remained for a longer period, presumably having convinced Philip's allies that he was with them. On February 9 Job returned to Cambridge and reported on several raids that the Narragansett were planning, after which he was sent back to Deer Island.

In February 1676 Major Thomas Savage requested a group of Christian Indian guides to accompany his 600-man army on a defensive mission and instructed his soldiers to select "six of the fittest men" from Deer Island. Once again Job Kattenanit was picked along with his former companions James Speen and James Quannapohit, again described as "principal men."[26] The February muster is the last mention of Job by name in Gookin's account of the war. It is unknown if he returned to Magunkaquog after the fighting ended.

The Indians interned on the Boston Harbor islands were allowed to leave in mid-May 1676. Most traveled to Cambridge for the summer to plant fields along the Charles River under colonial supervision. Through the fall and winter Native people began to move back to their homes. Gookin described seven places where Indians met during winter 1676 for regular Sabbath services and schooling: Nonantum, Punkapoag, Natick, Medfield, Concord, and Chelmsford; Magunkaquog and Hassanamesit were not mentioned. When winter ended, Gookin wrote that "the praying Indians most of them repaired to their plantations at Natick, Magunkog, and some planted at Hassanamesit; but not long after, they withdrew from thence and gave over tending their corn, for fear of the Maquas [Mohawk]."[27]

Magunkaquog residents had been ordered to leave their settlement in July 1675 at the start of King Philip's War, but several records suggest that some did not. Gookin's description of Mohawk raids during and especially toward the end of the war indicates that Native settlements located along the western edge of Massachusetts Bay Colony were occupied by "friendly" Indians on and off during this period.

Three months before to the Indians' release from Deer Island, a violent incident occurred near Magunkaquog. Thomas Eames was one of two men assigned to lay out and survey Magunkaquog in 1669. His house and farm were located about three miles to the east.[28] On February 1 or 2, 1676, Eames traveled to Boston for supplies and ammunition. While he was away, a group of Magunkaquog Indians allegedly raided the farm, captured and killed members of the family, and burned the house and barn to the ground, reportedly in retaliation for an earlier theft of stored Magunkaquog corn.

The Eames family tragedy is important to Magunkaquog's history because the documentary record provides very specific information about the men supposedly involved in the raid and their relationships to both Natick and Magunkaquog. Colonial records also support the contention that Native peoples were living at or near Magunkaquog during the period when they were supposed to be confined to one of the other praying towns or interned on Deer Island.

A petition dated July/August 1676 ordered the keeper of the prison in Boston to "take into yr custody William Jackstraw & Joseph his [son] & [Apurnatquin] [name illegible] Indians and late inhabitants of Moguncock, being committed for Burning Thos. Eames house & barn, killing & captivating his children in a barbarous & [cruil] manner."[29] William Barry's nineteenth-century history noted that on August 11 Thomas Danforth issued a warrant for the arrest of "Joshua Assatt, John Dublet, son-in-law to Jacob, William Jackstraw and two of his sons, the name of the one Joseph, also Jackstraw's wife, all of them late of Moguncog Indians."[30]

The Massachusetts Archives include a confession by three of the accused men, whose names are written as "William Awannuckkow, Joseph Awannuckkow and John Appamabahqoon." The document begins with a plea by the accused to "hear & consider our supplication" and notes that the men had turned themselves in to the colonial authorities in order to clear their names.

> Indeed we do acknowledge it we were in the company of those that Burnt Goodman Eames his house But we did not act in it, It was done by others, who are slain in the wars . . . , as for our part we came along wth that company upon a nessesary & Just occation, to get our corn w$^{ch}$ we had planted gathered and put up at Magungoog But finding our corn taken away we Intended to Return But [Neetus] and an other Man that were our [traders] Ernestly Mov'd to Go to Goodman Eames farm for to get corn, and they said they did Believe he had taken our Corn. But we were unwilling to goo, But they By [their] persuasion and threatening carried us wth y$^{m}$ But as we said Before we neither kil'd nor Burned nor take away any thing there But were Instrumental [to] Save Goodman Eames his children alive.[31]

The accused men identified themselves as separate from Neetus, a man whom Temple and Barry both described in their local histories as leader of the raid, whom Temple called "once a ruler at Natick, but not a resident of Magunkook."[32] The record also clearly indicates that corn had been planted, harvested, and stored at Magunkaquog in the previous summer and fall, despite the fact that the residents had been ordered to leave in July 1675.

Barry reported that all of the individuals at first denied involvement. Joseph apparently offered to confess on August 14 after Danforth convinced him that he would "speak to the Governor to spare his life, in case he would tell me plainly how all the said matter was acted." Writing after the confession in a petition by Danforth dated September 18, 1676, Joseph admitted that he and the other named men "were provoked" by their missing corn.[33] Barry's nineteenth-century history (a secondary source), based on the original petition at the archives cited above, makes no mention of earlier statements by the three Nipmuc men that they were not willing participants in the raid. Barry must have read the petition, which he cited as the source of the men's confessions, but decided to leave out the statements where each denied burning the house, committing murder, or taking hostages. This translation of events related to Magunkaquog is one example of how history can be redefined over time.

The result of the trial was not reported in Danforth's manuscript or in archives records, but Gookin mentioned it in a November 1676 report, writing of the Natick Indians: "such as are left . . . above thirty are put out to service to the English; three were executed about Thos. Eames his burning; about twenty rann away; and generally, such as remaine are of those Indians y$^{t}$ formerly (before the war) lived under our government at Hassanamesit, Magunkog, Marlborouh, and Wamesitt."[34] Gookin associated the three convicted men with Natick, although they had apparently identified themselves to Danforth as being from Magunkaquog (unless three separate men from Natick were later charged).

## Magunkaquog in the Post–King Philip's War Period: 1676–1715

During King Philip's War Magunkaquog appears to have fared like most other praying towns: fields were left untended, other Indians and/or colonial soldiers pilfered belongings, and (as the Eames story indicates) stores of food were gone. Gookin reported that at least some people returned to Magunkaquog in spring 1676, although with no details about how many individuals resided in the area or the condition of their homes.[35]

Mohawk raids on praying towns throughout the war continued after the Massachusett and Nipmuc Indians returned to their homes. In June 1678 twenty-two Indians were kidnapped by Mohawk while working in one of the Magunkaquog cornfields and taken to Albany. Their arrival was recorded in a June 27 letter by a Captain Salisbury to Commander Anthony Brockholls, who was the acting governor of the New York colony. He wrote, "Hon$^{d}$ S$^{r}$, This day there arrived here a troop of 60 *Maquas* with 22 Prisoners, to witt 3 men 17 women 2 Boys & 2 *Crounes* who say they are frind Indians of y$^{e}$ English, whereupon I called . . . to send y$^{e}$ Secretary & *Aernout* y$^{e}$ Interpreter to y$^{e}$ Prisoners, to examine them from whence they were, who doe say they are *Natick* Indians frinds to y$^{e}$ *English* & under the command of Major *Guggine* and say they were taken in a Indian Cornfield called *Magaehnak* 6 mile from *Suddberry*." The Mohawk apparently justified the capture by saying the Nipmuc "were taken about 6 miles from any *English* Place & therefore [they] did take them to be there enemies."[36]

Although the Mohawk leader promised to keep the hostages safe, Salisbury was dubious and appealed to Brockholls for advice on how to handle the situation. He concluded the letter by noting of the captives, "I doubt not if y$^{ey}$ be frind Indians (as they say) but you or I will Receive Letters there anent Speedily . . . but I doe Presume they are of there Praying Indians, because there is one amongst them that brought y$^{e}$ Indian Bible here in Govern$^{r}$ *Nicolls* time."[37]

In response to the capture, Samuel Ely and Benjamin Waite were sent as Massachusetts Bay Colony agents to meet with the Mohawk directly, without consulting New York officials, to "tell them y$^{t}$ y$^{e}$ Gov$^{r}$ and all the *Inglish* in these pairts . . . think it strange & can not but tak it very Ill that Last act of Hostilitie at *Maguncog*, where they killed three & carried away Captive Twentie four of our friend Indians, who are his Ma$^{ties}$ Subjects wth out any cause given by them y$^{t}$ wee know off, or any Complaint made to use by the *Macquas*." The order made specific mention of the Mohawk's former agreement that "they would not kill or hurt anie of our Indian friends Especially any of those belonging to *Natick*, which those did." Ely and Waite were told to "be verie Carfull to understand all thar answers clearly and fuly, which you are to Sett doun in writing."[38]

Salisbury sent another letter to Brockholls on July 25, warning of impending trouble over the Magunkaquog issue. The Massachusetts agents had either arrived or were known to be coming, and Salisbury received information that the captives were likely already dead and the Mohawk were "procuring beavers . . . to make, an Exscuse for there Misstake."[39]

On August 1, 1678, six Mohawk sachems met with Ely and Waite in the Albany courthouse to provide their account of the Magunkaquog raid. After asserting their alliance with Massachusetts Bay Colony and reiterating their treaty to leave Christian Indians alone, the sachems stated:

> You say there is a fault Committed in takeing away of those Indians at *Magoncog*, tis true we acknowledge it, Butt in who lyes y$^{e}$ fault? it may be in our young Indians who are like wolves, when they are abroad; Possibly in y$^{e}$ North Indians that live among us; and y$^{e}$ Indians of *Magoncog* are not ye lesse to blame, they not dwelling as frind Indians in y$^{e}$ Woods, haveing a Castell so well fortifyed wth Stockadoes, which frind Indians need not have, therefore did Imagine them to be Enemyes, for these Indians that live in or about y$^{e}$ *English* Plantations, w$^{t}$out fortificacons, we did never any harm too.[40]

This reference to a fortification at Magunkaquog is one of the key details used to interpret the foundation excavated on Magunco Hill (see Chapter 3).

The Mohawk were asked to meet with Massachusetts Bay Colony officials again to return the prisoners, but this had not happened by October 1680, when the Massachusetts General Court sent Colonel John Pynchon to Albany to meet with New York's Governor Sir Edmund Andros and the Mohawk to address continued attacks on New England Indians. Pynchon was given a detailed list of items to present to the Mohawk that included "requiring the deliuery of the Indian captiues taken in June, 1678, at Magunchog, vnto which they returned dilatory & dissatisfactory answers."[41]

The Mohawk explanation was at least partly rhetoric designed to explain the raid and pacify Massachusetts agents questioning them. New York officials had already discussed the Mohawk sachems' plan to "make, an Exscuse for there Misstake," and it would certainly make sense to present the raid as an innocent case of mistaken identity. Whether Magunkaquog really had a palisade or fenced enclosure,[42] it was located well away from any other English towns and may have been "in y$^{e}$ woods." The Mohawk description also suggests that Magunkaquog more closely resembled a traditional Native settlement or at least one not easily recognized by English-style structures or other features.

These documents help piece together the period just after King Philip's War and indicate that the Nipmuc had returned to Magunkauog after the war once again to tend to their cornfields. The capture of women, children, and several men also suggests that family groups were at Magunkaquog. Available documents give no indication that the captives ever returned, and the New York officials concluded that they had been killed soon after their arrival in Albany. It is unknown if those Magunkaquog Indians who were left merged back into the Natick community or if other Native people took over the maintenance of the cornfields and resided near Magunco Hill.

## The Magunkaquog Purchase

The interest of Harvard College in the Magunkaquog lands in the early eighteenth century is not surprising, given the close association of Eliot, the school, and its charter mission to educate clergy, missionaries, and even the Indians themselves. Harvard's administrators viewed land holdings and rents as a critical source of revenue from the earliest days of the college. The reasons for the college's aggressive acquisition of Magunkaquog are not as easy to understand, though.

Edward Hopkins, who had served as governor of Connecticut, left behind a large legacy worth 800 English pounds when he died in England in 1657. In 1708 the New England Company became aware of the money and made an inquiry as to the disposition of the Hopkins estate. Hopkins had been a member of the company but left no specific legacy to the group. In 1710 the lord chancellor was asked to award the £800 to the New England Company commissioners. The Court of Chancery issued an order for the money to be invested "in the purchase of lands in New England in the name of the College and Grammar School at Cambridge."[43]

A final agreement was reached in 1712: the funds were to be invested with the newly established "Trustees for Managing the Charity of Edward Hopkins, Esq." The trustees held their first meeting on January 14, 1713, recorded by treasurer Samuel Sewall and attended by fellow trustees, including Cotton and Increase Mather, Joseph Dudley, John Leverett, Jeremy Dummer, Daniel Oliver, and Thomas Fitch.[44] Although the college and the company had taken great pains to set up an official group to manage the Hopkins funds, the Massachusetts Court refused to release the money until a specific land purchase was approved.

The Hopkins funds were finally transferred to Samuel Sewall in spring 1715 and totaled more than £1,250. The Massachusetts legislature granted the trustees' petition to purchase the Magunkaquog lands on July 21, 1715. Samuel Sewall wrote to notify the New England Company that he had visited the land but added, "The Indians, at present, shew some Indisposition to part with it. This arises, as I conjecture, from the Influence of English-men, who hanker after it themselves. But I hope that Difficulty will be surmounted, when the Natives shall be perswaded to consider that the Purchase-Money is to be husbanded by the Commissioners, for the benefit of the Indians, especially the inhabitants of Natick."[45]

The legislature's resolution authorized Sewall, on behalf of the trustees, "to purchase of the Indian Inhabitants of Natick a Tract of Wast Land commonly known by the Name of Maguncoog belonging but not inhabited nor improved by the said Indians."[46]

This document suggests that by 1715 the people who had been living at or near Magunco Hill were no longer there. It also states that the bulk of the 8,000-acre praying town was not cleared or otherwise "improved,"[47] a contradiction to the late seventeenth-century descriptions of the Mohawk raid describing tended cornfields and a palisaded village. The record is also clear that the Natick Indians had authority over the disposal of the Magunkaquog lands during this period, at least for the purposes of this sale and according to colonial officials.

On August 9 the trustees of the Hopkins Charity met to "order and execute" the Hopkins legacy. A group of trustees was appointed to survey the bounds and "meet with the Indians of the Plantation of Natick, and acquant them of what is above, and desire the company of their Select-Men to see the said survey; and thereafter to proceed to open the Business of the purchase to them, and assure them of the Justice & Friendship of the Trustees to them."[48]

The Natick Indians also documented the Magunkaquog negotiations and on September 24, 1715, met and voted "that the Lands of Magunkook be sold to the Trustees of Mr. Hopkins Legacy" and that "Capt. Thom. Waban, Sam. Abraham, Solomon Thomas, Abraham Speen, Thomas Pegun, Isaac Nehemiah and Benjamin Tray be a Committee or Agents for the Proprietors of Natick, and be and are fully Impowered to Act in behalf of the said Proprietors . . . for ye Sale of the Lands of Magunkook."[49]

On September 28, 1715, Sewall "went to Cambridge to meet the Natick Committee . . . Accomplish the Bargain for Magunkaquog Land, and paid Fourteen pounds in part." The purchase was noted in Sewall's diary on October 11, 1715: "Went with Mr. Daniel Oliver to Natick . . . At Natick the Indians of the Committee executed the Parchment Deed for the Land at Magunkaquog: and paid the Proprietors Three pounds apiece."[50]

The original Magunkaquog deed of sale is preserved in the Harvard Archives. The oversized, heavyweight parchment was obviously scripted ahead of time, with a small box left blank for the amount of money to be finalized at the time of signing. The deed reads:

> This indenture made the eleventh day of October Anno Domini One Thousand Seven Hundred and Fifteen. . . . Between Thams Waban, Samuel Abraham, Solomon Thomas, Abraham Speen, Thomas Pegun, Isaac Nehemiah and Benjamin Tray a Committee or Agents for the Indian Proprietors of the Plantation of Natick. . . . in Consideration of the Sum of [six] hundred pounds in good Bills of Credit on the Province. . . . Commonly called and known by the Name Magunkaquog containing

> by Estimation Eight Thousand Acres. . . . Together with all the Singular the Housing Ediffices buildings fences trees woods. . . . Saving out the sd granted Land the former of Moses Simpson and Parker's Farm So Called.[51]

The deed was individually signed by the seven Native men mentioned above.

The Magunkaquog purchase was recorded on October 11, 1715, in the *Harvard Donations Book*: "Captain Sewall, President Leverett and Mr. Daniel Oliver . . . went to Natick and finished the purchase of Maguncoog and Donations were distributed to the Indians to their great satisfaction."[52] A subsequent legislative order for establishing the new town of Hopkinton from Magunkaquog noted the "good Advantage & universal Satisfaction of the Indians late Proprietors of the said Land."[53] As with other places discussed in this book, the renaming of this place after the Englishman whose money enabled the transfer from Native to Euroamerican "ownership" commemorates him, rather than those who lived here for thousands of years before him.

While the deed suggests acceptance of the settlement's sale and all involved being satisfied, other documents suggest a very different story. Sewall had earlier alluded to the unwillingness of the Natick Indians to part with the land but suggested that was due to trouble-making on the part of other English parties. One letter preserved in the Hopkins Charity collection clearly states the position of some of the Native inhabitants:

> Rec'd of Solomon
> Thomas at Maguncok
> Sept. 6 1715
> Natick September 5th day 1715
>
> Mr. most hai and ounorabol Samuel Souwall and all the jin gentlemon that is with you we had the touwn meting monday last and we dasire you [consl] us that we are boor indias we are nto will to sal our landes or to debate with it any ways
>
> Abram Spoon (his mark), Josiah Spoon (his mark), Isaac Spoon (his mark), Solamon Thomas (his mark), Israll Rambot[mas] (his mark), Simon Ephraim (his mark), Benjamin Tray (his mark), Samuel Sokomcho, Israel Weel (his mark), Daneal Weel (his mark), Samuel Weel (his mark), Jospth Wuttipbomso (his mark), Jospth Sokomcho, Samuel Boman (his mark), Samuel Omptowanon[54]

This letter was written less than three weeks before the Natick Indians voted to sell the Magunkaquog land. Solomon Thomas, Benjamin Tray, and Abraham Speen signed the letter above but on September 24 were instructed to act as agents in the Magunkaquog purchase negotiations with Sewall. What events had unfolded in the short time to change their position? Were the Natick residents really divided into two groups, those agreeable to the sale and those not? Were the Sewall letter signatories residents of Magunkaquog or individuals who had a more vested interest in this territory than in Natick? The September 5 letter seems very unambiguous and suggests that the majority of the community had discussed the purchase at a "touwn meting" and were in agreement that the Magunkaquog lands were not for sale.

Sewall's diary entry for October 12, the day after the Magunkaquog deed was signed, adds further doubt to the "great satisfaction" of the Indians.

> Solomon Thomas acquaints me that Isaac Nehemiah, one of the Committee, had hang'd himself. Ask'd what they should doe. I sent him to the Crowner. A while after I went to Cous. Gookin's in order to go home [Sewall had spent the previous night in Sherborn]. When there, Solomon came to me again, and earnestly desired me to go and help them. . . . So I went, Mr. Baker accompanied me. The Jury found Isaac Nehemiah to be *Felo de se*. Hang'd himself with his Girdle, 3 foot and 4 inches long buckle and all. 'Twas night before had done, so went to Sherbourn again, and log'd at Cousin Gookin's.[55]

This chilling description marks the end of Sewall's references to Magunkaquog or the purchase in his diary and in general marks the end of the Indians' presence in the written history of the Magunco Hill area.

There is no explanation for Isaac Nehemiah's suicide, nor any indication from Sewall that this tragic event was linked in any way to the sale of Magunkaquog lands. Sewall was still serving as one of the commissioners of Indian affairs in 1715. His notation that Nehemiah had died "*Felo de se*," literally "a felon of himself," was likely a legal finding of suicide that he made as a colony official. Isaac Nehemiah was one of the designated deed signatories but had not signed the protest letter to Sewall. He was also known as Isaac Wuttasukoopauin and was probably a grandson of the Eliot-era Natick leader known as "Captain Tom."[56] Isaac's brother Thomas was listed as a Natick resident in 1740, suggesting that the family maintained its connections to leadership positions throughout much of the town's history. This family history also documents the inseparable connections between Natick and Magunkaquog within Nipmuc homelands.

One of the most astonishing aspects of the Magunkaquog purchase documentation is that the Indians' protest letter was actually archived by the trustees and has been maintained within the Hopkins Charity papers. The preservation of this document seems almost counterintuitive. It clearly contradicts the claim of Sewall and others that the Natick Indians endorsed the Magunkaquog purchase, and it seems that the trustees' detractors could have used the letter to discredit their arrangement and use of the legacy money. An explanation may lie in the prevailing attitudes of the day. It is possible that the colonial administrators simply did not feel that a letter signed by a handful of Natick residents had any merit or that any other colonial authority would find it a worthwhile document. The letter's presence among other Hopkins Charity papers indicates that Sewall shared it with other trustees and possibly even discussed it privately, although there are no official records (other than Sewall's 1715 comment) indicating that the negotiations and purchase did not go smoothly or that anyone objected. No other sources refer to the Indians' letter or to any controversy surrounding the sale. Even Sewall's diary entry regarding Nehemiah's death seems unrelated to anyone not familiar with the September 5 letter.

## Postpurchase Events

The £600 recorded on the Magunkaquog deed was likely not turned over to the Natick residents themselves but rather deposited with the commissioners (Sewall was not only one of the designated representatives but also the treasurer) for expenses related to "oversight" of the Natick Indians. Sales of land for the "benefit" of Natives was a common practice of dispossession in colonial New England and then across the country over time.[57] Less than half of the charity award was used to pay the Natick Indians. More than £300 went to expenses involved in the purchase, including survey and travel costs. The remaining £300 was earmarked for the construction of a meetinghouse and support of a minister in the town of Hopkinton, officially recognized on December 13, 1715. The trustees intended to maintain an income for Harvard's benefit from the Magunkaquog lands by renting them out to colonial farmers.

No documentation exists on the actual abandonment of Magunkaquog by Native inhabitants; nor is there any indication that the trustees formally requested anyone to leave. The first lease of the land was not issued until 1719. The Natick Indians invested the Magunkaquog purchase money with their Euroamerican trustees and received an annual income, known as "the Magunkaquog rents."

Between 1719 and 1723 the Hopkinton land was leased out to planters at three pence an acre, with Harvard and the trustees paying three-quarters of the province taxes. The lessees were unhappy with the arrangement, and the trust did not realize any profits. In 1729 the trustees petitioned the General Court for more land, because the Magunkaquog property had proved so unsuccessful an investment.

The Hopkins trustees struggled with this parcel until 1742, when they legally terminated all of the 99-year leases originally granted. Revised contracts were used to lease land to non-Native planters in Hopkinton until the lease system was abolished in 1832 and the landholders were granted free title to their plots. One of the lessees during this period was Captain James Gooch, who acquired two parcels in 1742, including 270 acres that were almost "all of the Magunco Hill section, with land extending nearly to the Sudbury River on the north, and across present Union Street."[58]

On November 25, 1749, Gooch's entire tract was sold to Sir Henry Frankland. Like other Euroamerican men before him, his presence in Ashland (formed in the nineteenth century from part of Hopkinton) is well documented in the historical record, prose, and local legends. His estate and large home dominated the property. Historic maps of the town through the nineteenth and twentieth centuries indicate that the area around Magunco Hill remained undeveloped and was part of Frankland's wooded estate. Settlement continued along Frankland Road and Union Street, but the area around Magunco Hill remained woodland until the housing development described in Chapter 3 was proposed.

## Conclusions

The documentary history of Magunkaquog helps to weave together a more vivid, detailed picture of the past, where individual acts, even from hundreds of years ago, evoke an emotional response. The record is punctuated by a single violent act: the suicide of Isaac Nehemiah recorded by Samuel Sewall. Nehemiah was associated with the Natick community and had been designated by the Native leadership as a member of the committee entrusted to broker the sale with Harvard. Sewall was involved in the Magunkaquog purchase through his dual positions as Harvard trustee and head of the commissioners of Indian affairs in Massachusetts. The individual actions of these two men at the time of the takeover exemplify the history of Magunkaquog as a place with very different meanings for Native people and Euroamericans. They also serve as powerful symbols of Native identity and colonialism nearly a century after the first Europeans settled in New England.

Magunkaquog's documentary archaeology must also be interpreted within the larger cultural context of the seventeenth-century missionary movement, but a close examination of this one settlement suggests that it functioned independently with little, if any, non-Native oversight. Although individual colonial records consistently describe Magunkaquog as a model praying town, few Euroamericans actually visited or knew the individuals who lived there. Repeated orders for Native people to abandon the lands around Magunco Hill in the period of King Philip's War were ignored, despite a clear threat from armed colonists and hostile Indian invaders. Clearly the 1715 sale of Magunkaquog was not supported by all Natick-area Native residents. Even after the land was officially under Harvard's control the documentary and archaeological records suggest that Native people still lived here.

Taken as a whole, the history of Magunkaquog documents Native American cultural continuity before, during, and after a period of intense colonial and missionary activity designed to control and subvert the indigenous population of Massachusetts.

The association of the Magunkaquog place-name with the topographic feature that still bears its name in present-day Ashland (Magunco Hill) is a testament to the enduring importance of the landscape, both physical and cultural. This association of place also provides a context within which to interpret events at Magunkaquog.

Native American connections to Magunkaquog are documented prior to, during, and after the designation of Eliot's praying town of the same name and up to the present day in the Nipmuc Tribe's continued connection to this place as an important part of its history. Magunkaquog also serves as an example of Native autonomy in Massachusetts after King Philip's War. Despite popular history, Native people clearly occupied the lands at Magunco Hill after the conflict ended and the original missionary network was disabled. The supposed "conquest" of King Philip's War had not severed the relationship between Magunkaquog's occupants and their fields.

The suicide of Isaac Nehemiah on the night of October 11, 1715, is a powerful record of dissent available today. Although it is impossible to know the circumstances of this man's death, his act stands out in the documentary record as a very visible sign of protest, in addition to the earlier letter protesting the land sale. Nehemiah may have felt powerless when he was appointed to act for the Natick proprietors and again when he signed the Magunkaquog deed. Refusing to do so would not have changed the minds of his community leaders (if, indeed, they also supported the sale) or stopped Harvard from acquiring the land. His action, taken alone, may have been the only way that he could outwardly express his feelings to other Native people. The Natick community must have been affected by the death of one of its members. Sewall noted that Solomon Thomas had twice come to him the day after the incident. Other than these minimal references, however, the individual responses to Isaac Nehemiah's death were not written down.

Documents that describe the Magunkaquog settlement record the shifting nature of colonialism over time and across many different cultural interactions. Although Native histories of this place have been consistently presented from Euroamerican perspectives, Native voices are far from silent. Native histories, memories, and knowledge of Magunkaquog have always existed and are only "invisible" when we do not look for them (or perhaps when we don't expect to find them).

Historians, anthropologists, and especially archaeologists have attempted to understand seventeenth-century Native New England history in non-Euroamerican forms. Oral tradition and material culture are among the most popular choices for this task and do in fact offer the possibility of documenting information not recorded in the typical historic form: as written documents. But this reliance on traditional or native forms of culture transmission presents its own bias. In simple terms, it implies that a "factual" Euroamerican history was written down while an "authentic" Native American history was not. There is a danger in assuming that colonial-era documents did not record the individual and collective actions and reactions of Native people. The documentary archaeology of Magunkaquog includes a highly "visible" and continuous Native presence at this place; it did not need to be discovered or excavated, it just needed to be read.

Magunkaquog continues to be a meeting place in the present. An important part of the documentary archaeology has been the development of a strong collaborative relationship between archaeologists and members of the Nipmuc Tribe on whose homelands the site is located. The historical documents associated with Magunkaquog take on a richer meaning when viewed and discussed in the context of Nipmuc individuals and families who have lived in the area over the generations and today. This collaborative relationship contextualizes the importance of place and community, of individual action and reaction, and makes centuries-old texts relatable in the modern world. The stories of Magunkaquog preserved in the documents are being used to educate and inform Native and non-Native scholars and the next generations and to foster ongoing conversations about how we interpret this history.

## Notes

1. John Eliot, transcribed in Biglow 1830, 34–35.
2. Historical Records Survey (HRS) 1942, 14.
3. Collection of the Charity of Edward Hopkins (CCEH), 1668–1958.
4. See, for example, Ford 1970 [1896]; Kellaway 1961; Weis 1959; Winship 1967 [1920].
5. These records were compiled, transcribed, and published in an edited multivolume set (Shurtleff, 1853–1854). The Massachusetts State Archives holds a set, but the records are also available elsewhere.
6. Like the records cited above, another published set of early Massachusetts records is maintained at the Massachusetts State Archives (Acts and Resolves 1869–1922).
7. The Original Indian Record Book (OIRB) is maintained by the Morse Institute Library, Natick, Massachusetts, and is available on microfilm to researchers.
8. The published tracts include Eliot 1671, 1834, 1846, 1865, 1882a, 1882b; Eliot and Mayhew 1834; Shepard 1834a, 1834b; Whitfield 1834a, 1834b.
9. Gookin's texts have been published in two volumes: Gookin 1970 [1792] and Gookin 1836 [1677]. The citations in this chapter are taken from these two editions of Gookin's writings.
10. Sewall 1973 [1878].
11. The original records associated with the Charity of Edward Hopkins are cited as CCEH. Charles Bowditch was a trust administrator who published a history of the fund in 1889, and several authors have discussed the records in the context of the missionary movement (see McCord 1957 and Simpson 1957).
12. Trumbull 1881, 18–19, cited in Tooker 1901, 26–27.
13. From an original document transcribed in Biglow 1830, 34–35.
14. Shurtleff 1853–1854, 4(II), 465.
15. Gookin 1970 [1792], 78–79.
16. John Eliot, letter to Robert Boyle, cited in Ford 1970 [1896], 29.
17. Eliot 1671, 8.
18. Gookin 1970 [1792], 78–79.
19. Temple 1887a, 62.
20. Temple 1887a, 62.
21. HRS 1942, 7–8.
22. These are all Nipmuc settlements in the central portion of Massachusetts, in and around present-day Worcester County.

23. Gookin 1836 [1677], 470.
24. Gookin 1836 [1677], 480–481.
25. Gookin 1836 [1677], 486.
26. Gookin 1836 [1677], 501.
27. Gookin 1836 [1677], 518–519.
28. Barry 1847, 24.
29. Massachusetts Archives (MA) n.d., 30:212.
30. Barry 1847, 28.
31. MA n.d., 30:216.
32. Temple 1887a, 65.
33. Cited in Barry 1847, 28–29.
34. Gookin 1836 [1677], 532.
35. Gookin 1836 [1677], 518–519.
36. Fernow 1881, 520.
37. Fernow 1881, 520.
38. Fernow 1881, 521.
39. Fernow 1881, 527.
40. Fernow 1881, 528.
41. Shurtleff 1853–1854, 5:300.
42. A palisade is not identified in any other description of the settlement, but there is evidence of a possible fortified feature in the archaeological record, as discussed in Chapter 3.
43. Cited in McCord 1957, 296.
44. Bowditch 1889, 67.
45. Unpublished manuscript cited in Kellaway 1961, 185–186.
46. Acts and Resolves 1869–1933, 9:410.
47. Clearing, bounding, building, and other forms of landscape modification were seen by colonists as visible indications of land ownership. As such, many colonists used the lack of these visible "improvements" as signs that Native peoples did not own or otherwise value land. See Cronon 1983 for a detailed discussion of this concept.
48. Original document on file, CCEH.
49. OIRB, cited in Biglow 1830, 27.
50. Sewall 1973 [1878], 800–801.
51. Original document on file, CCEH.
52. Cited in HRS 1942, 14.
53. Acts and Resolves 1869–1922, 9:440.
54. Original document on file, CCEH.
55. Sewall 1973 [1878], 801–802.
56. O'Brien 1997, 129–130.
57. See O'Brien 1997 for a detailed discussion and Gould 2010 for an example at Hassanamesit.
58. HRS 1942, 17.

# 5

◎ ◎ ◎

## The Archaeology of Hassanamesit Woods

HEATHER LAW PEZZAROSSI AND STEPHEN A. MROZOWSKI

As the story of the Nipmuc continues beyond King Philip's War and into the eighteenth century, we shift our focus from Magunkaquog to Hassanamesit. Hassanamesit, now known as Grafton, lies only 30 miles west of Magunkaquog and was also the site of a praying town in the seventeenth century. The people who became known as the "Hassanamisco Indians" are the descendants of seven Nipmuc families who returned to Hassanamesit after the war and negotiated the sale of Hassanamesit to English settlers in 1727 for £2,500 and plots of land for each of the seven families. This chapter is the chronicle of one of those families, through the eighteenth and into the nineteenth century, based on archival and archaeological evidence.

Sarah Robins was one of the seven Nipmuc landholders to retain land at Hassanamesit following the sale of 7,500 of the 8,000 acres set aside for the praying town in the mid-1600s. She was likely a descendant of Petavit, alias "Robin," one of the praying town leaders before King Philip's War. Sarah was allotted 106 acres on the eastern slope of Keith Hill in 1727 and took possession of the property in 1728, beginning more than a century of residence on that land for her and her descendants. When Sarah Robins died in 1749, she left her land to her daughter, Sarah Muckamaug. When she died in 1751, she in turn left the family land to her own daughter, Sarah Burnee. Sarah Burnee left her land to her daughter Sarah Philips (better known as Sarah Boston) in 1824. And when Sarah Philips/Boston died in 1837, she left the land to her daughter Sarah Mary Walker (Table 5.1). Female inheritance of land was practiced within this family for over one hundred years, as the family land passed down from one generation's Sarah to the next. The daughter who inherited the land was not always the first female child; instead the important criterion seems to have been that she was born on the family land in Hassanamesit and carried forward her mother's given name. It was clearly a deliberate and coordinated tradition that helped the Sarahs retain their land for as long as they did. How old this practice may have been is not clear, although it was a practice shared by other Nipmuc families during the same period (see Chapter 7 for further discussion).

The site of the Sarahs' homestead, known as the Burnee/Boston Homestead site, has provided archaeologists with an opportunity to study over 100 years of continuous occupation by one Nipmuc family at a time when many Nipmuc families did not stay in one place for very long. With this constant in place, we can more easily make observations about the continuities and changes to Nipmuc lifeways in the eighteenth and early nineteenth centuries, the period following King Philip's War before the tribe's focus on preserving the final piece of land across town (Chapter 7).

Much of what we know about the lives of the Nipmuc people in the more recent past is informed by archival research. As a condition of Hassanamesit's sale, the English assigned overseers, or guardians, to the tribe. These men (assigned in groups of three by the colony's general court) were a mechanism of control and management of the wealth of the indigenous population of Massachusetts, so they kept detailed records.[1] As with the sale of Magunkaquog, guardians held the principle amount from the 1727 sale of Hassanamesit in trust and were responsible for managing these funds and distributing interest shares to each of the seven Hassanamisco families on a yearly basis. They also managed the sale of Native lands when the court granted Native families permission to sell. While the records they left behind have been very helpful for historians and archaeologists in understanding genealogies and tracing land ownership, they also reveal a specific Nipmuc history as seen from an administrator's perspective of privilege and power. They focus on financial transactions and land holdings, recording in detail events such as sickness or debt that put Nipmuc people at the mercy of the colonial and state government for the rights to sell their lands. The documents provide a clear picture of the government exerting control over the Nipmuc community, sequestering their financial assets, and keeping them in poverty, so that they were forced to sell their lands for survival.[2]

The story of these five generations of Sarahs, told from the archive, is a narrative of indigenous decline. Petitions written by the family to the Mas-

Table 5.1. Five generations of Sarahs at Hassanamesit Woods

| | |
|---|---|
| Sarah Robins | (unknown–1749) |
| Sarah Muckamaug | (unknown–1751) |
| Sarah Burnee | (1743–1824) |
| Sarah "Boston" Phillips | (unknown–1837) |
| Sarah Mary Walker | (1820–1879) |

sachusetts General Court reveal that they sold land often, at least once a decade, to build and keep up their home, pay medical debts, and carry them through lean times. For example, records indicate that Sarah Muckamaug began selling pieces of the family land in the late 1740s, first to build a house on the property and buy a cow.[3] In the summer of 1751 Sarah Muckamaug died in the care of Hezekiah Ward, an English settler, who was reimbursed for her care through her estate and the sale of more of her land.[4] Sarah Muckamaug's daughter, Sarah Burnee, sold a substantial portion of her land to neighbor Silas Fay in 1802 for money to repair her house.[5] As she grew older, she relied on at least two additional land sales to pay for her care.

Documents also cover the division of lands between family members. The Sarahs divided their lands at least twice: once in 1771, after a lengthy legal battle between Sarah Burnee and her half-brother Joseph Aaron (see below),[6] and then again in the 1820s, when siblings Sarah and Ben Philips divided land that Sarah Philips had inherited from their mother.[7] Both Joseph and Benjamin sold all of their lands in their lifetime, resulting in substantially diminished landholdings within the family. These divisions speak to the clash between the Nipmuc practice of female land inheritance and the paternalistic views of the colonial and state government; they also highlight that the women of this family really were the stewards of the family land. This was a continued practice among Nipmuc women (see Chapter 7).

The archive also contains evidence of debts that Native families owed to the guardians. Entire microfiche rolls are scattered with receipts for everything from blankets to coffins, dry goods, meat, cloth yardage, buttons, shoes, schoolbooks, wood, nails, shingles, and more.

Members of the Nipmuc community, having no direct access to the funds inherited from the sale of their homelands, often found themselves in debt for the basics of everyday life to those who held their funds. These debts were settled by rerouting interest payments back to the guardians, who diligently recorded every expenditure and reimbursement in their records.

In the case of the Hassanamesit land sale, funds were also mismanaged and stolen by guardians entrusted with them.[8] Throughout the eighteenth and nineteenth centuries Nipmuc tribal members often addressed the power imbalance between the community and the guardians, and those efforts are also fairly well documented in the archive. Several petitions, signed by various descendants of the original seven Nipmuc families, contain appeals to the court in Boston to overrule the guardians. A 1785 petition stands out because it shows that members of the community were aware of the long-term abuse that they suffered at the hands of the guardians. Together, Sarah Burnee, her father, Fortune Burnee, and Sarah's half-brother Joseph Aaron—along with three other Nipmuc community members—petitioned the General Court in Boston for a review of the accounts of the guardians (or trustees). They claimed that over the past six or seven years they had "not received one quarter part of [their] interest so due to [them]."[9]

A general review of the books was ordered on their behalf, but there is no indication that the records were ever actually presented at court. When the matter was reopened in 1788, the court found that "said Trustees have done as well in all respects by the said Indians as the nature of the matter would admit of."[10] Although that investigation was inconclusive, John Milton Earle later reported that by 1841 over 1,300 dollars of the Hassanamisco trust fund had been lost, stolen, or otherwise misspent during the years in which guardians were responsible for it.[11]

The picture that emerges from archival sources is one of struggle on the part of the Nipmuc and conflict between the tribe and the colony (and later the state). Archaeological investigations associated with the Hassanamesit Woods Project have helped us to see beyond this narrative of struggle, revealing a more complex picture of daily life continuing amid these difficulties. The richness of that picture is a testament to the power of archaeology to rediscover the intimacies of everyday life that round out—and even challenge—stories revealed through documentary sources, to see beyond the colonial standpoint focused on debt, loss, and the subjugation of generations of Nipmuc people.

## Revealing Nipmuc Spaces

The Hassanamesit Woods Project is an ongoing research initiative between the Fiske Center for Archaeological Research, the Nipmuc Nation, and the town of Grafton, Massachusetts. Between 2006 and 2013 the Hassanamesit Woods Project conducted an archaeological investigation of the property that belonged to Sarah Robins and her descendants.[12] One of the study's primary goals was to get a firm understanding of the spaces within the property, as it was used and defined by the Nipmuc family in the eighteenth and early nineteenth centuries. These foundational understandings were paramount in the formation of more nuanced conclusions in the later stages of research.

The archaeological research carried out at the Burnee/Boston Homestead site looked at three different levels of space: the house itself, the yard immediately around the house, and the outlying lands surrounding the homesite.

The dwelling itself was used by Sarah Robins and her descendants for over 100 years. After their occupation ended in 1837, the building sat unoccupied for several decades. As it collapsed, an orchard was planted around it. Shotgun shells found within the cellar cavity dating from 1898 to 1906 suggest that local hunters used the remains of the building and foundation as a hunting blind during that time. The cellar cavity and foundation were completely filled and covered after the 1938 hurricane that devastated the region, essentially erasing what remained of the dwelling from the hillside.

As excavations intensified in 2007, the foundation was relocated by John Steinburg using ground-penetrating radar. Subsequent excavations confirmed a deep, dry-laid foundation that had been built into the east side of Keith Hill (Feature 37 in Figure 5.1). Much of the foundation fill was removed by hand; this task took several field seasons, carefully removing layers of soil and rock that had been pushed into the cellar cavity by a bulldozer as part of hurricane clean-up efforts in the fall of 1938.[13] Although the foundation was consistently six to eight feet deep from the surface, it was clear that the easternmost wall of the building would have been open to air, as opposed to the western portion of the foundation that may have only risen a foot or so above the ground surface.

Based on analysis of soil micromorphology carried out by Dennis Piechota of the Fiske Center at UMass Boston, it appears that the foundation was surrounded by a shallow drip line evident as a dark stain that would have formed when water dripping from the roof mixed with organic matter around the edge

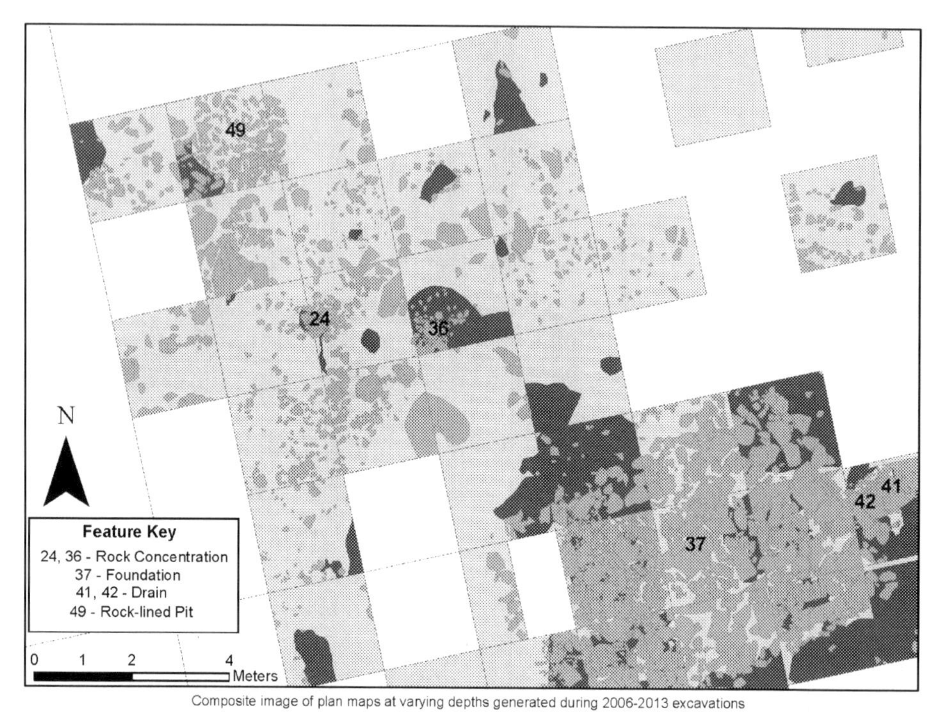


Figure 5.1. Yard area map, Burnee/Boston Homestead site.

of the house. The break in this deposit along the western wall of the foundation indicates that there may have been a small lean-to addition. A concentration of brick and wood ash inside the western wall of the foundation suggests that this was likely the spot where a cooking hearth and chimney were maintained inside the house. There is no evidence of a chimney base, so we assume that it was made of stone and only attached to one side of the building. One of the most interesting features of the foundation was a stone-lined drain that ran through the floor of the cellar west-to-east and downslope of the main yard area of the home lot. The southwestern section of the foundation wall had a break to funnel water into the drain (Features 41 and 42) and no evidence of a stone or brick-lined cellar floor was uncovered. In fact, it seems that the drain kept the cellar area cool and moist, a perfect environment for keeping liquids, fruits, and vegetables fresh.

Surrounding the dwelling was an area that served as a yard (Figure 5.1). With archaeological traces of an outdoor hearth, food consumption, a garden, and a midden located downslope from the dwelling, this was an active and heavily used area. A small concentration of ceramics included several reconstructible vessels as well as a much larger midden deposit that extended over much of the downslope directly east of the foundation (Feature 36). The yard also included the remains of a small hearth (Feature 24) that paleobotanical analysis (conducted by Heather Trigg) revealed contained ash and charred corn.

Intensive excavations within the foundation and yard area found a wide range of cultural materials dating to the period when Sarah Burnee and Sarah Boston lived on the hillside. Close to 120,000 artifacts were found throughout the yard, in the midden, and throughout the foundation. The assemblage contained a wide range of materials, including ceramics, glassware, metal eating utensils, animal bone and plant remains, iron tools, architectural remains such as window glass, brick, nails, and building hardware as well as many personal items such as jewelry, buttons, shoe buckles, and smoking pipes.

Beyond the home site were three additional pieces of Nipmuc land. The first was the home lot, the area immediately surrounding the yard that probably held the barn, where animals were husbanded. This was bounded on the north, south, and eastern sides by stone walls (Figure 5.2). A combination of geophysical testing, soil chemistry, archaeological survey, and large block excavation identified areas along the southern wall where animals probably made their daily trek to the South Pasture, just south of the home lot. We also found several areas of loosely packed stones that appear to have been used to form pathways—again apparently for animal use—from a possible barn area southeast of the dwelling site. The South Pasture contains little in terms of architectural or landscape features beyond its surrounding wall and a single short wall that appears to have served as an eating area for the domestic animals. Further south was the interesting area whose name, Swago, has been communicated through time and appears on an 1886 deed map of Keith Hill produced by Royal Keith (for whom Keith Hill is named).[14] Swago was an area of large, glacially transported boulders with several streams running through from west to east. In her analysis of "vernacular histories" Law Pezzarossi found reference to Sarah Boston collecting herbs in the area.[15] Its wet conditions still nourish a rich understory of small shrubs and wild herbaceous plants. A mix of geophysical testing, soil chemistry, vegetation survey, archaeological survey, and excavation has provided a picture of the general use of these spaces. In some instances, such as the South Pasture and

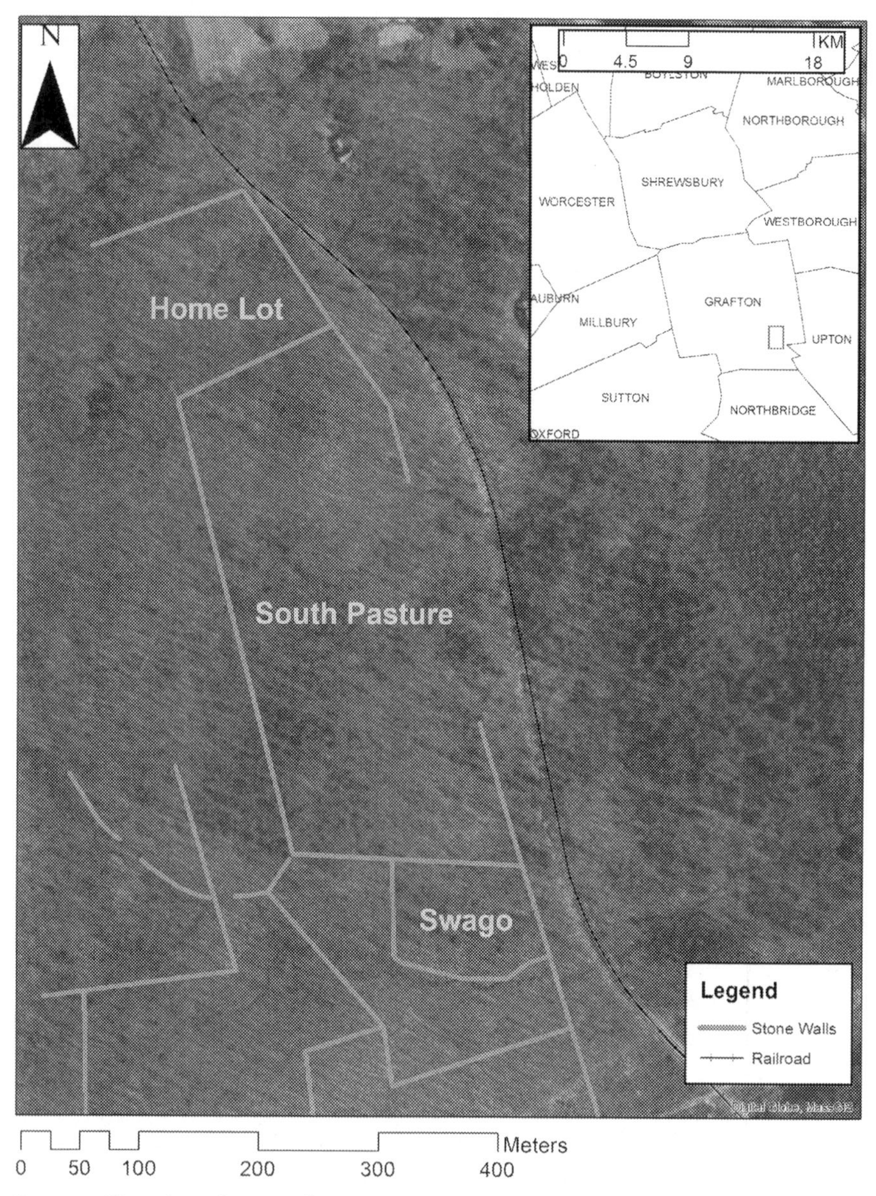


Figure 5.2. Home lot and surrounding area, Burnee/Boston Homestead site.

Swago, our study involved little more than archaeological survey searching for concentrations of material culture and overall landscape recording of walls. The plant remains suggest a patchwork of agricultural fields, access to fields allowed to go fallow, and mature stands of hardwoods and softwoods.

## Challenging Dominant Histories

The remainder of this chapter looks at the history of this Nipmuc family through the materials recovered archaeologically from the Burnee/Boston Homestead site. These objects tell equally important stories about different dimensions of the Nipmuc community and emphasize the contributions that archaeology can make to the enrichment of Nipmuc historical narratives and of the present-day tribe, which has embraced learning more about this site and its occupants through the Hassanamesit Woods Project.

The objects discussed here range from microscopic particles to animal bones, ceramics, and farming tools. Some are housed in museums, while others await further analysis in an archaeological lab. Still others will shortly be returned to the soil where they were recovered a decade or so ago. Unlike the documents that have largely guided the direction of Nipmuc history to date, many of these materials were forgotten or left behind in the family home as its occupants died or moved on. Others are mere traces of eighteenth- and nineteenth-century life, left unknowingly and inadvertently as a by-product of decades of routines and everyday habits. Today these objects form part of a growing and invaluable assemblage, recovered through archaeological research, with the ability to tell a more intimate story of the richness of lives lived despite the constant surveillance of the guardians, the struggle for autonomy, and the pressures of debt.

The following passages detail three of the most important lessons learned from the archaeological research, using several lines of evidence to support each claim. These lessons, and the methods by which they were brought to light, are examples of how archaeology can be what indigenous and postcolonial scholars call a "decolonizing methodology."[16] That is, these conclusions support the further study of alternative historical narratives that challenge, subvert, and in some cases enrich histories constructed through documentary research alone.

### Occupational Diversity

Countering narratives of indigenous decline often requires specifics about indigenous survival. As we have seen, at several bottleneck moments in Nipmuc history the dominant historical narrative tells us that the indigenous people of central Massachusetts were unable to thrive or even survive: the onslaught of disease in the early years of colonial incursion,[17] the shift in control represented by defeat of the Native peoples in King Philip's War,[18] the pressures of the American Revolution and the strain of industrialization, and difficulties in maintaining indigenous identities in a modernizing world.[19] Indeed, just consulting the archive would suggest that these challenging times often corresponded with petitions to sell land or pay debts, indicating financial strain on families. But these are not failings. Rather, these are moments when families were challenged and had to (and did) find new ways forward. With evidence of 100 years of continuous occupation at the Burnee/Boston Homestead, we can look at some of these moments for clues about how this family negotiated them, providing direct evidence for the kinds of survival strategies that Nipmuc people used to weather difficult moments in their history.

Sarah Muckamaug and her husband, Fortune Burnee, built a barn and bought their first cow around 1750. Sarah, who had grown up as a domestic servant in Providence, had recently relocated to Hassanamesit, where she was caring for her young son and daughter and her elderly mother, Sarah Robins. Her husband Fortune Burnee probably worked as a laborer on other surrounding farms. When Sarah Robins died in 1749, Sarah and Fortune made a bold decision to depart from at least two generations of experience in service and began farming for themselves, a decision that likely held the promise of more autonomy and potentially greater earnings, given their substantial landholdings at the time. Archaeologically, we have recovered evidence that Fortune Burnee had some success in his agricultural pursuits after the untimely death of his wife in 1751. Faunal remains of cattle, sheep, and pigs all show evidence of each level of butchery being carried out on the farm, implying that the animals were husbanded on site. Likewise, a broad range of age profiles are present in the faunal remains of cattle and sheep, implying that some cows were used for dairying, while others were raised for meat; some sheep were kept for wool production, and some lambs were slaughtered for consumption or sale at market.[20]

Archival records indicate that the family was also raising wheat and rye in the fields.[21] Rye could be sold for grain or for straw, depending on the harvesting technique used. Two large scythe blades recovered from the site were likely used by Fortune Burnee, his daughter Sarah Burnee, and his stepson Joseph Aaron to harvest their grain crops. They would have used the scythes to cut the mature grass, working together to wrap it in small bundles called sheaves and then stacking them in larger upright clusters called shocks to dry in the fields.

After about a week the grain would be stored in the barn and then threshed throughout the fall and winter months by beating it with stick or a flail, separating the heads from the straw. The straw could then be stored and used or sold for animal bedding or roof thatch. The chaff/grain mixture would then be winnowed to rid the berries of chaff and dust by tossing it in the air from a tray or basket. The grain was likely stored in barrels to keep it cool and dry before it was fed to livestock, milled for flour, or, in the case of rye, boiled, fermented, and distilled for whiskey.

While grain could be a lucrative crop in New England, it required a lot of labor and effort at harvest time. When Sarah Burnee inherited the family farm in 1765, she was twenty-one years old. Shortly after she took over the farm, her half-brother Joseph Aaron came to live with her, helping with the planting, harvesting, and husbandry. When Sarah married in 1771, her husband Prince Paine and her brother did not get along. The discord led Sarah and Joseph to agree to divide their farm equally. This division of land left Sarah the house, "the olde Barne," and several of the rye and wheat fields.[22] As part of the terms of this division, the court ordered that Joseph deliver to Sarah one-quarter of the rye each year after it had been threshed and cleaned, but it seems that Joseph may not have upheld his end of this bargain for long before the American Revolution disrupted life on Sarah's farm even further.

The dispute between Sarah and Joseph highlights one of the more complicated parts of life for Native women. Among indigenous groups such as the Nipmuc land normally passed through the female line, as seen repeatedly within the Hassanamisco community. This is one reason Nipmuc women such as Sarah Burnee and later Sarah Boston often initiated dialogue with the Massachusetts General Court, reflecting their roles as political leaders. Similar actions were taken by Sarah Arnold Cisco and her granddaughter Sarah Cisco Sullivan (discussed in Chapter 7). English law and culture was much more paternalistic, giving men most of the power and almost exclusive rights over the inheritance of property. It is not clear from the documentary record whether the troubles between Sarah and Joseph were complicated by clashing cultural practices surrounding the inheritance of land, but it seems safe to assume that they added to the challenges experienced by indigenous women such as Sarah at this time.

Archival sources suggest that the years surrounding the American Revolution were especially difficult for Sarah Burnee. Sarah and Prince had no children before the war. During the Revolution her husband, her father, and her half-brother Joseph joined the navy. The following year her other half-brother, Fortune Burnee Jr., joined them in enlisting in the local militia.[23] The mostly female community at the homestead tried to hold things together. In 1776, acting on a petition written by Sarah Burnee and other members of the tribe, the General Court found that absentee guardian Artemus Ward had recently been employed in the "Continental Service," while the other two entrusted guardians had "neglected to relieve these Indians."[24] Joseph Aaron returned to Grafton after the war with serious injuries that prevented him from working his land or his sister's. By 1777 Prince Paine was dead. Sarah was left a widow.[25]

Between 1771 and 1777 Sarah's lands had diminished by half, her husband had died, and her brother was disabled. This stunted the productivity of Sarah's farm and put a great deal of pressure on her to find other ways to survive. Between 1775 and 1786 she maintained the family homestead on her own. She sold some of her remaining lands. Archaeological evidence suggests that she may have taken in washing for extra income. Between 2010 and 2013 block soil samples were removed from several floor sections in the cellar. When the soil blocks were excavated under controlled conditions in the lab, the soil micromorphology from the sample just east of the foundation showed microlaminations and sand grains capped with silt on the upstream side, indicating a high likelihood of some kind of regularly repeated washing activity (Figure 5.3).[26] This evidence, combined with the hundreds of mismatched buttons recovered from the yard, suggests that perhaps Sarah Burnee took in washing for income when times were especially difficult.

Life may have gotten a bit easier for Sarah when she met Boston Philips in the 1780s. Little is known of him or how he and Sarah met. There is a record of a "Boston Phillips, alias Philip Boston" who served as a private in the American Revolution for three years between 1776 and 1779. He enlisted for the town of Holden, mustered by the Worcester County muster master, and was sworn in at Providence.[27] This is thought to be the same "Boston" who in 1754, at the age of twenty-five, was sold by Jonathan Harrington to Nathan Harrington of Holden for £50.[28] He may have been of African or Native ancestry or both. Together they had two children and were married in 1786. Her children Sarah and Ben were farmhands from a young age, helping their parents and taking on extra chores on neighboring farms as well. But when Boston Philips died in 1798, the family members were once again back on their heels. An aging Sarah Burnee sold more land to repair the home and provide for her adolescent children. Archaeological evidence suggests that, as the family landhold-

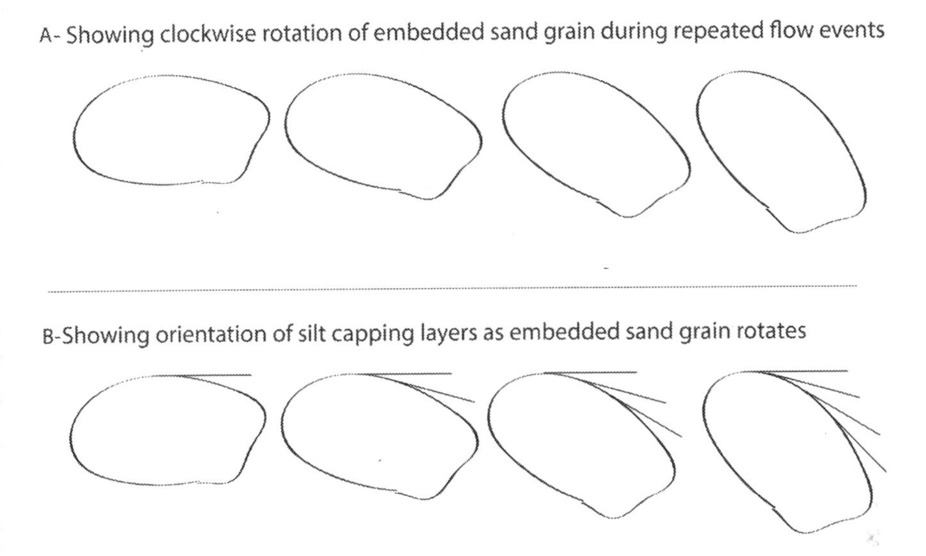


Figure 5.3. Soil micromorphology from the Burnee/Boston Homestead site.

ings continued to shrink and an agricultural lifestyle became less and less tenable, Sarah's daughter, Sarah Boston, became involved in the budding industry of Native basketmaking, in which indigenous artisans began reorienting the centuries-old practice for a settler market.

In the years following the American Revolution, many Native people in Southern New England developed a trade in basketmaking, chair-caning, and broom-binding that they mobilized by selling their wares throughout the countryside (discussed further in Chapter 6). This trade was not common or universal. Decorated baskets and other closely affiliated tasks and goods were widely accepted as distinctly Native things that emerged from distinctly Native abilities and knowledges, adapted for settlers' needs and tastes in the early nineteenth century. Baskets were made from wooden splints acquired by removing a year's worth of growth from an ash or oak log and cutting the thin layers into uniformly sized strips that could be woven together into anything from a small "berry" basket to a large storage basket.

Material from the site analyzed by Heather Law Pezzarossi suggests that Sarah Boston adapted the tools she had on hand to build herself a basketmaking

Figure 5.4. Axe artifact from the Burnee/Boston Homestead site.

tool kit. These are some of the same tools found at the Magunkaquog meeting house described in Chapter 3. Sarah used the butt end of an axe, for example, to pound the ash logs until the growth rings released. What remained of the axe was recovered from the yard during excavations; it was warped in the back, into a concave shape that revealed years of repetitive log pounding (Figure 5.4). She had the family scythe bent into a drawshave to shape her splints; that tool was found in the cellar feature. She also likely used knives and shears that were found on the farm, possibly used originally in tasks of butchery or sheep shearing. She also may have made brooms, perhaps from a small continued harvest of rye or wheat straw. She had special drill bits used in chair caning also recovered from the cellar feature and special shoe attachments called "ice-creepers" that helped her travel her routes and sell wares in the winter months.[29] These objects were mostly agricultural tools, probably acquired when Sarah Burnee and her father and half-brother worked the land, yet they were repurposed successfully into a basketmaking toolkit to support a new livelihood when the family's agricultural pursuits began to fail. These tools speak very clearly to a moment in Nipmuc history when a decision was made, a change was implemented, and the family and its home survived as a result.

## Gathering and Community

Community cohesion has always been extremely important for the Nipmuc. Of course, it is crucial for any group to communicate and share time and space together to ensure continuation of their shared identity. But for the Nipmuc (and other Native communities in the United States), their recognition and support from the federal government in the present is dependent on their ability to demonstrate the continuous cohesion of their community over time.[30] As noted in Chapter 1, for groups in the Northeast like the Nipmuc, who have been subject to colonial rule for over four hundred years, this can be a daunting task, especially if they rely on documents alone. Archaeology can help.

In the case of the Burnee/Boston Homestead site, evidence of community cohesion came from the study of foodways. A meal can be a very functional, practical ritual. After all, we eat to nourish ourselves, to stay healthy, and for energy to complete the tasks of the day. In that vein, we have worked to reconstruct a dietary profile based on faunal and botanical remains to the extent to which the preservation conditions allow. But the study of foodways is more than just what people ate; it also encompasses economic, social, and historical conditions surrounding food production and consumption. For example, sharing a meal with others is a social practice, bringing together families and indeed larger communities in times of celebration and scarcity alike through tasks of food preparation and the act of consumption. Sharing a meal can even bridge boundaries and help forge stronger relations with the people who surround us. People often have important rituals and traditions surrounding food, its procurement, its preparation, and its consumption. These may be traditions that have ancient heritage or they may be more contemporary.[31] Perhaps, as is often the case, they are a combination of the two, in which people perform old traditions in a new way. With this is mind, we can look at the archaeological traces at the Burnee/Boston Homestead site for a more complete picture of Nipmuc foodways in the eighteenth and early nineteenth century.

Thankfully, food preparation and consumption tend to leave many archaeological traces. From faunal remains to charred botanical material and patterns of refuse disposal, to ceramic tableware, utensils, glassware, and cookery, these things are all identifiable in the archaeological record. In the case of the Burnee/Boston Homestead site they can all be brought into conversation together to paint a bigger picture of Nipmuc community in the eighteenth and nineteenth centuries.

The recovery of faunal remains can be difficult in the New England climate, as many of the bones left behind erode in the cycling of hot and cold, arid and humid conditions. Trampling can also be an issue in areas of refuse that were also high-traffic yard areas and/or later became plowed fields. However, the animal bones at this site still provide some important clues. Many of the bones and bone fragments recovered from inside the foundation and surrounding yard area were from domesticated animals such as sheep, goats, pigs, chickens, and cattle, like those raised on the farm. The faunal assemblage also included a rich collection of wild animal remains, indicating that hunting and trapping were part of the household economy. Amélie Allard's analysis of the animal bone notes the presence of wild fowl such as ducks, turkeys, and pigeons that were probably eaten on a regular basis by the household's residents. An abundance of turtle remains also indicates that these prized animals were being trapped in the many streams and wetlands surrounding the homestead site. Remains of nine individual turtles were recovered, which suggests that they were much prized and actively sought after. Evidence also exists of trade and/or travel between the household and coastal communities to the east of Grafton in the form of saltwater fish remains recovered during excavations.[32]

Easily the most abundant materials recovered from the homestead site were ceramics. From coarse earthenware (often used in food preparation and storage) to refined white earthenware (predominantly tableware) to porcelain (more costly and often reserved for special occasions) to stoneware (a heavy, durable material often used for liquid storage), and even some handmade coarse earthenwares made in the precolonial indigenous style, ceramics made up 65 percent of this site's entire material assemblage, numbering over 80,000 sherds.[33] While many of the ceramic sherds were small—only a few centimeters in size—the analysis of these artifacts in the laboratory effectively classifies each one, determining what object they belonged to, what part of the object they made up, and when the object was manufactured.

The ratio of coarse earthenware to refined earthenware varies from context to context and site to site. In places where more people are fed regularly, it makes sense that tableware (refined ceramics) would outnumber food preparation vessels (coarse ceramics). This is precisely the case at this site: the ratio of coarse earthenware to refined earthenware is substantially lower than at surrounding farms.[34] For example, the ceramic assemblage from the neighboring Pratt-Keith Farm, a Euroamerican farm from the same period, contained about 75 percent coarse earthenware, while coarse earthenware was only 47 percent of the Burnee/Boston Homestead assemblage. Here refined earthenware (predominantly tableware) composed 56.6 percent of the entire ceramic assemblage, indicating that this household regularly fed a larger number of people than their neighbors did.

The specific kinds of objects identified on this site also support this conclusion. A refined earthenware minimum vessel count conducted by Guido Pezzarossi from only a 30 percent sample of the site identified 106 individual vessels, including 4 punch bowls, 9 plates, 13 tea cups, 5 tea pots, 8 mugs, and 3 tankards, suggesting that entertaining was a major activity here.[35] Minimum vessel counts of glassware from the same 30 percent sample revealed 15 to 20 tumblers and between 1 and 5 decanters as well as over 50 eating utensils (knives, spoons, and forks).[36] Studies of the types and numbers of cast-iron cooking vessels revealed that the Burnee/Boston household was equipped with several skillets, kettles, and a Dutch oven. The household had quite a variety of sizes of cookware as well, with some small enough for personal use and some large enough to cook for a crowd.[37]

Overall, when the site's food preparation and consumption artifacts were compared with other archaeological assemblages from the same time, we found that the sheer number of eating and drinking vessels, plus utensils, was more comparable to a tavern than a homestead.[38] In her study of probate inventories from late seventeenth- and early eighteenth-century New England taverns, Kathleen Bragdon proposed that while tavern keepers kept large quantities of drinking and serving vessels for their patrons, colonial-era yeomen farmers often did not.[39] A solely domestic assemblage would have more food preparation and storage vessels (like coarse redware vessels), along with relatively fewer drinking vessels. Sarah Boston's assemblage, like that of the taverns in Bragdon's study, seems to lean heavily toward accommodating large numbers of people eating and drinking.

Initial faunal analysis carried out by Ryan Kennedy in 2010 suggests that the household tended to rely on head and foot parts of the domesticated animals represented, with fewer long bones recovered in comparison. This suggests that they often used the many kettles recovered for long, slow braising or stewing in the preparation of soups, stews, and potages ideal for feeding larger groups.[40] The distribution of faunal remains also suggests that feeding large numbers was a priority. A comparison of faunal materials from the yard area to those from the foundation found that both food preparation and food consumption occurred in the yard, while only food preparation occurred inside the structure.[41] This is important and suggests that people may have regularly eaten outside, especially when large groups were present.

Archaeologists often use a technique called Mean Ceramic Dating to determine the average period of manufacture for the ceramics in a given assemblage. In the case of the Burnee/Boston Homestead site, the Mean Ceramic

Date for refined white earthenware, or tableware, falls between 1795 and 1810, allowing for the extra fifteen years of lag time suggested for acquisition in rural contexts.[42] Based on archival records, the maximum number of official occupants in the home always hovered around four to six individuals, further supporting the idea that the Burnee/Boston site was likely a place of gathering for the Nipmuc community in the late eighteenth and early nineteenth centuries. This date range correlates well with the mature adulthood of Sarah Burnee, who died at the age of eighty-one as "the oldest proprietor of the Indians in that town," as reported in the *National Aegis* (Worcester, Massachusetts) in June 1824. Given the documented Nipmuc traditions of looking to elders for leadership and gathering around community elders in times of difficulty and celebration, it makes sense that the Hassanamisco community would have regularly met at this homestead during that period and that it would have been a central place. These dates also correlate very well with the beginning of the basketmaking industry, which raises two probabilities: (1) that the new business pursuits provided them with an influx of income; and (2) that the Hassanamisco people approached basketmaking as a community. Shared Hassanamisco stamp patterns found on curated baskets tend to support the assertion that basketmaking was done in groups and often served to reinforce a shared Native identity and celebrate community bonds.[43]

## Heritage and Memory

The archaeological material from the Burnee/Boston Homestead site has helped us understand many things about Nipmuc life in the eighteenth and nineteenth centuries, but perhaps its most profound lesson has to do with how we see and identify indigeneity in the archaeological record. Archaeologists struggle with the push and pull of continuity and change. Objects that communicate antiquity and the maintenance of ancient traditions tend to be labeled as a triumph of endurance for Native cultures. For example, we recovered two fragments of an ancient stone bowl from the site's yard. This bowl, carved from steatite, has distinct lug handles that helped date it to the Late Archaic period, about 3,000 years ago before the adoption of pottery when bowls such as these were common in the Northeast.[44] Before it broke it was likely used with a pestle to grind plants for food and medicine or used for food storage. The fact that it was found in and around the rest of the kitchen refuse from the eighteenth- and nineteenth-century occupation of Sarah Burnee and

Sarah Boston implies that they deposited the bowl fragments there, just as they had other refuse. The bowl fragments are considered by archaeologists to be objects of great importance in the study of Nipmuc continuity. They communicate the owner's acknowledgment and sense of belonging to an ancient Nipmuc heritage, which is of course noteworthy and important.[45]

Other artifacts also speak to long-standing indigenous traditions and technologies that were adapted to eighteenth- and nineteenth-century life. For example, we recovered a thick tumbler base with clear evidence of flaking on the broken edge. The full length of the piece had been worked using lithic technology, creating a curved and bifacially worked cutting tool. Sarah Burnee and Sarah Boston owned plenty of knives and had access to any number of iron tools, yet they chose to employ long-standing lithic technology on a broken piece of glass to achieve a function. This is important for two reasons: first, it speaks to the continued importance of indigenous knowledge in the everyday lives of the eighteenth- and nineteenth-century Nipmuc community; second, it speaks to the maker's ability to adapt this indigenous knowledge and apply it to a Euroamerican material, even several hundred years after contact. The historical depth of this knowledge is not clear; it was clearly common among the Nipmuc for thousands of years, but does this mean that it was viewed as an ancient practice by Sarah Burnee or Sarah Boston? Or was it a practice that remained part of everyday life rather than an old set of skills that they consciously sought to maintain? Both points are important considerations in the study of indigenous cultural persistence in the colonial and postcolonial era.[46]

Yet our considerations of heritage must not stop there. While the long arc of Nipmuc heritage before colonization is undoubtedly important, so are community, family memory, and heritage in the shorter term. When we think about a different scale of heritage within a more generational and multigenerational time frame, other objects also warrant the same kind of attention.[47] Take, for example, a silver-coated, seal-topped spoon found in the homestead's cellar feature (Figure 5.5). This kind of spoon dates to the second half of the seventeenth century, so it too stands out among a collection of late eighteenth- and early nineteenth-century things. With those dates, it may have a connection to the praying town period, when Sarah Robin's grandfather Petavit, as a community leader, interacted with goods brought by John Eliot to familiarize the tribe with an English lifestyle. Or it could have come from the home of Captain Whipple in Providence, Rhode Island, where Sarah Robins and her parents were held in servitude after King Philip's War (see Chapter 6). Perhaps she brought it with her when she moved to Hassanamesit as a memento of her time in Providence. The spoon shows little sign of wear, indicating that it was carefully curated during the eighteenth and early nineteenth centuries and kept for more than a century as an heirloom. While this object does not communicate indigeneity per se, it is still very important in a discussion of indigenous survival and continuity because it illustrates an unbroken connection with the family's past, celebrating either Petavit's leadership of the praying town community or Sarah Robins's hardship in servitude. In either case, this object celebrates Nipmuc heritage, albeit in a different way.

The same idea can be applied to a collection of matching eighteenth-century "bullet" buttons, most commonly found on Revolutionary War coats, recovered from the site. The presence of a number of these buttons suggests that Sarah Burnee and her daughter kept Joseph Aaron's Revolutionary War coat as a reminder of his military service. As mentioned above, the Revolution was an especially trying time for this family. Joseph fought in the war and sustained life-altering injuries. Because of these injuries, he was unable to work his land when he returned and had to sell it piecemeal to support himself and his wife in their old age. He essentially sacrificed his health and his land for the Revolution, making the coat a very important reminder of the price that Joseph—and

Figure 5.5. Silver-coated, seal-topped spoon from the Burnee/Boston Homestead site.

the family—paid for American independence. While American nationhood was (and remains) a direct affront to indigenous sovereignty, Joseph's involvement speaks to the complexity of his position. These buttons remind us that we all have multiple identities, some intersecting and some incongruous, without one negating the other. Rather than seeing themselves outside of the larger American community, Joseph, Sarah, and their descendants acknowledged their part within it, all without ever denying the indigenous community they still clearly remained part of. By the lifetimes of Sarah Burnee and Sarah Boston, being American *and* Native was a reality, as it was for so many other tribal people in New England by this time. Similar transitions had occurred for the Arnold/Cisco family across town (discussed in Chapter 7) as well.

We can take this concept of community one step further, using the China glazed tea wares found on the site as an illustration. Sometimes the things we find archaeologically were not meant to stand out as Nipmuc or even have special family significance but instead helped Nipmuc people find common ground with their neighbors and be a relevant part of the larger Grafton community, which is also an act of persistence.[48] China glazed tea wares were wildly popular between 1775 and 1812. These vessels were covered in a blue tinted glaze and painted with imitation Chinese patterns popularized by the more expensive Chinese porcelain that they were meant to reference.[49] Sarah Boston and her mother had several dozen. The China glazed tea wares found at the site were in fact significant in their "insignificance or commonness."[50] Virtually all the vessels are tea saucers or small shallow bowls, so it would seem that they played a prominent role in entertaining and in the social practice of taking tea in particular. The fact that Sarah and her mother participated in the consumption of English ceramics and Chinese patterns and drinking tea, just as their Euroamerican neighbors did, is noteworthy. After all, Sarah Boston and her mother Sarah Burnee did not experience their Nipmuc identity in a vacuum; they were also part of the early American experience, buying dishes and fabric and other goods that expressed their style and preferences, just like everyone else. These practices did not make them any less engaged or involved with their Nipmuc heritage, though, as other artifacts recovered from the site demonstrate.

## Discussion

As the collaboration between the Fiske Center and the Nipmuc Nation grew, it did so in a very organic way, much less formal than other such collaborations and built around listening and learning. Given our focus on chronology and the daily lives of those who lived with Sarah Burnee and Sarah Boston, it was easy to address a question that was important to the Nipmuc today: why had their petition for federal recognition been reversed in 2001? One of the reasons stated by the government was a lack of written documentation of community or political continuity.[51] For example, the federal government specifically questioned the written proof of Nipmuc political leadership between 1785 and 1808. The Nipmuc had argued, based on archival evidence alone, that Joseph Aaron, being prominent in petitions to the General Court, had adopted a leadership role in the community that likely continued until his death in 1808. The BIA countered in its denial of federal recognition in 2004, stating: "This FD [Final Determination] does not accept such an assumption as demonstrating 'substantially continuous' political leadership." The BIA further criticized that "from Joseph Aaron's death (in 1808) until the first petition submitted by John Hector in 1837 (Earle Papers), there ensued another period of 29 years where contemporary primary documentation of political authority or influence were lacking [*sic*]."[52]

We would argue that the archaeological evidence of community-centered foodways at the Burnee/Boston Homestead site corresponding with the period surrounding the BIA's doubts of political leadership makes a sound and robust argument for tribal leadership from both Joseph Aaron and more importantly his sister, Sarah Burnee, both elders in the community at this time. Archaeological evidence of the transition from farming to basketmaking further supports that, together, Joseph and Sarah brought the community through a very difficult postwar period and helped them find ways forward in an increasingly industrialized Blackstone River Valley. The totality of this empirical evidence represents a substantial contribution to the argument for political and community continuity of the Nipmuc in the nineteenth century and further strengthens their claim to legitimacy.

Archaeological evidence challenges the dominant and overly simplistic narrative of indigenous decline in New England, a narrative deeply engrained in popular culture (as discussed elsewhere in this book as well). It shifts the perspective from an administrative point of view to a more intimate and quotidian view of Nipmuc life that can reveal the creative and maybe inconspicuous things that the Nipmuc did to survive in times of hardship. It challenges the idea that change and transition in the Nipmuc community after colonization were tantamount to loss. Specifically, through evidence of occupational diversity and economic survival, combined with evidence of the maintenance of both long-term and short-term indigenous heritage, the archaeological work at the Burnee/Boston Homestead site demonstrates how constant change actually supported continuity of the community itself in a very real and important way.

The combined archival and archaeological evidence provides a highly detailed portrait of a household linked to its neighbors, Nipmuc and Euroamerican alike. This was not a marginalized group who lived in relative isolation from the rest of the households around Keith Hill and Worcester County more broadly (also evident at the Cisco Homestead site discussed in Chapter 7). The various economic and social strategies that the household adopted drew on both long-standing indigenous technologies, cultural practices, and knowledge and newly introduced ones. This combination of change and continuity was the earmark of a people facing a lifetime of struggle and the type of adaptation and culture change that we could expect to see with any population. But while land was lost through slow but deliberate dispossession (through legal instruments wielded by English colonial and United States governments), the Hassanamisco Nipmuc have successfully weathered colonialism to continue their struggle for political recognition and sovereignty. If the archaeology at Hassanamesit Woods aids that struggle, we believe that is the best use of our work that we can imagine.

## Notes

1. Kawashima 1969, 42–56.
2. See O'Brien 1997 for a detailed discussion of this practice.
3. Massachusetts Archives Collection (MAC) 1701–1750, 694.
4. MAC 1750–1757, 592.
5. Earle 1652–1863, Box 1, Folder 3.
6. Earle 1652–1863, Box 1, Folder 4.
7. Earle 1861.
8. Earle 1861, 87–99.
9. Earle 1652–1863, Box 1, Folder 5.
10. Earle 1652–1863, Box 1, Folder 1.
11. Earle 1861, 96.
12. Law et al. 2008.
13. Gary (2005) interviewed the operator of the bulldozer. Several photographs of the event are still held at the Grafton Historical Society.
14. 1886 Deed Map of Keith Hill copy housed at Fiske Center, UMass Boston.
15. Mrozowski and Law Pezzarossi 2015.
16. Tuhiwai Smith 1999.

17. Snow and Lanphear 1988.
18. Calloway 1997.
19. Law Pezzarossi 2019; O'Brien 2010.
20. Allard 2015.
21. Earle 1652–1863, Box 1, Folder 4.
22. Earle 1652–1863, Box 1, Folder 4.
23. Quintal 2005, 77.
24. Earle 1652–1863, Box 1, Folder 1.
25. *Providence Gazette*, 14, no. 703: 4.
26. Piechota 2015, 124.
27. Massachusetts, Office of the Secretary of State 1904, 311.
28. Estes 1894, 406.
29. Law Pezzarossi 2014a, 353.
30. See 25 CFR Part 83, US Department of the Interior, Indian Affairs (June 29, 2015), https://www.bia.gov/as-ia/raca/revisions-regulations-federal-acknowledgment-indian-tribes-25-cfr-83-or-part-83.
31. See, for example, Gould 2013.
32. Allard 2015.
33. Pezzarossi 2014.
34. Pezzarossi 2014.
35. Law et al. 2008, 158; Pezzarossi 2014.
36. Law 2008, 100; Law et al. 2008, 172.
37. Pezzarossi et al. 2010, 217.
38. Bragdon 1988; Rockman and Rothschild. 1984.
39. Bragdon 1988.
40. Pezzarossi et al. 2010, 217.
41. Allard 2015.
42. Adams 2003; Pezzarossi et al. 2010, 217.
43. McMullen 1987, 102–123.
44. Truncer 2004.
45. Bagley et al. 2015.
46. Law 2008, 109.
47. Silliman 2009.
48. Pezzarossi 2014.
49. Samford 2014, 32.
50. Pezzarossi 2014, 165.
51. See Proposed Finding against Federal Acknowledgement of the Nipmuc Nation (2001), https://www.federalregister.gov/documents/2001/10/01/01–24513/proposed-finding-against-federal-acknowledgment-of-the-nipmuc-nation.
52. 2004 Nipmuc Nation Final Determination (June 18, 2004, 91), https://www.bia.gov/sites/bia.gov/files/assets/as-ia/ofa/petition/069A_npmcna_MA/069a_fd.pdf.

# 6

## Movement and the Nipmuc Landscape

### The Legacy of Sarah "Boston" Philips

HEATHER LAW PEZZAROSSI

Archaeologists get a very specific view of the lives of the people they study. This perspective is based on intimate knowledge of a specific place and logically restricted in scale and scope. While these perspectives are valuable in the study of Nipmuc archaeology, the study of Nipmuc landscapes benefits from a complementary consideration of the different ways people occupy a place, to make it their own and continue to reside upon it regardless of ownership. This is especially true given the documented patterns of movement practiced and land loss suffered by Nipmuc people after King Philip's War (1675–1676). For many scholars, the loss of King Philip's War is viewed as a turning point, when Native people in southern New England no longer maintained an advantage over the settler population.[1] Native communities were forced to make drastic changes in their livelihoods to survive.[2] These strategies often included dimensions of mobility and impermanence that are difficult to find through archaeology. This chapter combines an archaeological perspective with a broader consideration of Nipmuc residence to gain a better understanding of the cultural landscapes of a Nipmuc family in the Blackstone River Valley through the last decades of the colonial period and into the nineteenth century.

In 2005 I joined the Hassanamesit Woods Project, a collaborative effort by the Nipmuc Nation, the Fiske Center for Archaeological Research at UMass Boston, and the town of Grafton, Massachusetts. The goal was to investigate the remains of a homestead that belonged to a Nipmuc woman named Sarah "Boston" Philips in the early nineteenth century. She was a well-known Nipmuc basketmaker until her death in 1837 and a celebrated member of the Grafton community. The remains of her home sat buried under a twentieth-century apple orchard, now a thickly overgrown forest, tangled with vines and scattered with traces of old stone walls.[3]

With a little research, we learned that Sarah "Boston" Phillips had a very important family history. Her matrilineage shows that her great-grandmother Sarah Robins was allocated over 100 acres of land at Hassanamesit in 1727 on what became Keith Hill in the town of Grafton. According to colonial records, Sarah Robins established this plot of land as a home for her family and began a tradition of passing the land down through the female line. Sarah Boston's grandmother, Sarah Muckamaug, inherited the land from her mother, Sarah Robins, and oversaw construction of the family home before passing it to her young daughter Sarah Burnee at the time of her death in 1751. Sarah Burnee (Sarah Boston's mother) lived for eighty-one years on Keith Hill, serving as a matriarch to the Nipmuc community throughout the Revolutionary War and beyond. Sarah Boston herself became a well-known basketmaker and farm-hand who appears in many local histories.[4] She grew up on the family property and inherited her family's land in Grafton at the time of her mother's death in 1824. She lived there her entire life, just as her mother and grandmother had done before her. While this research covers just over 100 years (between 1727 and 1837), Sarah Boston's great-grandmother's role as one of seven Nipmuc proprietors involved in the transfer of Hassanamesit to settlers (and its re-naming to Grafton) hints at an even deeper familial connection between the Nipmuc people and the Hassanamesit landscape.

And in fact Sarah Robins's familial connections to Hassanamesit extend far further into the past. She likely descended from one of the most well-known Nipmuc families that in the seventeenth century had cultivated one of the most amiable and prosperous relationships with the English in all of southern New England. The man believed to have been her grandfather (Petavit, alias Robin) was a leader at Hassanamesit when it was a praying town; he died in 1674. Her father and uncle, Petavit's sons Joseph and Samson, both came to be trusted figures in the community and eventually left Hassanamesit to become religious teachers at Wabbaquasset and Chobonokonomum, respectively. They played key roles as mediators during King Philip's War and were among the seven families that returned to Hassanamesit after the war to regain what they could of their former homeland.[5] Another prominent family from this time, the Printers, also returned to Hassanamesit and was part of the 1727 land division. That decision resulted in the Nipmuc Tribe holding on to a small parcel today known as the Hassanamisco Reservation (discussed in Chapter 7). At first glance, this Nipmuc story seemed very much to be about one very specific plot of land, the Robins's parcel.

◙ ◙ ◙

Our excavation began in the summer of 2006. I belonged to a team of graduates and undergraduates conducting a field school at Hassanamesit Woods in search of Sarah Boston's home. We accessed the site by lugging equipment a quarter-mile down the defunct Providence and Worcester Railroad lines then trudged halfway up the eastern slope of the hill and set to work clearing underbrush, vines, and leaves from the forest floor. We established a grid to organize the excavation, working within the old stonewalled plots to find logic in the historic landscape. What we hoped to find was continuity, maybe something connecting the eighteenth- and nineteenth-century occupations to the seventeenth-century praying town or a satisfying layering of colonial and precolonial occupations.

In the second season we uncovered the corner of Sarah's stone house foundation under a brittle old apple tree. The next five summers were spent carefully exposing the footprint of the house, mapping and gingerly lifting rocks out of the old cellar to define its walls. When the house foundation was clear, we looked for the barn. What animals did Sarah have? How did she use her land? Could we see generational changes in how the landscape was used? We designed further studies of landscape features and recovered material culture and animal and plant remains to answer these questions. The site was excavated in 2 × 2 meter blocks, 10 centimeters at a time, sometimes with shovels and buckets, at other times on hands and knees with trowels and dustpans. Each excavation unit often took several weeks to excavate. Some, like those deep into what was once Sarah's cellar, took years of careful rock removal, mapmaking, and stratigraphic analysis, as the field schools were limited to summer. Throughout the excavation we came across objects hinting at lives spent far beyond the bounds of the family plot: a set of "bullet buttons" from a Revolutionary War coat, a fancy silver coated spoon, some boot spikes for more effective foot travel in the winter.

Archaeologists can focus narrowly on one place—in this case, the Burnee/Boston Homestead—and tend to minimize the importance of lives lived in a broader landscape. We wanted to find a contained history, but what we found instead was a clip, just a node of a larger history of the Nipmuc's occupation of their ancestral landscape that we could not hope to find in that one place.

The story that we pieced together is unique to this family, but it speaks more broadly of the Nipmuc's occupation of their homelands in what today is called the Blackstone River Valley during the colonial period (until 1775) and beyond. It challenges us to think about how we make and maintain landscapes as our own. The relationships that people have with important spaces and places are not necessarily bound by ownership in a legal sense. While they may not belong to us in title, they can belong to us in other, arguably more important ways. "Dwelling" in this sense, or the occupation of a place, includes all kinds of residence, including personal land ownership, land ownership as a collective, landscapes of familiarity created through continuous practices of movement and work, landscapes of confinement, landscapes formed through the maintenance of social relationships, and the maintenance of memorial landscapes through continued practices of storytelling. Places formed and maintained in these ways challenge the taken-for-granted values and sentimental notions that accompany Western-style sedentism and land ownership, especially in colonial and settler colonial settings.[6] Places of dwelling include renting, squatting, and the familiarity that comes with traveling a landscape over and over and laboring within it. These kinds of landscapes challenge us to consider the full experience of occupying a place that is more complex than residing in a house or owning a plot of land.[7] They must involve reconsiderations of scale, of movement, and perhaps most importantly an overlapping and simultaneity of landscapes (for example, indigenous/colonial or ancient/modern) that may or may not be compatible with one another yet nonetheless coexist.

◎ ◎ ◎

We worked on site in the summers. I flew home from my graduate studies in Berkeley, California, each May and settled into my sister's attic in Providence, Rhode Island. Each morning I packed my kit and hurried out the door into an idling station wagon driven by our field director. We made our way from Providence to Grafton, a journey of about 40 miles northwest, spanning nearly the entire length of the Blackstone River Valley. The river, once known as the "Nipmuc River," begins as a trickle of streams in the hills of Worcester, Massachusetts, and terminates in Narragansett Bay, just north of Providence. When I first began this commute, I had no idea of the significance of this geography in Nipmuc history, but as my research progressed I began to appreciate the parallel between my own daily commute and the historic landscape of Sarah Boston's family. In the following passages I have chosen to juxtapose my own habitual movement through the Blackstone River Valley with my understanding of the dynamics of Native landscapes over the course of the eighteenth and nineteenth centuries in this same geographical place. Of course, I am not attempting to define or bound these Nipmuc landscapes; nor am I claiming to understand Nipmuc landscapes because I traveled through the valley myself. I only seek to acknowledge my own situated perspective and illustrate the intimate ways in which places and routes become important in the framing of histories.

The Blackstone River Valley has always been an important place for the Nipmuc and other indigenous communities. Whereas European settlers often use(d) rivers to mark boundaries between places, Native people in the Northeast have long used rivers as central arteries and thoroughfares of trade and communication.[8] Similarly, the riverine uplands of southern New England have always been places of movement for the indigenous peoples living there. Archaeological evidence points to ancient practices of seasonal movement in and out of the woodland valleys—designed to maximize the resources of each locale—that composed the rhythm of the indigenous semisedentary lifestyle dating back several thousand years.[9]

The English who first settled in the area made early attempts to convert local indigenous people not only to their religion but to their way of life, including English practices of sedentary habitation and intensive agriculture (see the discussion in previous chapters). The praying towns of the early Massachusetts Bay Colony were some of the most well-documented attempts to accomplish this wholesale conversion,[10] as earlier chapters in this book discuss. These fourteen praying towns, scattered about modern-day central and eastern Massachusetts and northeast Connecticut, were located strategically on important paths between the colonies. Hassanamesit sat about halfway between Boston and the Connecticut colony but also atop the Blackstone River Valley, connecting it with the Rhode Island colony and Narragansett Bay. While these positions made it relatively easy for John Eliot and his English overseers to travel in and out (keeping close tabs on each community's status), the conversion effort itself was based on confinement of indigenous occupants. While being trained in the catechism and the English style of farming, residents were kept apart from surrounding communities to gain the effects of full immersion.[11] The success of these tactics has been questioned by modern scholars.[12]

When King Philip's War erupted in 1675, English support of the praying town experiment ended abruptly. Members of Sarah Robins's family—along with the other so-called friendly Indians—were in an awkward position. The English did not trust them and attempted to keep praying town residents confined to designated areas, eventually shipping many to Deer Island in Boston Harbor to die of starvation (see Chapter 4).[13] During this period and for some time after King Philip's War, Hassanamesit, while undeniably rich in Nipmuc heritage, once again became a landscape of confinement, defined by Euroamerican boundaries and often difficult to move in and out of. Native mobility (specifically up and down the Blackstone River Valley) was often the best advantage against these tactics of confinement. In a letter to the Massachusetts Council, Captain Daniel Henchman reported that "all the Indians were in continual motion," some moving "towards Narragansett, others toward Watchusett [north of Worcester], shifting gradually, and taking up each other's Quarters," staying "not above a Night in a Place."[14]

In the fall of 1675 a group of 300 of Philip's men set siege to Hassanamesit and coerced its inhabitants, including Sarah Robins's father and uncle (Joseph and Samson), away to Philip's winter encampment at Manemesit (now Barre, Massachusetts), about 30 miles northwest of Hassanamesit. Joseph and Samson continued to bounce between camps in the Watchusett area throughout the war, providing council to King Philip and acting as mediators with the English.

In the aftermath of King Philip's War movement was still a practical and important part of survival. Nipmuc groups and individuals traveled south to join the Mohegan in Connecticut, while others traveled west to take refuge with their Mahican neighbors at Schaghticoke. Still others went north to Penacook territory and found shelter there. Records indicate that many Nipmuc traveled to Boston, Providence, and Hartford and surrendered there.[15] Local officials sold most of these women and children into "involuntary indenture" for a period of years based on their age at surrender. Colonial records indicate that Sarah Robins and her mother chose to travel with other Nipmuc families from points in Massachusetts through the Blackstone River Valley to Providence, where sentencing for war captives was comparatively lenient.[16]

◙ ◙ ◙

As we found our way out of Providence each morning to head to the site, we descended College Hill, passing many of the oldest buildings in the city. In the late seventeenth century long waterfront plots extending up College Hill were granted to some of Providence's founding families: the Browns (who founded Brown University), the Wickendens (who established one of the oldest churches on the East Side), and the Whipples (who helped build Rhode Island's shipping industry).[17] Many of these buildings still serve as cornerstones of Providence's urban landscape. As a long-time resident of New England, it struck me that certain historic landscapes, especially the ones constructed by the powerful elite, are so visible, so omnipresent, as to be iconic. I can't help but wonder how much of our understanding of these cities' histories is colored and warped by the privileged remains that we see each day. By looking past or perhaps even through these names and grand structures, we can construct a more inclusive landscape that considers indigenous lives and landscapes not truncated or erased by the colonial incursion but coexisting in conjunction, opposition, and negotiation with it.[18]

Documentary evidence suggests that Sarah Robins was just a small child when she was indentured in Providence to the Whipples. The Whipples were an important family in Providence and factor greatly into the story of Sarah and her descendants. Captain John Whipple served in several influential roles before King Philip's War: he was a councilman, tavern-owner, deputy to the General Assembly, selectman, treasurer, surveyor, and moderator, all in the town of Providence between 1666 and 1676.[19] His house and tavern stood on North Main Street, a few hundred yards from where the Roger Williams Monument stands today. Then it was prime waterfront property in the very center of Providence's rapidly expanding landscape; today an awkward intersection bustles in front of a modern-style condominium complex just north of Star Street, where Whipple's two-story, stone chimneyed house once stood (see Figure 6.1).[20] Whipple's home and tavern served as the meeting place for the Providence Town Council before King Philip's War, and Roger Williams preached there. Many residents fled when war erupted in 1675 and Providence was all but destroyed, but Whipple stayed. His home was spared, making it one of the oldest buildings in the city until it was destroyed in the early twentieth century.

In 1676 Whipple, "who stayed and went not away" during the war, was both appointed to the committee that decided the sentencing of indigenous captives and granted a "share" of their servitude for himself.[21] Sarah Robins, who had a documented relationship with the Whipples later in life,[22] was likely granted

Figure 6.1. Captain John Whipple house, Providence, Rhode Island. Howard W. Preston, photographer. (Courtesy of the Rhode Island State Archives, Preston Collection)

to John Whipple and/or his family by John Whipple himself, essentially as a spoil of war. As such Sarah would have spent her childhood in service to the Whipple family, for John Whipple Sr., his son John Jr., or his grandson John III. Together these men owned several properties including two taverns and at least two homes, all near Star Street and North Main.[23] Sarah, like many other young Nipmuc captives in post–King Philip's War New England, likely grew up washing dishes, cleaning, laundering clothes, and working in one of the Whipples' taverns. While male-centered histories tend to ignore the role that people (especially women of color) played in the history of early Providence, Sarah's presence here was an important part of a broader and more inclusive Nipmuc colonial history. As such, Providence is an important place in the study of historic Nipmuc landscapes.

While Sarah Robins was growing up in Providence, Nipmuc families began returning to Hassanamesit by the 1680s or 1690s, led by James Printer, after the threats of Mohawk raids had abated. Beginning in the early eighteenth century, the colonial government again made several attempts to confine Nipmuc families to the old praying towns. Following King Philip's War, in 1677 all Native people except servants and apprentices were ordered to report to Natick, Punkapoag, Wamesit, or Hassanamesit.[24] In 1706 the New England Company petitioned the General Court for stricter guarding of the boundaries at Natick, Punkapoag, and Hassanamesit, warning the court that Native people "pass through the Towns & Travile into the Woods without Licence from authority."[25] In 1708 the court again ordered stricter enforcement of the boundaries around the former praying towns with the knowledge that "the friend Indians do still Presume to Travel into the Woods, & amongst the Frontier towns, contrary to the Order of the Court."[26]

Given their initial land allotment in 1727, Sarah Robins likely had an active presence in Hassanamesit, despite her continued work obligations in Providence. With such restrictions and regulations placed on the inhabitants of the former praying towns, Sarah's status as a servant may have given her the freedom that others in her community did not have to move in and out of Hassanamesit. With movement restrictions eased for servants and apprentices (by the 1677 regulation), it would have been beneficial for the Hassanamesit community to have members in indentured servant roles, if for no other reason than to increase the potential flow of goods, information, and people in and out of the community in a safe and reliable way. Sarah likely traversed the length of the Blackstone River Valley many times to return home to Hassanamesit, possibly delivering food and other goods as well as valuable information during the insecure postwar decades. This means that she was familiar not only with the budding urban landscape of Providence and her ancestral home at Hassanamesit but also with the routes between.

Sarah Robins's familiarity with both Hassanamesit and Providence is a starting point to imagine one example of the scale of the colonial Native landscape. Her world included spaces of labor and privilege, complex racial and cultural spaces, and urban and rural spaces alike that were occupied by both Native people and Euroamerican settlers in the decades following King Philip's War. It also included landscapes learned by moving successfully through them, negotiating colonial boundaries and restrictions in the process. Her life, as well as other Native lives, played out not in the margins of the colonial world but right in the middle of it. Sarah Robins not only lived her daily life in urban places like taverns and the homes of the wealthy and powerful (she was a stone's throw from a bustling wharf in one of the most important ports of colonial New England) but also had important connections to the countryside and an intimate understanding of the Blackstone River Valley.

◙ ◙ ◙

In 1727 the General Court of the Massachusetts Bay Colony allotted Sarah Robins and her husband Peter Muckamaug 106 acres on the eastern slope of what later became Keith Hill following the sale of 7,500 acres of Nipmuc land to establish the town of Grafton. Six other Nipmuc families were also allotted properties in the surrounding countryside, including Moses Printer (see Chapter 7). Sarah and Peter, likely in their fifties or sixties by that time, left Providence the following year to claim their land and presumably to reside in Hassanamesit more permanently.[27] They seem to have had two children—a son George and a daughter Sarah—while they were living in Providence.[28] When they left for Hassanamesit, they left their grown daughter Sarah Muckamaug in service in the Whipple household, now headed by Captain Whipple's grandson John III.[29]

Young Sarah Muckamaug, like her mother, spent her early years working as a domestic servant, facilitating the privileged and extravagant colonial lifestyle of the Whipples. Probate records show that the Whipples rejected the Puritan values of their predecessors and embraced a lavish way of life, surrounded by the finest china, furniture, and clothing with many servants and several slaves.[30]

The same year that her parents left, Sarah Muckamaug married one of the Whipple's slaves, Aaron Whipple, in the home of William Page.[31] Aaron was owned by John Whipple III's uncle, Joseph Whipple, and resided in the same vicinity on North Main Street.[32] Sarah and Aaron had four children: two daughters, Rhoda and Abigail, and two sons, Abraham and Joseph. We have no dates for the births of the first three children, but the fourth, Joseph Aaron, was born in Providence around 1740 with the help of a midwife named Hallelujah Brown Olney.[33]

Shortly after the birth of Joseph Aaron, Sarah Muckamaug's father, Peter Muckamaug, died.[34] She left Providence for Hassanamesit with her infant to help her mother, leaving her older children (Rhoda, Abigail, and Abraham) in

Figure 6.2. Richard Brown house, Providence, Rhode Island (Library of Congress, Prints & Photographs Division, HABS RI-31)

Providence, just as her parents had done with her, in the service of the Brown family.[35] They lived and worked on what was then known as the Grotto Farm owned by Richard Brown.[36] His brick farmhouse still stands on the grounds of Butler Hospital on Swan Point Road, the oldest brick house in the city (Figure 6.2). It too has a celebrated past, filled with white men who played important roles in the establishment of Providence and later in the American Revolution. Yet the focus on such landmarks neglects the role of the people of color who lived and labored in these same spaces, making them just as much Nipmuc and African American landscapes as they are Euroamerican ones.

⊙ ⊙ ⊙

Working our way out of Providence, we join traffic onto Route 146, a modern four-lane highway that zips up the Blackstone River Valley from Providence to Worcester with efficiency. This nondescript interstate highway provides little evidence of the historic and geographic importance of its route. Travelers cannot see the river from the road; nor can they really make out the valley from the tree-lined highway. In fact, the road was built to circumvent the peculiarities of the Blackstone River Valley that make it so historically significant. It curves gracefully above mill villages and skirts awkward town centers for the sake of efficiency. While the highway itself is relatively new, its path is not. It was constructed in the shadow of a far older path, known in the colonial era as the Great Road. In the seventeenth and eighteenth centuries the Great Road was one of two main routes through the Blackstone River Valley from Providence to southeastern Massachusetts. Constructed between 1660 and 1683, it followed a similar path as the modern highway, winding roughly along the west bank of the Blackstone River, leading farmers and lime miners in and out of the countryside surrounding Providence.[37] It was eventually connected to Worcester in 1737. Yet the Great Road was not a new path even then. It followed the Shawomet Path, an important indigenous thoroughfare that traced the banks of the Blackstone, linking the Nipmuc, Narragansett, and other indigenous communities long before it served European settlers.[38]

Sarah Muckamaug traveled this road, like her parents before her, in 1740 on her way home to Hassanamesit with her infant son, Joseph. Thanks to a detailed investigation into the legitimacy of Sarah Muckamaug's marriage to Aaron Whipple some twenty-five years later,[39] colonial records contain several in-depth accounts of Sarah Muckamaug's actions during this time. Mary Wilkinson claimed that Sarah set up a temporary shelter for herself and her child on her farm in what is now Lincoln, Rhode Island.[40] The Wilkinson land sat about a half-mile "from the Blackstone River on the main road from Providence to Woonsocket Falls, three miles from the latter place, and twelve from the former."[41] Nineteenth-century descriptions report that the Wilkinson homestead was situated on a hill on the west side of the river, facing east with a view of both the river below and Cumberland Hill beyond. The walk from North Main Street in Providence, where her employer John Whipple III lived, to the Wilkinson farmstead is now about a four-hour walk, but the journey may have taken twice as long, considering that she was traveling with a child in road conditions that colonial officials called "rough, hilly, crooked and indirect."[42]

Mary Wilkinson attested that Sarah had asked to build a "hut," which she then lived in "for some time."[43] It is possible that she had learned to make this journey, and build such shelters, while on previous trips to and from Providence and Grafton with her parents, Peter and Sarah. We know little about what this "hut" looked like, yet its existence is crucial to our discussion of historic Nipmuc landscapes. It points to the continuation of an important tradition of mobility within the Nipmuc community of the mid-eighteenth century, a kind of semipermanent practice of dwelling (on land owned by a third party) that would rarely have resulted in any official documentation and likely left a small and ephemeral archaeological trace equally difficult to find. This tradition was carried out by a woman who, by all accounts, spent most of her life in service to a privileged white family in an urban environment, yet she still had the knowledge to do it successfully alone with an infant.

These are the kinds of places—whether we call them homes, or shelters or just stopping-over places—that made the continued practice of traveling the Nipmuc landscape possible in the colonial period. Keep in mind that the Blackstone River Valley was likely a place of great uncertainty in the eighteenth century, so these are not necessarily places of nostalgia. While at first glance they seem to fulfill a straightforward need for shelter, they may often have been necessitated by anxiety about the changing countryside and the settlers who were beginning to occupy it in greater numbers.[44]

After her stay at the Wilkinson farm, Sarah Muckamaug would have continued her journey along the course of the Blackstone River on the Great Road, stopping for the night again somewhere near Uxbridge. Then she crossed to the eastern side of the river closer to Grafton at Andrew Abraham's "ford way" at the confluence of the Blackstone and Quinsigamond Rivers or at one of the bridges built by Elisha Johnson in the 1720s.[45] There she would connect to the Mendon Road, taking her right to the base of the hill of her family's land.

◎ ◎ ◎

We descend from the high ground of the interstate and roll gently down Sutton Street in Northbridge, Massachusetts, passing several nineteenth-century farmsteads. It is easy to romanticize these landscapes; contemporary narratives of early American history encourage us to venerate them as part of our American heritage, thoughtfully conserving old homes and taverns as idyllic reminders of a colonial landscape. We are not often reminded of the indigenous landscapes that these colonial ones overlie; nor do we often see the complex ways in which Native people were involved in forging this American rural landscape.

Joseph Aaron was only an infant when his mother carried him from Providence to his grandparent's land in Grafton around 1740. There Sarah Muckamaug married her second husband, an African American man named Fortune

Burnee, and together they constructed a home for Joseph and his young half-sister, Sarah Burnee (born in 1743), before Sarah Muckamaug died in 1751.[46] But unlike his sister, who lived out her entire life on the family farmstead in Grafton, Joseph had a more complex path. His story challenges us again to ask how Nipmuc people continued to occupy their homelands—not just the lands they owned, but a much broader landscape defined just as much by colonial restrictions and motivations as indigenous heritage.

When Joseph's mother died he was only eleven. A year after her death his stepfather, Fortune Burnee, sent Joseph to serve as an apprentice at David Daniels's farm in Mendon, Massachusetts.[47] Life on the Daniels farm, however, was not an isolated rural existence. Joseph was likely involved in the Daniels enterprise as a caretaker of stagecoach horses associated with an important tavern and stopover point on the Mendon Road called Coverdale Stand.[48] It was located not far from the Daniels farm at the halfway point between Providence and Worcester (Figure 6.3).

Figure 6.3. Coverdale Stand on the Mendon Road, ca. 1905–1915. Theodore Clemens Wohlbruck, photographer. (Courtesy of American Antiquarian Society, Worcester, Mass.)

Archival records indicate that during his time at the Daniels farm, Joseph Aaron maintained active social ties in Grafton and in Providence. For example, his presence is recorded in Grafton in 1763, at the age of about twenty-two, when Timothy Paine paid him and his sister six shillings through the Grafton General Store.[49] Yet in 1768 the midwife who delivered Joseph in Providence in 1740 remembered him having spent much of his life in Providence.[50] Given his recorded activity in both locations, Joseph likely used his association with the Coverdale Stand to travel relatively freely throughout the Blackstone River Valley when he could, maintaining connections with both his father and siblings in Providence and his sister and stepfather in Grafton.

As a grown man Joseph returned home to Grafton, establishing his own farm at the base of the hill after settlement of the lengthy and contentious court battle with his sister Sarah over division of the family land.[51] After only a few years of raising rye, Joseph left again. In 1774 he was "gone to sea," prompting his wife to rent their pasturelands for income.[52] In 1778 he left again, enlisting as a soldier in the American Revolution under a Captain Warren in the 15th Battalion.

Joseph Aaron served his Nipmuc community faithfully after the Revolution, often signing as lead petitioner on pleas to the General Court for more just treatment of the Hassanamisco Nipmuc.[53] But by the time he returned to Grafton, he had sustained injuries that plagued him the rest of his life. Unable to maintain his farm, he began weaving baskets and selling off sections of his land for income. Joseph Aaron's final parcel of land was willed to neighbor Silas Fay at the time of Joseph's death in 1808, in return for care that he and his wife received in their old age. For the Nipmuc community in the late eighteenth century, this practice was all too familiar. A similar sale across town fifty years later left the Arnold family with just over three acres (discussed in Chapter 7), the last Nipmuc parcel in Grafton.

Many Hassanamesit families found themselves dispossessed of any land they held earlier through Euroamerican tactics of indebting Native residents to their settler neighbors. Native families often paid for basic needs like health care and home improvements through the only means they had, the sale of their land.[54] Seemingly well-meaning neighbors often offered to pay these expenses in return for a portion of land abutting their own farms. By the time the American Revolution was over, many Native families like Joseph Aaron's had little left to sell.

Joseph's story reminds us that many Nipmuc people spent their lives in motion not necessarily by choice but rather as an outcome of the historical and economic circumstances that they found themselves in. Joseph likely did not choose to leave Grafton when his mother died or sacrifice his health and subsequently his land for the American Revolution. However, his cumulative legacy is an excellent example of how Nipmuc people inhabited the New England landscape in the eighteenth century. If we just looked in one place, we would miss a great deal of Joseph's story. We might glimpse the roles he played within the Hassanamisco community and see his story as rather tragic, resulting ultimately in an unfortunate loss of land for the Nipmuc. But we would miss his involvement in the African American community in Providence and would never appreciate the connections he must have made within the Blackstone River Valley as part of the stagecoach community on the Mendon Road. We might not appreciate the great sacrifices he made: first his health for the early republic, then his land for the care of his wife. His story challenges us to think of the Nipmuc community not as an entity to which an individual belonged(s) in isolation but as one dimension of a complex set of relationships with all kinds of people, with nations both ancient and formative, that ultimately shaped the spaces that he inhabited.

As we come to the center of Northbridge on our way to the site, we see water spilling efficiently over one of the old dams abutting the many mills that lined the Blackstone River in the early nineteenth century. The Industrial Revolution took hold in the Blackstone River Valley beginning in 1793 with Samuel Slater's textile mill in Pawtucket, Rhode Island, then grew exponentially as mills and their associated villages cropped up on the Blackstone's riverbanks.[55] Many of the mills are now abandoned, creating a postindustrial landscape of gravel yards set against the ruins of stone and brick structures. Some mills crumbled; others are still occupied. Businesses that still inhabit these structures—places like the Curtain Factory and Braid Rug Depot—hint at the once vibrant textile industry that transformed the area from an agrarian farmscape to an industrial nexus in the early nineteenth century.

Often indigenous histories and landscapes get lost in this premodern, early industrial narrative. Indeed, it was a difficult time for the Nipmuc, as it was for many people living in the Blackstone River Valley after the American Revolution. By the time Sarah Burnee's daughter Sarah Boston inherited her land in 1824, so much had been sold over the years that it was untenable as a farmstead.[56] While this was a common problem for the Nipmuc, it became widespread even within the Euroamerican community in the early nineteenth century. As land inheritances grew smaller, and space for spreading out became scarce, many families of all ethnicities had to find other ways to make a living.[57]

Like many of her neighbors, Sarah Boston was forced to imagine new ways forward, new ways to survive in a world that was changing at a rapid pace. Sarah and many of her Native contemporaries across New England were part of a movement in the late eighteenth and early nineteenth centuries to establish a trade in basketmaking, chair caning, and broom-making that they mobilized by selling wares throughout the rural countryside.

Native basketmaking in New England has a rich history that extends from the precolonial era to the present day. Yet the basketry developed in the post–Revolutionary War era was unique because it was intended specifically for sale to the settler community. Women often worked together in groups, making baskets in fall and winter and traveling regionally in the warmer months, selling their wares.[58] They established regional routes on which they sold baskets to the same households year after year.[59] The Native practice—initiated by precolonial practices of regional and seasonal mobility yet transformed by motivations specific to the early years of the Industrial Revolution—provided a lucrative enterprise and a way to maintain social networks among widely dispersed Native families. They offered a material justification for Native people to continue to inhabit a landscape that they no longer owned.[60]

Baskets from this developing trade are well known and well studied. Scholars of Native New England basketry have established that their decorative motifs and unique forms and materials can be traced to specific networks of Native artisans.[61] Rather than claim that only certain geographically defined Native factions used particular patterns, colors, and forms, more nuanced scholarship acknowledges more complex distinctions. While proximity and tribal politics do influence designs, their similarities and differences more accurately reflect communities of basketmakers that probably had multiple tribal allegiances who by necessity moved broadly across a social landscape of their own making (and may have also had intertribal kinship ties). These communities shared time together, sheltered one another on their travels, and likely influenced one another's skills and creative decisions, resulting in the distribution of different basket styles and baskets themselves far beyond established tribal homelands. This is also how Nipmuc people today understand the landscape of southern New England, as a network of places connected over time and space by kinship and community.

Yet in this context the baskets did even more than connect Native artisans to one another. They also served very effectively to create lasting relationships between indigenous artisans and their settler customers, whose business made their livelihoods possible. Small decorative baskets satisfied an emerging craving for domestic order, beauty, and cleanliness. The chosen size and form, in combination with the ornamental floral patterns, appealed to Euroamerican women as efficient yet ornamental storage solutions for clothing and other home goods.[62] Distinct styles signaled an "authentic Indianness" that continued to gain currency in popular culture and politics as the American historical narrative developed in the early decades of the Republic. These styles helped Native women establish repeat and reliable customers within their widespread networks.

The landscapes that Native basketry facilitated in the nineteenth century were multidimensional. They both strengthened Native communities and further developed the relationships that Native people had with the surrounding settler community.

◎ ◎ ◎

As we reach Grafton, we turn right on Old Upton Road, leading up the eastern slope of Keith Hill, and park in a hay field lined with stone walls running parallel to the now defunct Providence and Worcester Railroad tracks. The tracks curve gracefully through the Grafton forest, skirting what is now Hassanamesit Woods on their way to Worcester. After distributing equipment among the crew, our daily quarter-mile march down the tracks begins. We match our steps with the placement of railroad ties, grateful for the slightly awkward yet direct path right to the edge of the Burnee/Boston Homestead site. The rail lines, established in the mid-nineteenth century, replaced the short-lived Blackstone Canal as a cheaper and more reliable means of transporting people and goods from Providence to Worcester through the Blackstone River Valley. In 1847 the Providence and Worcester Railroad constructed its main line through Grafton. The track wound around the base of the hill not more than 100 yards from Sarah Boston's recently vacated home.

Sarah Boston was remembered locally as the "last descendant of King Philip." Indeed, her death in 1837 and the subsequent sale of her remaining land in Grafton in 1854 tend to mark an end point for this Nipmuc family's historical narrative. From both an archaeological perspective and an archival one Native visibility is very closely tied with land ownership and continuous occupancy. But ending our story with Sarah Boston can be particularly harmful for the broader narrative of Nipmuc persistence in the nineteenth century. Shrinking Nipmuc landholdings and decreased archival visibility have been interpreted by historians as a general diminished presence—or even a "vanishing"—of the Nipmuc in the Blackstone River Valley.[63] If we studied broader trends in the volume of Nipmuc landholdings in the early nineteenth century, we might be tempted to draw this conclusion. But this assumption needs to be challenged.

The Industrial Revolution and its accompanying modernist attitude had an enormous impact on the perception of Nipmuc persistence.[64] As the network of railroads expanded in New England, Euroamericans moved to Worcester and other urban centers in record numbers. They were eager to differentiate their own newfound mobility from the "aimless" mobility that they had falsely identified and spent the last century rebuking in their Native neighbors. They saw their movement as a product of modernity, a result of the burgeoning industrialism and cosmopolitanism in the region, aided by the arrival of local rail systems and justified by the inevitable expansion of the American frontier. When Native people sold their land and moved westward or toward New England's cities, however, they were considered "uprooted" or even "vanished." [65] By extension, their claims to Native persistence on the landscape, and even Native identity, were considered baseless.

In the mid-nineteenth century, as Nipmuc landholdings became scarcer and scarcer, many indigenous people, like their Euroamerican and African American counterparts, found work as soldiers, laborers, and baggage-handlers; others took jobs in the many factories along the Blackstone, becoming tanners and shoemakers. Many Nipmuc people, like Sarah Boston's daughter Sarah Mary, and John Hector (see Chapter 7), moved to Worcester to find work, live with kin, and make new homes for themselves in a city that was considered a relatively safe and prosperous place for people of color at the time.[66]

Sarah Mary Boston (1820–1879) joined an already vibrant community in Worcester, composed of at least nine former Grafton families also with ancestral ties to Hassanamesit. She met and married an African American named Gilbert Walker. They adopted a child named Sarah Ellen Walker.[67] Gilbert Walker was recorded in the 1850 census as a barber, a common profession among African American men at the time. He was born a slave in Maryland, escaping north to Worcester as a young adult.[68] In 1853 Sarah and Gilbert petitioned the Massachusetts General Court to sell Sarah Boston's remaining land in Grafton to purchase real estate in Worcester.[69] Far from abandoning their Nipmuc connections, however, they were using their resources to settle into a growing and integrated Nipmuc and African American community.[70] Walker was actively involved in Worcester's vibrant abolitionist movement in the 1850s. In 1855 Gilbert and Sarah Walker lived near 60 Union Street. They shared this neighborhood with the Reverend John Mars of the Zion Methodist Church (the first African American church in Worcester) and Ebenezer and Hepsibah Hemenway, a Nipmuc/African American family who helped escaped slaves like Isaac Mason (who went on to write one of Worcester's slave escape narratives) find places to settle in Worcester.[71]

In 1856 Gilbert Walker opened his own barbershop underneath the Bay State House at the corner of Main and Exchange Streets in Worcester (Figure 6.4), only one block from Nipmuc barber and perfumer James Johnson.[72] In 1859 Sarah and Gilbert drew her family in closer, petitioning the state to care for her uncle Benjamin Phillips in his old age.[73] When the Civil War was imminent,

Figure 6.4. The corner of Main and Exchange Streets in Worcester, Massachusetts, where Gilbert Walker's barbershop once stood. (From the collections of the Worcester Historical Museum, Worcester, Massachusetts)

Gilbert joined William Brown, another member of a mixed Nipmuc and African American family and abolitionist, in recruiting for the 54th Colored Infantry and providing free haircuts for volunteers.[74] In an 1865 Independence Day parade celebrating the end of the war, Walker rode on a wagon, cutting a girl's hair to advertise his business underneath a banner that read, "The black man has shed his blood for the Union, he claims equal rights before the law!"[75]

It is easy to see how the Nipmuc community in Worcester may have become more difficult to trace in the mid-nineteenth century. Stereotypical assumptions of Native people residing only in rural, isolated settings were aggravated by the fast and loose administrative labeling of Native and African American people on census records in the mid- to late nineteenth century.[76] These factors, combined with the nation's ideas about Native blood quantum versus the African American "one drop" rule,[77] might make it seem that the Nipmuc dimension of the community was overshadowed at this time. But that would be a mistake. This emergent, blended, intermarried, urban community (still present today) is in fact not evidence of a coming together of two previously separate communities but rather a florescence of a community hundreds of years in the making. Sarah Mary Walker's great-great-grandmother grew up in urban Providence. Her great-grandfather was a free black man who fought in the American Revolution and involved himself in the Nipmuc community his entire life. Her great-uncle, Joseph Aaron, was the son of a slave, again from an urban and affluent home in colonial Providence. Her family and her Nipmuc identity survived these generations in urban settings, with African ancestry, without question. If Sarah Walker lost anything, it was the yoke of Euroamerican paternalistic guardianship and oversight, which (while convenient for archival research) mostly served to regulate the economic oppression of Nipmuc people for centuries and granted Native legitimacy based solely on dwindling landholdings.

◙ ◙ ◙

This chapter provides a few limited sketches of how one Nipmuc family occupied the Blackstone River Valley throughout the seventeenth, eighteenth, and nineteenth centuries. Sites from the elite households of colonial Providence to a stagecoach stop in the Mendon countryside to a barbershop in downtown Worcester are Nipmuc places because they have helped to anchor and animate a living Nipmuc landscape. I hope that this chapter has helped in thinking about what residing, or "dwelling," in a certain place might mean for the Nipmuc people. Sometimes it does involve a very specific and meaningful plot of land that is owned outright, such as the Burnee/Boston Homestead, or occupied, like the Cisco Homestead (in Chapter 7). But in other cases the scope and scale of occupying a place might be different and more difficult to identify.

For the Nipmuc these places include—and have included for centuries—both urban and rural environments, sites of confinement and conscripted labor in juxtaposition and simultaneous coexistence with routes of habitual and necessary mobility. They include spaces of colonial privilege and routes of entrepreneurship and emancipation. Rather than existing outside of a broader American society, they existed within it and among others and in that way played a crucial role in the formation of the American landscape as a whole.

## Notes

1. I use "settlers" instead of "Euroamericans" in this case to mean people or their descendants who came from elsewhere and settled in New England. They were not necessarily European, but they were specifically not indigenous.

2. Calloway 1997; Mandell 2010.

3. For more about Hassanamesit Woods, see Chapter 5; see also Mrozowski and Law Pezzarossi, 2015.

4. While Sarah Boston appears in many local histories, by far the most prominent is Forbes 1889.

5. A 1698 document for the sale of land between "Hassinnomoskok and Makonkock" is signed by James Printer, Zachariah Abram, Ammi Printer, and Joseph Robin. Massachusetts Archives Collection (MAC) 1643–1775, Petitions, vol. 105, doc. 32a.

6. For more on the biases of sedentism, see Malkki 1997.

7. Silliman 2009.

8. Brooks 2008.

9. Chilton 2002.

10. Mandell 1991.

11. Tinker 2003.

12. Documentary evidence suggests that Native praying town dwellers found ways not to practice all aspects of an English lifestyle. For example, when reporting on Hassanamesit, Daniel Gookin reported that "they have a meeting house for worship of God after the English fashion of building, and two or three other houses after the same mode; but they fancy not greatly to live in them" (Gookin 1970 [1792], 45).

13. Pulsipher 1996.

14. Temple 1887b, 87–88.

15. Lauber 1913, 129.

16. Rhode Island did not sell its captives into slavery as the Massachusetts Bay and Plymouth colonies did; instead they were indentured for a set period (see Lauber 1913, 129).

17. Cady 1957, 10, 14.

18. Scholars of New England history have been documenting this coexistence for decades. See, for example, Baron et al. 1996; and Doughton 1997.

19. Austin 1887, 221.

20. Whipple and Carroll 2003.

21. Austin 1887, 221.

22. Based on depositions collected in 1771, we know that Sarah Muckamaug, Sarah Robins's daughter, worked for the Whipple family in her young adulthood. While Sarah Robins may indeed have been working for another family, it is reasonable to assume, given Whipple's documented role in the appointment of Native captives after King Philip's War, that her mother likely was also involved with this family. Earle 1652–1863, Box 1, Folder 4.

23. Cady 1957, 14; see also Whipple and Carroll 2003.

24. Mandell 1996, 29.

25. MAC 1603–1705; Mandell 1996, 67.

26. MAC 1701–1750, 53. See also Mandell 1996, 67.

27. Earle 1652–1863, Box 1, Folder 2.

28. "George Muckamuck alias George Read" was baptized January 5, 1734–1735 at the age of twenty in Grafton (Rice 1906, 94).

29. Earle 1652–1863, Box 1, Folder 4.

30. Whipple and Carroll 2003; McLouglin 1986, 69.

31. Earle 1652–1863, Box 1, Folder 4.

32. Whipple and Carroll 2003.

33. Earle 1652–1863, Box 1, Folder 4.

34. MAC 1701–1750, 53.

35. Earle 1652–1863, Box 1, Folder 4.

36. Rhode Island Historic Preservation Commission 1989, 8–9.

37. Diamant et al. 1987.

38. "Great Road History," Blackstone Valley Historical Society, http://www.bvhsri.org/our-environment/greatroadhistory/, accessed August 28, 2017.

39. In the late 1760s and early 1770s Sarah Muckamaug's daughter Sarah Burnee and her son Joseph Aaron entered into a lengthy legal struggle over the division of family lands. See Earle 1652–1863, Box 1, Folder 4. Sarah Burnee and her husband at the time, Prince Paine, attempted to stop Joseph Aaron from claiming his land rights by questioning the legitimacy of their late mother's marriage to Aaron Whipple. Depositions were solicited by Sarah Burnee and Prince Paine to question whether they were ever married at all. Depositions solicited by Joseph Aaron sought to prove the validity of the marriage. Along with a wealth of information about this particular family, this record of strife brings to light an important trend of Native/African American intermarriage and the tensions that it precipitated in colonial New England. See Mandell 1999.

40. Earle 1652–1863, Box 1, Folder 4.

41. Wilkinson 1869, 104.

42. Diamant et al. 1987, 13.

43. Earle 1652–1863, Box 1, Folder 4.

44. Law 2014, 20–22.

45. Brigham 1835, 13.
46. MAC 1750–1757.
47. Earle 1652–1863, Box 1, Folder 4.
48. "Joseph Daniels," Daniels of Massachusetts Bay Colony.
49. Earle 1652–1863, Box 1, Folder 3.
50. Earle 1652–1863, Box 1, Folder 4.
51. Earle 1652–1863, Box 1, Folder 4.
52. Earle 1652–1863, Box 1, Folder 5.
53. Earle 1652–1863, Box 1, Folder 5.
54. O'Brien 1997.
55. Prude 1999.
56. Mrozowski and Law Pezzarossi 2015.
57. Prude 1999, 56–58, marks a rapid rise in the number and diversity of local businesses in rural Massachusetts from 1810 to 1830—mostly established by newcomers—as people clambered to find trades other than husbandry. "The categories of shops . . . embraced not only the familiar ventures like stores, taverns, blacksmithies, and nail-making works, but also unprecedented projects: two shoemaking shops, a bakery, a stove factory, chaise and bobbin making manufacturers, and textile machine works."
58. McMullen 1987; Ulrich 2001.
59. Lester 1987. See also Ulrich 2001.
60. Law 2014; Law Pezzarossi 2014b.
61. Handsman and McMullen 1987; Tantaquidgeon and Fawcett 1987; Turnbaugh and Turnbaugh 1987.
62. Phillips 1998, 207.
63. Doughton 1997.
64. Law Pezzarossi 2019.
65. O'Brien (2010, 84). O'Brien points out the ironic contrast between Native and Euroamerican mobility: "English notions about fixity and place figured centrally in dispossessing Indian peoples. While scheduled Indian mobility rooted in a seasonal economy offered a justification for English colonialism in the seventeenth and eighteenth centuries, in the nineteenth century New Englanders cast Anglo-Saxon mobility as normative."
66. McCarthy and Doughton 2007.
67. Earle 1861.
68. *Proceedings of the Worcester Society of Antiquity*, 146.
69. Massachusetts Anti-Slavery and Anti-Segregation Petitions 1853.
70. Doughton 1997.
71. McCarthy and Doughton 2007, xlv.
72. *Worcester Directory* 1852 and 1856.
73. Earle 1861.
74. McCarthy and Doughton 2007, xlv.
75. Greenwood 2010, 92.
76. Starna 1992.
77. Garroutte 2003.

# 7

# The Cisco Homestead and Hassanamisco Reservation

## Past, Present, and Future of the Nipmuc Nation

D. RAE GOULD

In the small town of Grafton, Massachusetts, a parcel with three and a half acres and an old house sits at 80 Brigham Hill Road. It would be unknown to most and easily overlooked on this busy road, except for a street-side sign reminding all who pass by that this is an "Indian Reservation . . . [that has] never belonged to the white man, having been set aside in 1728 . . . [in] the praying Indian town of Hassanamesit" (Figure 7.1). This sign, erected in 1930 by a state committee, continues centuries of recognition of a special place on the landscape and the people associated with it: the Nipmuc Tribe. Like Magunkaquog and the Burnee/Boston Homestead site, the Hassanamisco Reservation and Cisco Homestead in Grafton provide an opportunity to explore life histories and events through documents and archaeology associated with an evolving New England landscape. As at the Burnee/Boston Homestead site, documentary and archaeological evidence has helped us better understand the lives, activities, and motives of the women who lived here over the generations—also named Sarah—and how their efforts enabled the preservation of this place and the continuation of the Nipmuc Tribe into the twenty-first century. This parcel is the only one still occupied and managed by Nipmuc people following the loss of Sarah Boston's parcel on the other side of town in the 1850s.

The building and land around it evolved into a tribal reservation and center of Nipmuc culture between the 1850s and the early twentieth century. Known for the past 150 years as the Cisco Homestead, the building is believed to be the oldest surviving timber-framed structure built for and continuously occupied

Figure 7.1. Sign in front of the Hassanamisco Reservation erected in 1930 by the Massachusetts Bay Colony Tercentenary Commission. Photograph by Margaret Haynes-Lamont. (Courtesy of the Nipmuc Nation Archives)

by Native Americans in the region. Today this place is recognized as an Indian reservation by non-Native people, the State of Massachusetts, and the federal government,[1] as well as by the Nipmuc and other Native people. During the last half of the nineteenth century, female tribal leaders from the Cisco family emerged at this location as Sarah Robins's descendants ended their presence across town. Cisco women became stewards of this land and actively pursued its preservation, ensuring its continuous occupation and that it was not lost to non-Natives as Sarah Boston's homestead was. Accepting the role of tribal leadership came with living on the last piece of tribal land.

In 1857 Nipmuc John Hector sold his parcel of tribal land on Brigham Hill Road. He wanted to pursue opportunities in the nearby city of Worcester, where other tribal members and kin had already relocated to (as discussed in Chapter 6). Following the 1857 sale, Hector's niece, Sarah Arnold Cisco, continued to live next door; her home and the surrounding land became the last piece of Nipmuc land remaining from the Hassanamesit settlement of their ancestors dating back to well before John Eliot's visits in the 1600s and Euromerican settlement of the area. Her decision to stay and fight to keep this tribal land for future generations became the foundation of the Nipmuc Tribe—and the Hassanamisco Reservation—that exists today. Through the determination and fortitude of Sarah Arnold Cisco, her granddaughter Sarah Cisco Sullivan, and great-granddaughter Zara CiscoeBrough, today the Nipmuc people have a small reservation with a 200-year-old homestead that is the touchstone of their tribal life, community gatherings, and cultural practices.

This chapter primarily explores the documentary evidence related to this site and preservation efforts dating back to the moment of John Hector's sale in 1857. It also discusses some of the archaeology conducted at the site. The reservation and homestead have been on the National Register of Historic Places since 2011, which was only possible due to both modern-day and nineteenth-century efforts to preserve this Native American cultural landscape surrounded by non-Native, privately owned land since 1857. The documents, and the stories they tell, demonstrate political, social, and community activism by generations of Nipmuc women (including myself), as at the Burnee/Boston Homestead site (see Chapters 5 and 6). Women leaders from the Cisco family played critical roles in the preservation and transformation of this land base that by 1857 was symbolic of the continued presence of Nipmuc people in southern New England. Because these women were descendants of Moses Printer (occupant of this parcel during the 1727 division of Hassanamesit), and because they identified as Nipmuc throughout their lives, their roles were in many ways predetermined once the decision to save the Printer parcel and Cisco Homestead on Brigham Hill Road was made in 1857.

My study of this site has focused on interpreting and preserving the memory of this place and the family associated with it, while developing a deeper understanding of its history, meaning, and centrality to the Nipmuc Tribe. The Hassanamisco Reservation is a cultural landscape defined by personal, familial, and cultural knowledge passed from one generation to the next. Cultural landscapes and the histories associated with them are not always a subject studied by archaeologists and anthropologists. Interpreting multilayered landscapes (such as those discussed in this book) involves documentary research, archaeology, architectural history, and oral history (and oral tradition) to understand all components that contributed to the creation and meaning of these places. Archaeology provides just one part of the history. In this case, an archaeology of the building was also an important tool for re-creating the lives and activities of those who lived on Brigham Hill Road over the generations.

Concepts of memory and persistence are central to a cultural landscape like the Hassanamisco Reservation. All people have connections to the places where they live, work, and play. They form relationships with these places and find comfort in the sense of belonging created by those bonds. For a tribal community, this sense of belonging is central to the meaning and connection that develops to a place over centuries and millennia. Research focused on tribal communities (or any community) and on places important to them needs to be community-based, with the goals, needs, and interests of the tribe always central.[2] Indigenous scholars and activists have been asking for decades why non-Native scholars have assumed an inherent right to define tribal cultures and histories without consulting tribal people about their conclusions.[3] Until a few decades ago, archaeology has continued on this track. Over the past few decades Native people have taken more active roles in a discipline that defines their past; indigenous contributions are now categorized properly as indigenous *knowledge*.

I am one link in the chain of tribal members whose knowledge has contributed to the understanding, remembrance, and transformation of this place, helping to preserve our heritage for future generations. This is a place to be remembered, because encased within its walls and boundaries is a history that few outsiders have known or correctly interpreted. For Nipmuc tribal members today, the Cisco Homestead and Hassanamisco Reservation represent both the beginning point of our modern history and culture and a physical reality that we can pass on to the future. At the same time, they are the single piece of our past that has withstood all attempts to characterize, define, marginalize, and erase the memory of the Nipmuc Tribe that was present on the landscape long before John Eliot and other colonial settlers arrived. This small cultural landscape continues to be the center of tribal social, political, and public activities. It is where powwows are held each July, where tribal leaders lived for generations, and where the tribal office has been located, as well as a place that outsiders have recognized as marking Nipmuc presence in the region. This landscape is an important mnemonic device providing a physical location for

Nipmuc tribal members to go to and take from it a sense of identity, history, and cultural values. In many ways, it is exemplary of a history that has a future.

## Indigenous Cultural Landscapes

The concept of cultural landscapes (introduced in Chapter 1), and indigenous cultural landscapes in particular, is central to understanding the sites discussed in this book and the connections (and spaces) between them. The concept is explored further in this chapter. Landscapes are often defined as large-scale properties composed of multiple linked features that form a cohesive area or place but can be small-scale as well. The Magunkaquog meeting house, Burnee/Boston Homestead site, and Hassanamisco Reservation are examples of smaller cultural landscapes significant to the Nipmuc people over time and space. They are also part of the larger landscape of tribal homelands in southern New England that Nipmuc people have moved throughout for thousands of years. Similar to the other sites discussed in this book, the Cisco Homestead and Hassanamisco Reservation hold deep cultural and historical meanings for those who have traveled to and from them, occupied and used them, and woven them into generations of cultural practices. The way the Burnee/Boston Homestead functioned as a touchstone for the Nipmuc community is another example of this (see Chapter 6). Because their meanings are specifically tied to indigenous uses, meanings, and histories, the sites discussed in this book are defined as indigenous cultural landscapes.

As part of an archaeological site, and at a most basic level, a cultural landscape can be defined as a feature created through a shared set of values.[4] Other definitions of cultural landscapes focus on their roles as vernacular spaces, shared places, and places associated with identity, social relations, and cultural meaning. Cultural landscapes can also be bounded places, both physically and politically, where social and economic order can be studied, and as places connected to memory (serving as mnemonic devices).[5] The Hassanamisco Reservation and Cisco Homestead compose a cultural landscape encompassing all of these definitions, integrating an architectural structure, its land base and occupants, and the broader Nipmuc population over hundreds of years and beyond. The reservation and the 200-year-old homestead also function as a cultural landscape because they connect present Nipmuc people with their past, in addition to communicating meaning and history to both outsiders (non-Natives who visit or know of this place) and other Native people.

Every landscape is an accumulation, a rich source of data about the peoples and societies who created it over time.[6] This is especially true for indigenous cultural landscapes. The reservation and homestead originated as an everyday (or vernacular) landscape that transformed into a politically charged, bounded place that is today a rich source of information about the Nipmuc and Native people in southern New England. For some this place represents a silenced population no longer present, or inauthentic (not "real") at best, in its present form because it does not look like the western Indian reservations that we know from movies, the media, and other sources. For tribal people, this place is a symbol of our continued existence and active participation in the modern world, as a people who have changed with the times and are no longer defined by stagnant definitions created by others. The history and meaning of this place, which is so closely tied to *our* history and meaning, must be understood within the context of the multiple meanings a place can have over time and to different populations.

## Engaging Indigenous Cultural Landscapes in Archaeology

Although cultural landscapes have long been a topic of study, including among archaeologists, the way they are integrated into the practice of archaeology is still evolving. The widely publicized events associated with the Dakota Access Pipeline in 2016 and 2017, for example, demonstrate that a chasm still exists between how indigenous people view and regard the land they have been connected to for generations and competing economic, development, and political interests. Those potentially working with landscape-level properties can learn to recognize them in several ways, in addition to consulting with the communities associated with them. A first step is recognizing that indigenous cultural landscapes may include broad areas well beyond the conventional area of a site. This requires looking up and not being site-specific and myopic. Archaeology and historic preservation professionals are often involved on a daily basis in Section 106 review and decisions regarding criteria for the National Register of Historic Places; being able to recognize landscapes is critical to their work.[7]

For example, Traditional Cultural Places (TCPs; often cultural landscapes) can be encountered during cultural resource surveys or archaeology projects.[8] The National Park Service (which oversees the National Register of Historic Places) uses the term "Indigenous Cultural Landscape (ICL)" for areas with indigenous connections to landscapes, explaining that they are not confined to house sites, towns, or settlements (the more traditional archaeological sites explored). Indigenous perspectives on "homelands" are holistic, rather than compartmentalized into discrete site elements typically used by archaeologists and others (through terms such as hunting grounds, camp, domestic site, midden, settlement, or village).[9] The National Park Service's focus on Indigenous Cultural Landscapes is a good example of how expanding understandings of landscape are informed by tribal people who know their homelands best. These landscapes can be smaller, as noted above, and often provide information about what is called the "built environment." The three sites in this book all have built environment components central to interpreting their uses. While the Magunkaquog and Burnee/Boston Homestead sites have only archaeological remains left, the Cisco Homestead provides a rare standing structure that can be interpreted over time through studies of the structure itself, which is in the process of being restored by the tribe (see Figures 7.2 and 7.3).

Through a nomination generated by tribal members and consultants, the property was placed on the National Register in 2011 under Criterion A (con-

Figure 7.2. The Cisco Homestead (2010) before restoration. Photograph by Margaret Haynes-Lamont. (Courtesy of the Nipmuc Nation Archives)

Figure 7.3. The Cisco Homestead (2017) with exterior restoration nearly complete. Photograph by D. Rae Gould.

tributing to broad patterns of our nation's history) under the significance area of ethnic heritage. Having a standing Native homestead in New England from the early nineteenth century has greatly contributed to the property's significance and recognition by outsiders, in both the past and present. The nomination focused on how the survival of this structure kept the land from being sold to non-Nipmuc people and preserved the tribe's base for its annual powwows, tribal museum, and cultural practices. The property is not associated with any famous people, but with everyday people less documented in American history, who struggled to make ends meet and maintain a presence as Indian people in a world that challenged their continued existence, just as at Magunkaquog and the Burnee/Boston Homestead site. Their stories are the more uncommon ones associated with National Register cultural landscapes and the field of Historical Archaeology.[10]

The remainder of this chapter shares some of the history, stories, and meanings of this small cultural landscape from the nineteenth century through the present, providing details on its importance to the Nipmuc Tribe and how it functions as an important connection linking past, present, and future.

## History of the Hassanamisco Reservation

The Hassanamisco Reservation is the remaining land of the Nipmuc settlement Hassanamesit (meaning "place of small stones"), which became an 8,000-acre praying village in the 1650s, recognized by the Massachusetts Bay Colony (see Figure 1.1). Located along what became known as the "Great Trail," Hassanamesit was approximately the same area as present-day Grafton and was one of numerous Nipmuc settlements in modern-day central Massachusetts, northeastern Connecticut, and northwestern Rhode Island that English settlers encountered as they expanded westward from the coast after 1620. Written documents connected to this land date back to the time of John Eliot, who began preaching to Nipmuc people here in the 1650s (discussed in detail in other chapters). According to colonial records, seven Nipmuc families retained 500 acres following the transfer of 7,500 acres of Hassanamesit to English settlers in 1727 (as noted in previous chapters). The parcel at 80 Brigham Hill Road is the remnant of a 108-acre allotment to Moses Printer, one of the Indian "proprietors" involved in the division of the area between the English and Indian inhabitants who returned after King Philip's War.

In the years between the 1727 division of Hassanamesit and the last sale of Nipmuc land in Grafton by John Hector in 1857 (leaving three and a half acres), portions of Printer land were sold through guardians (or trustees) charged with managing Indian affairs in Massachusetts. Sometimes the guardians re-

Table 7.1. Hassanamesit Reservation Occupants, 1600s to 1988

| Occupants | Lifespan |
|---|---|
| Moses Printer | bef. 1665 to 1727/1728 |
| Sarah Printer Lawrence | ca. 1718 to 1771 |
| Patience Lawrence Gimbee | ca. 1745 to 1794 |
| Lucy Gimbee Arnold Hector[a] | ca. 1769 to 1843 |
| Harry Arnold | 1788 to 1851 |
| Sarah Maria Arnold Cisco | 1818 to 1891 |
| James Lemuel Cisco | 1846 to 1931 |
| Sarah Cisco Sullivan | 1884 to 1964 |
| Zara CiscoeBrough | 1919 to 1988 |

[a] Constructed the original homestead in 1801.

corded these transactions, but at other times they did not, leaving large gaps in the documentary record of Nipmuc land loss. Available records indicate that in the 130 years between 1727 and 1857, the 108-acre Moses Printer allotment corresponding to the modern-day 80 Brigham Hill Road parcel dwindled down through a number of transactions, the first as early as 1728 or 1729. By 1801, when the homestead was first constructed by Lucy Gimbee (Moses's great-granddaughter; see Table 7.1), numerous land sales had been recorded as Moses's descendants continued to divide the family land. During Lucy's lifetime a number of the family's parcels were sold off, seemingly to provide financial support to her and her family, just as Sarah Robins's descendants did across town (see Chapter 6).

Lucy's two sons Harry Arnold and John Hector remained on the family land after her death in 1843, but John's decision to relocate to Worcester and sell his share of the land in 1857 left Harry occupying the last piece of Nipmuc land in Grafton (the three and a half acres). Beginning with Harry's daughter (Sarah Arnold Cisco) the struggle to maintain this piece of Indian land is most clearly documented through her actions (and reactions). The letters she wrote were kept by her descendants for generations, suggesting that they also understood her struggle to keep this land; these letters survived to become part of the present Nipmuc Nation Tribal Archive, documenting much of the history associated with the reservation and tribe's leadership over the past 150 years. Combined with correspondences and documents from other Printer descendants, letters (and other archival material) from Sarah Cisco Sullivan (1884–1964) and her daughter Zara CiscoeBrough (1919–1988) provided the primary documents for research on this cultural landscape.

Beginning in the mid-nineteenth century the property came under the stewardship of the Cisco family, who descended from the marriage of Narragansett Samuel Cisco and Harry's daughter Sarah Arnold (1818–1891). By the early twentieth century the Cisco family had established themselves as tribal leaders through their role as stewards of this land, which was recognized as an Indian reservation by that time. By the 1920s Sarah Arnold Cisco's son, James Lemuel Cisco (1846–1931), assumed the role of chief of the Hassanamisco Indians. Following James, his daughter Sarah Cisco Sullivan and granddaughter Zara CiscoeBrough maintained a presence on this land base and also assumed tribal leadership, along with stewardship of the reservation and homestead. Today the reservation is managed and maintained by the Nipmuc Nation's traditional government under the leadership of Sonksq (Chief) Cheryll Holley.

As the location of tribal gatherings, powwows, and the home of tribal leaders in the past, the Hassanamisco Reservation and Cisco Homestead have continuously served as the focal point of Nipmuc cultural activities from the mid- to late nineteenth century to the present.

Although Lucy Gimbee's family was living in postcolonial New England, the control and sale of their land by white guardians continued a colonial mentality that Indians, as "wards of the state," could not properly manage their affairs or determine what was in their best interest. In many ways, the federal acknowledgment process of today continues this relationship, with the Bureau of Indian Affairs (BIA) and external "experts" determining the best course of action for tribes and even whether they are "real" tribes or not. Despite colonial and postcolonial attempts to erase Nipmuc people off the land and Euroamerican histories and actions like renaming (discussed in Chapter 2), this small parcel has survived when all other Nipmuc land occupied at the point of English settlement has been lost. The survival of the homestead from 1801 to the present is just as remarkable. Between 1801 and the mid-twentieth century the homestead expanded a number of times. By the time Zara CiscoeBrough occupied it from around 1960 until her death in 1988, it had expanded to a ten-room, multiuse structure. This homestead survived while others, like the Burnee/Boston Homestead and the seventeenth-century structure at Magunkaquog, did not.

The Nipmuc and other tribal people in southern New England gathered there throughout the twentieth century for regular meetings, ceremonies, and other political, social, and cultural activities. Somewhere between Lucy Gimbee's decision in 1801 to build an English-style home and her granddaughter Sarah Arnold Cisco's activism to preserve this land base (which continued with her descendants), the homestead and reservation became symbolic of Nipmuc presence and perseverance, transforming into what was widely acknowledged as an Indian reservation. In the case of Native American/indigenous cultural landscapes, the connection of specific land to ancestors, even if they are not buried there, is critical to the narratives, memories, and meanings that these places carry.

## Preserving the Hassanamisco Reservation through Memory, Activism, and Persistence

The loss of Sarah Boston's property in 1854 was a defining moment in the history of the Nipmuc Tribe. Following that, Moses Printer's land transformed from a domestic parcel for his descendants to an Indian reservation and by

1900 had become a source of strength for tribal people in southern New England who gathered here for meetings, ceremonies, and other activities. As with the Sarah Robins parcel, the women associated with the Printer land over the generations were central to its preservation as the stewards of land, history, and culture.

The current chief, Cheryll Toney Holley, is another link in the chain of female leaders who have maintained these responsibilities. She leads the tribe's traditional government that oversees the reservation, homestead, and cultural activities (such as the annual powwow, naming ceremonies, and repatriation efforts). The other half of the tribe's political structure has been the more outwardly facing tribal council, which has dealt with federal recognition, economic development, and tribal membership rolls over the decades. Both branches of the tribe's leadership supported my research on the reservation and homestead, which began when I served as a primary researcher for the tribe's federal recognition efforts.

Archaeology, documentary research, oral history, and oral tradition together can tell compelling stories, reconstructing life histories and regional histories in ways not possible through one source alone. Working for my tribe as an anthropologist provided opportunities for formal interviews and informal conversations with tribal members about their recollections of tribal events, people, and traditions from the twentieth century, back to the 1930s (oral history). Their knowledge also included information from parents and grandparents (oral tradition), providing recollections from 1860 through 1930 when this cultural landscape was evolving from a domestic to a more public tribal place. Memories and information from tribal members help connect the past and present in ways that other sources cannot.

In addition to information provided by tribal members, physical evidence at the reservation exists through the built environment: buildings, ground-level features (ceremonial fire, clambake pit), landscaping evidence, and other features visible through the archaeological record. Often the only opportunities to study Native structures involve excavations in and around abandoned foundations, as at the Magunkaquog and Burnee/Boston Homestead sites, but the reservation still has standing structures, including the Cisco Homestead. An architectural study provided information about the history of the building and its inhabitants, and about modifications made between the early nineteenth and mid-twentieth centuries, when the homestead reached its final configuration. Archaeology on the reservation revealed a number of things, including changes in how the land was used over time. The land immediately surrounding the homestead contained artifacts from different periods and soil that appeared to be jumbled fill. We believe that this was fill removed to create cellars (cellar ejecta) as the building expanded over the decades. And the area in front of the homestead was also purposefully filled, most likely to create a graded front yard as the homestead and reservation assumed a more public role.[11] These conscious decisions to alter the immediate landscape surrounding the homestead were connected to the important role of this place within the broader Nipmuc homelands by the late nineteenth century as it became the tribal reservation.

Added to these sources of information, documents from the last few decades of the 1800s reveal how Cisco family members increasingly viewed their home and the land around it as "Indian land" needing protection from non-Native neighbors. From 1857 forward, the family used this cultural landscape as a bounded, politically charged place to achieve certain goals, first as individuals then as tribal leaders. The most important of these was preservation of the land and homestead.

Earlier Printer descendants (beginning with Lucy Gimbee) also may have considered their home in this way, although they would not have used the term "cultural landscape" to define it. Lucy, for example, understood that living on the Printer parcel provided a special status to access funding (through the guardians) to construct the original homestead in 1801. Having a more visible presence could have been a conscious decision and motivating factor for her to construct an "English-style" house; it was more permanent than a wigwam or other cottage-like structure. The original 16- by 20-foot house was solidly constructed, as attested by its existence today within the original framing of the homestead. Without the continued presence of a building on the small land base, the land would likely have been sold long ago to non-Nipmucs, as the Robins parcel across town was.

Lucy's decision to construct this home is one example of how Native women in New England, like Native women elsewhere, are multifaceted, as Choctaw scholar Devon Mihesuah has noted. For Native women, the daily tasks of maintaining home, family, and work were compounded by additional demands of tribal responsibilities. This was especially true for the generations of women who built, expanded, maintained, and preserved the Cisco Homestead and land surrounding it, as it was with Sarah Robins's descendants discussed in Chapter 6. Unlike many mainstream feminists, Native women have often felt empowered in their domestic sphere, particularly when they are aware that their role contributes to cultural survival. Less concerned about how they are perceived by others, these women work to hold their tribes together,[12] as the Cisco women did through preservation of the reservation and as tribal leaders. The strong female leaders of the Nipmuc Tribe today continue to bind it together. In the case of this site the domestic landscape became one with the political, as the homestead served as tribal headquarters, tribal museum, and home, while the land surrounding it was a tribal reservation.

## Female Activism and Leadership in the Nineteenth Century: Sarah Arnold Cisco

The story of the homestead and reservation, and of the women responsible for its preservation, can be retold thanks to an extensive archive of correspondences, photographs, newspaper articles, and ethnographic material that they left behind. Over 3,000 documents in the Nipmuc Nation Tribal Archive dating back to the 1840s demonstrate that three main issues persisted throughout the nineteenth and twentieth centuries for these women: land, economic survival, and political activism. While they were activists and tribal leaders, the Cisco women were also well aware of their roles in the domestic realm, as noted above. Often a sense of tribal authority is born in this realm, as family and tribal responsibilities meld into one. Documents from the archive indicate that Sarah Arnold Cisco began the struggle to preserve the final piece of tribal land and attempted to involve other people in Grafton in her efforts to expand the land base and ward off neighbor John Sweeney's attempts to take the property.

In 1859 the family of Harry Arnold (Lucy Gimbee's son) lived in the homestead. They were threatened by the "white man" (Sweeney) who had purchased John Hector's parcel next door two years earlier and was now trying to infringe upon the last piece of Nipmuc land. Harry's daughters (Sarah and Patience Phidelia) sought legal action to protect it. Within two years of Sweeney purchasing the Hector parcel, Sarah and Phidelia began to challenge his legal right to acquire this Indian land. One particular struggle between Sarah and Sweeney revolved around a cart path that had existed on the Printer land for access to a spring and well (still visible today in the backyard). Sweeney assumed that he had a right to access the Cisco yard, judging by Sarah's complaints of his intrusions and documents focused on a right-of-way noted in deeds. Joint access would have made sense when the two brothers lived on the family land; but once Hector sold his half to Sweeney, Sarah no longer thought that he should have legal access to the spring on her family's parcel. Archaeology on the reservation in 2006 and 2007 revealed a cobbled area leading back to the spring, likely the remnants of this cart path that was the focus of this battle.

In her complaints about Sweeney's intrusions Sarah was clear that her home was on "Indian land" that retained a special status and was identified as the last piece "belonging to the tribe." Sarah and her family had become stewards of this land, a responsibility that she passed on to her descendants. One example of Sarah's continued proactive actions occurred a decade later, in 1869. She was still questioning the loss of land next door and, in this ongoing battle, was trying to expand the tribal land base and requesting more land due to her right as a Hassanamisco Indian. A letter from this time documents that she retained a lawyer and requested him to write a petition for more land, as long as it was "set off on Brigham Hill for the Indians" and as long as she claimed to be a descendant of the Hassanamisco Tribe of Indians of Grafton. Sarah understood the responsibilities associated with living on the last piece of Nipmuc land. Rather than make this appeal as an individual or for her immediate family, she claimed a right based on her identity as Hassanamisco Indian and "for the Indians." At the same time, her letter revealed the dire economic situation of the family, as she also requested more land so they could "raise a living" and keep one of their few vital assets: a cow providing food for the family.[13] This letter demonstrates an understanding of an inherent right based on Nipmuc ancestry and that Nipmuc tribal members understood the importance of using legal tools to protect their heritage. Earlier petitions (discussed in Chapter 5) demonstrate that this was long-standing knowledge dating back to the time of John Eliot.

Sarah also appealed to the public to support her request for more land based on Indian identity and was just as clear about her concerns regarding the last piece of tribal land. She claimed that Sweeney was trying to run her off the land in a letter that began: "I write this to let the public know my situation." Sarah described her precarious financial condition and complained that through loss of land (from the 1857 Hector-Sweeney transaction), "we had . . . been wronged out of some of our rights" by Sweeney. She protested that "ever since this man has . . . intruded upon us [he] has tried all ways to run us off what little we have."[14] John Sweeney sold his parcel on Brigham Hill Road around this time, possibly due to unending frustrations with his pestilent neighbors on the Indian land next door.

Following the 1857 sale to Sweeney, Sarah Arnold Cisco's struggle to remain on this land was twofold. She was poor and could have made an easier living had she moved to Worcester or Providence, where other tribal people lived or moved back and forth (as discussed in Chapter 6). And she had to battle her neighbor, who was apparently coveting the tribal land. Instead, Sarah chose to stay in Grafton and contend with these struggles, a conscious choice on her part, influenced by her knowledge that she lived on the last piece of Nipmuc land not yet lost to non-Indians and by her role as steward of this land. Future generations of Cisco women made the same choices (see below).

By the end of the 1800s outsiders also recognized the homestead and reservation as an important piece of the area's history and as the last piece of tribal land in the area. The disappearance of the land would signal the disappearance of the Nipmuc people in their minds, but the continued presence of the land and homestead on Brigham Hill acted as a steady reminder of the tribe's continued presence. In 1900 acknowledgement of the parcel as "Indian land" confirmed recognition of its status by outsiders. A deed from this year for land abutting 80 Brigham Hill Road referenced the "Indian land" next door.[15] A 1993 transfer of that parcel to a new owner (the Grafton Land Trust) maintained this language,[16] confirming the long-standing acknowledgment of the Indian land.

By the 1920s the 80 Brigham Hill Road parcel was unquestionably recognized as an Indian reservation with an established association with tribal activities and identity, where the annual powwow was held and leadership of the tribe was seated. The first *documented* public gathering here occurred on July 4, 1925, in the form of a clambake hosted by the Hassanamisco Indians at "Chief Lemuel Ciscoe's Wigwam" (Sarah's son). This July fourth gathering became the foundation of the modern annual powwow at the reservation held every July. By 1926 the gathering was referred to as an "annual powwow" and included speakers, games, and a dinner. This tradition was carried forward by future generations of Moses Printer's descendants and into the present by the tribe's traditional government.

## The Next Generations of Leaders

By the early decades of the twentieth century Sarah Cisco Sullivan (Sarah Cisco Arnold's granddaughter and daughter of James Lemuel Cisco) continued the annual gatherings. In her position as tribal leader, she used the homestead and reservation to manage tribal affairs, tribal and public gatherings, and other events. Tribal and intertribal gatherings at the reservation by the early 1900s demonstrated its separateness as a unique place—an indigenous cultural landscape—for Indians to meet and socialize and to confirm their identity and relationships. Sarah and her daughter Zara CiscoeBrough were the next two generations of Cisco women whose commitment and persistence enabled preservation of the reservation and homestead. Both were single women who faced the challenges of maintaining a household and leading the Nipmuc Tribe during a time when most tribal leaders were male.

Sarah Cisco Sullivan was born in the 1890s, a period in American history when Indians were being pressed into what some have labeled "marginality."[17] The Indian wars to the west and the 1890 massacre at Wounded Knee (South Dakota) that ended them were still recent events. Until her death in 1964 Sarah maintained a single focus: maintaining the small tribal land base on Brigham Hill Road where she led annual gatherings and served as the nexus for the tribe.

Sarah also led the Nipmuc Indian Chapter of Worcester, Massachusetts. This group emerged in the 1950s as a continuation of previous tribal social networks dating back to at least the 1920s. It provided public recognition of continued tribal status in a time when assimilation and termination of tribes became federal policy across the country.[18] Such leadership was not without difficult moments, however, as letters between female leaders in southern New England reveal. Male leaders wore the headdresses, signifying their roles as "chiefs," while women assumed less public leadership roles but did the day-to-day work to keep communities strong. Sarah struggled within this group and within her tribe, retaining the title "princess" (as her daughter Zara also did). In the 1950s the idea of a woman assuming formal tribal leadership was still uncomfortable for many, as was female leadership in American society generally. Sarah's authority, however, was never in question. As steward of the tribal land, it was understood that maintaining the reservation was the most important (and real) challenge that any tribal leader in New England faced. She was always at the heart of those struggles.

Even when living in a nursing home toward the end of her life and with her energy fading, Sarah's focus remained on preserving the tribal land base. In a 1961 letter to her niece, she worried about who would protect the reservation, writing, "By what seems to be cooking, they will take the place if I don't get home there soon . . . some of the people in town are just aching to get their hands on the place."[19] Written three years before her death, this letter demonstrates how aware of the real threats to their presence Native people in

New England had to be at all times: the loss of land that erased them from the landscape in the minds of non-Natives. In the 1960s losing the tribal land was just as potent a threat to Sarah as it had been a century earlier to her great-grandmother Sarah Arnold Cisco, who struggled to keep enough land for the family cow. The loss of Sarah Boston's parcel in the 1850s was etched into tribal memory as well, as were the experiences of other Nipmucs like Isaac Nehemiah at Magunkaquog 250 years earlier.

Sarah's ability to maintain authority both within her tribe and within the public realm was something that she passed on to her daughter, Zara Ciscoe-Brough (see Figure 7.4). Throughout the twentieth century both assumed roles as stewards of important places in their tribal homelands, including Indian

Figure 7.4. Zara CiscoeBrough (*left*) and her mother Sarah Cisco Sullivan, ca. 1960, in front of the Cisco Homestead. (Courtesy of the Nipmuc Nation Archives)

burial grounds in Grafton where tribal ancestors were buried. Zara was born in 1919 and assumed the reigns of leadership in the decade when modern-day Indian activism was born. Amid memorable events in the late 1960s and early 1970s, such as the occupations of Alcatraz, Wounded Knee, and the BIA building in Washington, D.C., Zara quietly fought her own battles on the New England home front as American Indian tribes moved toward an era of self-determination instead of termination.[20]

As an effective culture broker and negotiator, Zara worked hard to have a constant presence on a local level, while keeping her hand in regional and national events. Even though she also used the title "princess" as her mother did, Zara acknowledged that her role in actuality was as sachem and knew how to use the media to further the causes of her tribe. After permanently returning home in 1959 following successful careers as a clothes designer and engineer, Zara settled down to a life committed to serving as Nipmuc tribal leader until her death in 1988. A savvy business woman, fashion designer, artist, engineer, historian, writer, volunteer, and activist, she came back to her small New England hometown to lead the Nipmuc Tribe and maintain the reservation and homestead in the prime of her life, when many others would have chosen the prosperity and freedoms available elsewhere. These were the choices that tribal people had to make over and over again since the time of European settlement: relocate to places where kin and support existed and/or give up their land under pressure. Isaac Nehemiah, Sarah Robins's descendants, and John Hector made these decisions, just as Sarah Arnold Cisco, her granddaughter, and her great-granddaughter did.

While she selflessly gave her time, money, and energy, Zara was reminded of the obligations that led her back to Massachusetts. In a 1970 letter to her cousin she echoed the concerns of previous generations about preserving the reservation after she was gone, acknowledging that her eventual return was always understood: "I considered this my duty as I was made to understand from childhood thru Grandpa and Mother that someone had to care when they were gone. I have sacrificed my personal life for this, while the rest of the Family did as they pleased. You know this, but do the others? I sometimes wonder?"[21] This responsibility had been handed down for generations. Beginning as early as the lifetime of Sarah Arnold Cisco (and possibly with Lucy Gimbee), the occupants of the Printer parcel and homestead on Brigham Hill recognized that they were holding onto the physical representation not only of their past but also of the Nipmuc people's future.

The most defining element of Zara's identity was as Princess White Flower, leader of the Nipmuc Tribe. At the homestead on the small reservation, tribal members visited her on a regular basis, convened for the annual Indian Fair every July, and held regular meetings to discuss tribal business.[22] Throughout the 1970s Zara devoted her energy to visions for the tribe: an increased land base, formalized state recognition, and eventually federal acknowledgment. Federal acknowledgment would provide resources for housing, education and health programs, and other benefits.

Zara was the most charismatic and politically active of the women who lived on the reservation, using it as a center of activism in addition to a foundation for the tribe. She served on several committees in town, remained active in national and state Indian affairs, and had many friends, tribal members, researchers, tourists, school groups, and scout troops visit for educational programs or information on the Nipmuc and surrounding tribes. Newspaper articles regularly noted how Zara entertained visitors from the public interested in learning more about Nipmuc history and culture. The reservation and homestead were (and still are) the central mnemonic devices for retelling and connecting visitors to that past, while reaffirming the continued presence of the tribe by the very visit to a place that has survived to the present.

Lucy Gimbee in the first half of the nineteenth century, Sarah Arnold Cisco through the rest of that century, then Sarah Cisco Sullivan and Zara CiscoeBrough throughout the twentieth century are all examples of independent women (three without husbands for most or all of their lives) who built, maintained, and managed a place on the landscape that became increasingly important to the personal and group identities of Indians in southern New England. The occupants of the homestead and stewards of the reservation reappropriated the meaning of this place and told its history through *their* understandings of what it has meant to be Nipmuc and of Nipmuc history and culture. Through the use of the building as a museum and educational center throughout the twentieth century, Nipmuc women became another type of steward of our tribe's past, holding intellectual knowledge to transfer to nontribal members. This practice continues in my work as a scholar who can now retell our stories and support continuation of our tribal cultural knowledge.

I see this cultural landscape as a *history,* a place with a story that can be read to better understand the past, combined with information from documents and archaeology. The life histories of those associated with this place are central to this story, as they are at Magunkaquog and the Burnee/Boston Homestead sites. A cultural landscape can be "the result of many artifacts grouped together in particular relationships" that together communicate meaning but must be *read* to be understood.[23] Reading the landscape as a text of the past allows us to understand "the plots and subplots that have been written on the land by both the conscious and unconscious acts of the people who lived there."[24] One component of a landscape's reading (and its meaning) is the passing down of information about it through narratives recounted by those associated with it. Just as importantly, "to understand a landscape truly it must be felt, but to convey some of this feeling to others it has to be talked about, recounted, or written and depicted."[25] This, in effect, creates the memories that make a cultural landscape meaningful, as the case studies in this book demonstrate.

## Preservation Efforts in the Twenty-First Century

As a link in the chain of tribal members who have focused on preserving the homestead and reservation, I have used contemporary methods to achieve these goals. In addition to raising funds for the physical restoration of the homestead, completing the nomination for listing the property on the National Register of Historic Places was a key effort toward preservation. This is an example of how preservation of culture and place can be achieved without federal acknowledgment (which provides access to grants for preservation projects). National Register listing provides a degree of protection under certain federal and state laws and increases public recognition. For example, Section 106 of the National Historic Preservation Act requires federal agencies engaged in projects (and projects receiving federal funds or permits) to identify and assess the effects of their actions on properties eligible for or already listed on the National Register, including indigenous landscapes such as the reservation. States also have similar review laws.[26]

Efforts to restore the Cisco Homestead have also been outward looking and collaborative in several ways, just as work at Hassanamesit Woods has been. Tribal members have combined their knowledge, time, and resources to keep the effort moving forward, albeit slowly, with lack of funding as the biggest obstacle. The Town of Grafton has been instrumental to the restoration efforts, awarding the Nipmuc Nation several grants to complete phases of the exterior restoration (Figure 7.3). As of 2019 the exterior restoration is nearly complete; additional funds are now needed to begin extensive interior restoration.

The tribe's partnership with the Town of Grafton is one example of how the history, meaning, and cultural practices associated with this landscape can only be understood from consultation with tribal people. This is especially true in archaeology or academic studies in general. Beyond requirements of laws like Section 106, including indigenous knowledge develops stronger relationships between groups with overlapping interests and serves to educate on the local, state, and federal levels. While the Town of Grafton values the historic significance to the tribe of the homestead and reservation, this place has also been an integral part of the town's history and tourism over the years. Understanding the landscape-level significance, and our connected and intersecting histories, has been central to this partnership.

## Past, Present, and Future

After the 1857 sale of John Hector's portion of Moses Printer's parcel on Brigham Hill, the last piece of Nipmuc land (next door) evolved into a tribal reservation central to the Nipmuc Tribe. Today the reservation is recognized as an indigenous cultural landscape with a rich source of information. The events and activities that occurred there, and their meanings to Nipmuc culture and to outsiders, are an integral part of southern New England history. As the center of tribal social and political activities by the early 1900s, the homestead and remaining three and a half acres were preserved because of efforts beginning with Sarah Arnold Cisco that continued with the following generations of women in her family. The Nipmuc Nation continues this effort and recognizes the importance of the Cisco family to our cultural heritage and continued existence.

This place is one example of the cultural landscapes that exist all around us that need to be considered by archaeologists and preservation professionals responsible for interpreting and defining the American past. Many landscapes in this country have indigenous origins or are still used by tribes today, so the inclusion of indigenous perspectives and knowledge about these places in processes such as Section 106, research projects, and CRM archaeology is critical. Incorporating this knowledge may require rethinking Western notions of boundaries, history, and significance. Likewise, rethinking the Western distinction between natural and cultural resources also helps us to recognize, interpret, and record landscapes. One way to ensure higher visibility is through listing properties on the National Register of Historic

Places, which may help gain access to preservation and restoration funding and offers some protection.

This chapter provides an example of one indigenous cultural landscape that has been the touchstone of Nipmuc culture and history. Over the past 150 years the Printer parcel and homestead transformed from a domestic space in the small town of Grafton to a cultural landscape intimately connected to our identities as Nipmuc people and remains so today. The continued presence of the tribe in the twenty-first century is visible through the physical restoration of the homestead and the annual powwow held every July. It is less visible in the more private language preservation, cultural programs, and tribal gatherings that occur here or in the behind-the-scenes work to raise funds for the homestead's restoration, which are just as important to our cultural preservation.

My effort to tell part of our tribal history is also a response to a determination by the BIA in 2004 that the Nipmuc Nation does not constitute a tribe by the standards of the federal government, thus confirming for many non-Natives that we are not "real" Indians or genuinely connected to our past. Federal acknowledgment cases, in particular, demonstrate that interpretations of tribal history and culture by outsiders can greatly impact the lives of real people in the contemporary world. For example, the struggle to restore the homestead is much more difficult because we cannot access funds available only to federally recognized tribes. Our tribe also does not have the same standing in the Section 106 process that considers cultural resources in our homelands; often we find out about projects through neighboring tribes invited to the consultation process simply because they are federally recognized. Sometimes other tribes inform us about these projects; at other times they do not.

In the decision regarding federal acknowledgment, the BIA interpreted the homestead and Printer parcel as a private allotment (from the 1727 division that created Moses Printer's 108-acre parcel) and not an Indian reservation. This "either/or" mentality does not allow for this place with a complex history to serve as both: a home base for leadership on land that came to be regarded and used as an Indian reservation by both tribal members and outsiders. This type of myopic thinking is exactly what archaeologists and others who engage with cultural landscapes must avoid. Seeing the complete picture—the physical, political, and cultural landscapes within which history unfolds—first requires being able to understand that the landscapes are present. The next step is understanding their meanings as individual sites and their connections to other places within larger areas and, most importantly, to the people associated with them today and in the past. This is one of the most important steps that must be taken in rethinking places and spaces in indigenous homelands.

In the case of the Nipmuc Nation and this cultural landscape, many outsiders struggle to understand how New England tribes have continued their cultures and identities, after 400 years of engagement with non-Native people socially, politically, and economically and the acculturation processes that have been part of those engagements. The stories of men like John Eliot and Daniel Gookin have been diligently recorded and remembered at places like Pulpit Rock in Woodstock, Connecticut, while the stories of the Native people associated with these places require deeper scholarship, thought, and perspective, informed by indigenous knowledge of time and space. At the heart of this issue lies the question of whether adoption of Euroamerican customs (acculturation) by Native peoples equates to a loss of tribal identity and cultural cohesiveness (assimilation).

The Hassanamisco Reservation and Cisco Homestead provide a model for how to investigate other important Native places in this region and beyond, such as the Mohegan Tantaquidgeon Museum and Congregational Church, Narragansett Indian Church, and Mashpee Meeting House. These places are also central to their tribes' histories and have withstood time to provide statements about the continued presence of Native people in the region, despite the incorporation of non-Native elements.[27] For Native people of New England (and elsewhere), changed cultural practices such as the incorporation of non-Native building styles are not indications of inauthenticity; they are symbols of survival.

Like the Cisco Homestead, the Mohegan museum and church, Narragansett Indian Church, and Mashpee Meeting House are Euroamerican-style structures erected under colonial conditions, yet they connect tribal people to much deeper precolonial pasts. The meanings of these places are also embedded in the indigenous historical knowledge maintained by the individuals and tribes who built, maintained, and use these structures. They provide links to the past as the land of southern New England once did and are connecting dots on the paths throughout a broader southern New England indigenous landscape, like the paths from Providence to Grafton and Grafton to Worcester. These are only a few examples of many that demonstrate how the landscape is still used by Native people in this region to maintain important connections to place. These quasi-public buildings exist on tribal lands that have also dwindled, like the Printer parcel did, yet maintain a presence despite 400 years of encroachment.

For Native people, land and places such as these have always been anchors for kinship relations, tribal identity, and, more recently, definitions of sovereignty. Since colonization began over 500 years ago with the arrival of Columbus, indigenous peoples of the Americas have had to reconceptualize their relationships with land as they struggle to maintain land bases in Euroamerican societies that define bounded parcels as economic assets. Holding on to a land base, as the Printer descendants did, makes an important statement to the dominant Euroamerican culture about the connections between keeping land, history, and culture, rather than allowing these to be redefined by (or lost to) outsiders. Cultural landscapes, such as the one focused on in this chapter, often become communal spaces because the struggle to keep them requires more than one or two people. They represent one group pushing against the rest of the world in an attempt to preserve and maintain a sense of difference, rather than an economic asset to pass on to future generations, what Annette Weiner has described as an "inalienable possession."[28]

While maintaining a separateness, the occupants of the reservation and homestead were also able to establish a comradery and cohesiveness within the broader community and with their non-Indian neighbors, especially when seeking support to ward off threats like John Sweeney. Clearly the women who lived here used this network to further their goal of preserving the land and building, while also using legal tools and the media. Today this support network is stronger than ever due to recognition of the homestead and reservation's importance to our tribe and its historical significance to the Town of Grafton. In inviting public participation and seeking support to restore the homestead, there is an expectation that tribal members will reciprocate with involvement in events that celebrate Grafton's history and our shared past. Involvement of tribal people in parades, local gatherings, and other town-sponsored activities has occurred since at least the early decades of the 1900s. And more recently I (and other tribal members) have been involved in events as organizers and speakers. This is also a very public dimension to the Nipmuc Tribe's continued presence in Grafton, which, for all participants, provides a connection linking the past, present, and future. This type of collaboration has also occurred in the writing of this book by the four authors whose lives have intersected over the past few decades as we explored the three sites discussed here.

A major theme of this book has been to introduce three case studies that are both archaeological sites and parts of a larger story: American history told and retold through different lenses and different materials (artifacts and documents, combined with oral history and tradition). The Magunkaquog meeting house, Burnee/Boston Homestead, and Hassanamisco Reservation sites are significant places independently but are also connected through the larger landscape of Nipmuc homelands in southern New England. While the focus of an archaeologist is often to record a moment or period, that interpretation is often only a snapshot (or one component) of a much more complex history and culture. In the case of the Nipmuc, this stretches back thousands of years and into the future, as all of us have recognized through our work. If Harry Arnold and his daughter, and then future generations, had not fought to keep the small parcel on Brigham Hill Road, that future would not be as strong.

## Notes

1. Despite its refusal to formally acknowledge the Nipmuc Nation as a tribe, the BIA has included the Hassanamisco Reservation on a map of federal Indian reservations for decades (see Chapter 8).

2. Atalay 2012.

3. See, for example, Deloria 1969, 1970, 1992, 1999.

4. Deetz 1990, 2.

5. Bender 1993; Groth 1997; Jackson 1984; Lewis 1979; Meinig 1979a, 1979b; Rubertone 1986; Upton 1983.

6. Meinig 1979a, 44.

7. For more information on Section 106, see information provided by the Advisory Council on Historic Preservation at http://www.achp.gov/ (accessed May 27, 2019).

8. For more on the topic of TCPs, see National Park Service Bulletin 38, "Guidelines for Evaluating and Documenting Traditional Cultural Properties" (Parker and King 1990).

9. More information on how the National Park Service has defined and integrated the concept of Indigenous Cultural Landscapes is available at https://www.nps.gov/cajo/learn/upload/ICL-Banner-Update-April2015.pdf (accessed May 27, 2019).

10. For more information about the National Register nomination, see https://www.nps.gov/nr/feature/indian/2011/Hassanamisco_Reservation.htm (accessed May 27, 2019).

11. See Gould 2010 for a more complete discussion of archaeological investigations at the Hassanamisco Reservation.

12. Mihesuah 1996, 15, 18.

13. Nipmuc Nation Tribal Archive, Document H003.

14. Nipmuc Nation Tribal Archive, Document H003.

15. Sweetser to Woodward, Worcester District Registry of Deeds, Book 1670, 406–407.

16. Thomas A. Teal to Grafton Land Trust, Worcester District Registry of Deeds, Book 15301, 183.

17. Johnson 1994, 63.

18. See the Indian Relocation Act of 1956, House Concurrent Resolution 108 (1953), and Public Law 280.

19. Sarah Cisco Sullivan, 1961 letter to niece, Nipmuc Nation Tribal Archive.

20. Johnson 1994, 63, 71.

21. Nipmuc Nation Tribal Archive, Document H1788.

22. A number of the tribal members who provided oral interviews discussed their involvement in these activities dating back to the 1960s, following Zara's return to Grafton and assumption of tribal leadership.

23. Rapoport 1990, 137.

24. Yamin and Metheny 1996, xiii.

25. Tilley 1994, 31.

26. For more information on the National Register of Historic Places, go to https://www.nps.gov/subjects/nationalregister/index.htm (accessed May 27, 2019).

27. See Gould 2013 for a more complete discussion of these other tribal structures in southern New England.

28. Weiner 1986, 1992.

# 8

# Rethinking Native Spaces

## Connecting Pasts to Futures

D. RAE GOULD AND STEPHEN A. MROZOWSKI

Through the lens of the events, decisions, movements, and places connected to the lives of Isaac Nehemiah, Sarah Burnee and Sarah Boston, and Sarah Cisco Arnold and her descendants, the Nipmuc spaces across southern New England seem to tell new stories. The archaeological investigations and documentary research that the authors of this book have engaged in over the decades provide details about these individuals and their everyday lives—how they traveled, how they made a living, what they used for dishware—and about important decisions that changed the course of events for the Nipmuc people, individually or collectively. Selling the land at Magunkaquog clearly weighed heavily on the mind of Isaac Nehemiah in the moments before he took his life in 1715. With an ailing husband and resources scarce, Sarah Burnee knew in 1798 that she would soon be facing a similar decision regarding her family parcel in Grafton. Sixty years later and across town, Sarah Arnold Cisco would consider her options: relocate to Worcester as her uncle John Hector had done a year earlier or stay and try to hold onto the last piece of Nipmuc land in the region. Sometimes these individuals had agency and choice; sometimes they did not.

While these may seem like new stories, they have in fact been there all along, waiting to be told by unearthing the artifacts, discovering the documents, listening to information shared by modern-day tribal members, and having the time and patience to find the right people to tell them. Like the individuals discussed in the chapters of this book, Nipmuc spaces and landscapes have also persisted and have information to share, even if they have been written over by four centuries of change. The rivers, hills, mountains, and places (such as Hassanamesit and Swago) continue their presence across New England and Nipmuc people continue to be connected to them, as they have for millennia.

Through a type of double narrative, the authors in this book have shared two stories: those of the individuals from the past whose voices emerge through our work and those of our work over the past two decades, individually and collectively. By coming together over the course of the three projects at Magunkaquog, the Burnee/Boston Homestead, and Hassanamisco Reservation sites, we have made discoveries about these places, the individuals who occupied them, and ourselves. This book is a culmination of those discoveries, although we also intend for our individual projects and collaborative work to continue.

## Important Themes

Several themes are addressed in this book. Rather than place the spaces and people in the chapters above solely in the past (and echo the narratives of erasure that have pervaded discussions about Indians in New England), we recognize the direct connections between the past, present, and future. Understanding that Isaac Nehemiah, Sarah Burnee, Sarah Boston, Sarah Cisco Arnold, and her descendants were looking forward and knew that the decisions they made would have consequences is one example of this. For example, the decisions of Sarah Arnold to stay in Grafton and of her great-granddaughter Zara CiscoeBrough to return 100 years later were seminal points in the history of the Nipmuc Tribe that affected future generations and the very survival of the tribe. In this regard, the physical links of past, present, and future—of histories that have futures—revealed through our combined efforts mirror those of Nipmuc ancestors, unwilling to succumb through a perseverance evident in the continuing material presence on the landscape and in the documents preserved in archives.

Our work also continues the important effort of institutionalizing how studies of indigenous peoples and their spaces are conducted. That is, we are further influencing ways of thinking about indigenous peoples, their histories, and their cultures. As noted in the chapters of this book, these views have been changing for several decades—most notably through the incorporation of indigenous scholars into anthropology and archaeology—but it has been a slow and ongoing endeavor. Part of that change involved a growing awareness within the archaeological community that something had to change, that business as usual was no longer acceptable. Through collaborations non-Native scholars began to listen and to learn that their own views had to be modified; their own perceptions of how their work is conducted needed to be more inclusive and open to other voices. This book is one link in an ongoing process of decolonizing the study of indigenous peoples that rests at the heart of efforts to reconcile relationships forged as part of a colonial past that needed to be abandoned. In this regard it was necessary for both groups—indigenous and nonindigenous scholars—to find a new approach to their shared aspirations. In some instances this meant taking new approaches to old problems. Drawing on indigenous knowledge and oral histories is a good example of transcending what had previously been a closed system of inquiry reliant upon the notion of a detached scholar whose work seldom had any practical benefit. In other instances it meant using time-honored approaches such as stratigraphic interpretation and the refining of chronologies in the production of histories that were not only more democratic but more rigorous as well.

As a model for a decolonized archaeology, these case studies of Nipmuc spaces are also important for broader reasons. They help us reflect on the histories and meanings of places—and of the people associated with them—and address issues that provide a better understanding of the world we live in and cultural differences that exist, which can also be mediated through increased knowledge. In the more globalized world of today people are in constant contact with others who have diverse identities, histories, and cultural practices. The stories of the individuals and families in this book are about survival, loss, adaption, and the struggle to maintain a presence in an increasingly industrialized, capitalized, and globalized world that has favored Euroamerican values and culture and created a hegemonic relationship between the dominant culture and the "other." We can transpose these situations to apply to many groups around the world today who have been (and still are) affected by colonial structures, racial and ethnic discrimination, and written histories that have been defined by a dominant culture and claimed as truth. Anthropology and archaeology have historically been part of these colonial processes. But with an increasing number of non-Euroamerican scholars emerging over the decades, we are more often reconsidering how we tell the past and understand the present. The Magunkaquog, Burnee/Boston, and Hassanamisco Reservation sites are only three examples of this reconsideration.

Collaboration is perhaps the most important aspect of a decolonized archaeology. As Sonya Atalay has stated,[1] research on sites such as the ones in this book can only be done through working with, by, and for indigenous peoples. Collaboration is essential when engaging in projects with indigenous communities or any community whose past is being explored. These pasts are important on a host of levels; perhaps most importantly, the histories shared by members of a community are critically linked to their own identities. Who else should (or could) have the right to define those identities or inform this research?

In instances where institutionalized erasure has sought to silence voices in attempts to construct historical narratives of exclusion—part of broader attempts at genocide—archaeology can help rediscover the lives of those silenced, as long as it is conducted with decency and respect. For example, only through collaborative processes can archaeologists understand the cultural landscapes and homelands in a region and how people connect to them. Nipmuc spaces, whether entire homelands as a large landscape or the smaller places moved through over time, are examples of this. The histories they hold and pasts they embody can be reconnected to the descendants of those whose lives were devoted to continuing the communities that have persisted through struggle. These are the histories that have futures revealed through our work.

The important role of women in the persistence to preserve and maintain tribal land bases and cultures is also a central theme of this book. Women have long been the keepers of land as the producers of food for their families and tribes and the keepers of cultural knowledge who pass it from one generation to the next.[2] The women who occupied the Burnee/Boston and Cisco Homesteads actively rethought what their continued presence meant and consciously redefined it throughout their lives. Zara CiscoeBrough's return to Grafton to assume tribal leadership and stewardship of the parcel on Brigham Hill is one example of a point in her life when she redefined herself and her role as a tribal and community member. Two centuries earlier, Sarah Robins and her daughter Sarah Muckamaug had made similar decisions to return to Hassanamesit (then Grafton in 1735) and maintain a presence on the changing landscape of their homelands. Sarah Burnee continued to play an active leadership role through her petitions and her work that helped to maintain a space for community gatherings, as the artifacts from that site indicate. While these women in some ways were not very different from their neighbors—moving between rural and urban environments at different times, living in English-style houses with stone walls defining their boundaries—at the same time they were (and *needed to be*) very different. Maintaining this difference was critical to the survival of these Native spaces and of their occupants' identities as Indians. It is no mere circumstance that Nipmuc women played such an important role in history; this has been part of a cultural legacy that runs deep in their culture. With so many Nipmuc men having been lost or displaced beginning with King Philip's War in the late seventeenth century, Nipmuc women did what they had always done: maintained leadership posts and used their ingenuity to remain active in the local and regional economies while maintaining good relations with their neighbors.

The individuals discussed in this book also acutely understood the legal and political systems they were working either against or within, for better or worse. For Isaac Nehemiah, the system overwhelmed him, resulting in an ultimate sense of despair that ended his life. While Sarah Burnee and her descendants pushed against the system for several generations, the end result was also a loss of land that has now, ironically, been preserved through the town that replaced Hassanamesit (discussed further below).[3] The individuals connected through the stories in this book understood and used legal and social systems to their advantage when they could. They knew the importance of adapting to a changing world and using tools available to continue their struggles against racism and the steady dispossession of their homeland. This is most evident beginning with Sarah Arnold Cisco, who used a network of non-Native people to further her goal of preserving the land base and building on Brigham Hill Road. Today this support network is stronger than ever due to local recognition of the Hassanamesit Woods parcel across town and of the Cisco Homestead and Hassanamisco Reservation's importance to our tribe and to the local history.

Moving between these systems continues today for many tribes. While certain processes work against tribes (as the federal acknowledgment process did for the Nipmuc Nation), they can also result in another type of collaboration in addition to the work that the authors of this book have engaged in. As noted throughout the book, working with outside entities such as the Trust for Public Lands, Public Archaeology Lab (PAL), the University of Massachusetts at Boston, and the Town of Grafton, the tribe has participated in the preservation of a large piece of land holding an important archaeological site (Hassanamesit Woods) and in the interpretation of that site. The tribe has also been able to embark on restoration of the Cisco Homestead through grants provided by the Grafton Community Preservation Committee. While sometimes outside systems are oppressive and detrimental (as with the imposition of Christianity by John Eliot or the forced sale of Magunkaquog by Harvard College), understanding them was critical, as the petitions, letters, and actions by Joseph Aaron, Sarah Arnold Cisco, and others demonstrate.

Issues of authenticity and identity have also been an underlying theme throughout this book, through recognition of Native peoples' continued presence on the landscape, how their pasts are retold, and whose voices and knowledge systems are more authentic (for example, academic or indigenous knowledge, which are sometimes melded). Although the sites discussed in these chapters have different meanings to different people over time, the investigations and interpretations of them can only be complete through the braiding of indigenous and Western epistemologies. These knowledge systems are most powerful when informed by each other and by integrating different lines of inquiry (such as archaeology and oral testimony) with equal value.

Rather than adhering to rigidly defined boundaries, the combined scholarship that has emerged from our collaboration represents a powerful method for linking past, present, and future. Many of the methods applied during these excavations were cutting-edge approaches that sought an ever more refined understanding of a complex archaeological record. By combining the analysis of plant and animal remains with micro-stratigraphic soil profiles and a whole host of material culture studies, the authors have sought to reveal the most intimate details of lives lived in spaces that remain part of the contemporary landscape. A dialogue was maintained through it all (through meetings and social media), so that Nipmuc tribal members—elders and children alike—were kept informed and encouraged to participate. This relationship also included several visits by tribal members to the Burnee/Boston Homestead site over the course of the excavations so they could remain informed about the archaeology being conducted. While working on the Hassanamisco Reservation site during the summers of 2006 and 2007, Rae Gould hosted UMass Boston field school groups from the Burnee/Boston site so that they could better understand the connections between the two sites in Grafton and the tribe's broader history.

Also important is the interweaving of definitions of ourselves that we develop in relation to those we see as different from us. The case studies in this book are representative of larger identity struggles that everyone faces on a daily basis. Non-Native people have used their interpretations of Native peoples to construct definitions of themselves (in opposition to the "other") both in the past and today but have often done so without accurate knowledge of Native people as individuals or of the spaces that they have occupied. In the same way that Nipmuc people today ask, "What does it mean to be Indian in southern New England in the twenty-first century?" many Americans are asking themselves about their places in the world, their heritages and histories, and their futures in an increasingly globalized yet fractured world. Outside of this country, too, people everywhere seek "a past" that helps them define their place in the world today. Such identity issues require maintaining a separateness, while at the same time being integrated into and functioning in the world that surrounds us. Similar ambiguities also defined the people and spaces discussed in this book, with the main irony being that one place (the Hassanamisco Reservation) transformed into such a central space *because of* the land loss all around it, as it assumed greater importance as the last parcel of Nipmuc land held by the tribe.

The individuals explored in this book also defined themselves in relation to how they defined others. Lucy Gimbee did this, as did her granddaughter Sarah Arnold Cisco, and then Sarah's granddaughter and great-granddaughter (Sarah Cisco Sullivan and Zara CiscoeBrough). Sarah Burnee and her descendants Sarah Boston and Sarah Walker did as well. Two hundred years ago cultural divisions allowed Lucy Gimbee to use her status as a Hassanamisco Indian to construct an English-style house (through the guardian) on her family land. Her granddaughter Sarah Arnold Cisco used this same identity to hold onto the land and maintain it for future generations. Today these divisions allow Indian tribes to have successful tribally owned businesses and live on reservations with separate governments, police forces, health centers, schools, and other facilities. These spaces are clearly defined, bounded, and named, with multiple meanings depending on who is interpreting their histories and the context of their creation. To outsiders, Indian reservations are places where the exotic "other" lives, continuing "traditional" cultures connected to a romanticized past. Or they are places to consume Indian culture through purchasing arts and crafts or attending powwows, tours, and other publicly accessible events. For Native peoples, their reservations may serve as havens from a harsh outside world defined by a history of colonialism, oppression, and genocide, or they may be prisons where they cannot escape the harsh conditions of poverty, drug or alcohol abuse, and high suicide rates (the results of colonialism, oppression, and genocide).

The continued presence of reservations today—whether exoticized by outsiders or a daily reality for tribal members—underscores that connections to land are central to any narratives about Native peoples. Land has been part of their history and cultural identity long before the arrival of Europeans. Land (and landscape) is another theme central to this book. While Sarah Arnold Cisco was fighting to preserve the last piece of the Printer parcel in Grafton, Indian people further west were being killed and collected as "specimens" for emerging national museums,[4] all because of Euroamerican greed for land, its resources, and the concept of Manifest Destiny. For Native people, land has always been much more than a wilderness to be conquered and developed or a commodity to be bartered or sold. It is an anchor for kinship relations, tribal identity, and, more recently, definitions of sovereignty. Since colonization, Indian peoples have had to reconceptualize their relationships with land and struggle with decisions to maintain (or let go of) the land, as the individuals in this book did, often against a backdrop of violence. The cultural landscapes and places discussed in this book became communal spaces, either through their reconceptualization as praying towns or through becoming tribal gathering or reservation spaces. As communal spaces, they became what Weiner has described as inalienable possessions,[5] with cumulative identities through a series of owners who have "kept" them through time and through histories that are authenticated by cultural systems and practices.

These places are also considered to be valuable treasures requiring protection against all forces that could cause their loss.[6] This concept was clearly articulated in the responsibilities felt by Zara CiscoeBrough, who "was made to understand from childhood thru Grandpa and Mother" that the land and homestead needed to be protected and maintained for future generations of Nipmuc people.[7] This responsibility was also one that Isaac Nehemiah clearly struggled with. As the nineteenth century progressed, the Hassanamisco Reservation—as a cultural landscape—symbolized the continued presence of Nipmuc people in the area and was recognized as such by both tribal members and outsiders, as its presence in John Milton Earle's 1861 report and in local histories demonstrates.[8] Even though local histories and other sources (such as newspaper articles) claimed that the Indians of this region were a vanishing "race," the nagging presence of this land base and the homestead on it would not let them forget that the *people* associated with it also maintained a presence (even if small), which became more and more visible over the later decades of the nineteenth century and up to the present. Beginning with Sarah Arnold Cisco, tribal members refused to let this place or their presence be forgotten.

A paradox in the story of this cultural landscape is that the very process of seeking federal acknowledgment—even when unsuccessful—reaffirms a group's existence because the group is coordinating the effort and, once again, navigating complex legal and political systems to maintain a presence and secure resources for the greater good of the community. The individuals discussed in this book also demonstrated that they had the ability to work within repressive legal, social, and political systems that tried to define Indian people as less capable, less intelligent, and disappearing. In very sophisticated and conscious ways they sent the message "we are still here" as our homesteads, meeting houses, and reservations attest, despite substantial land loss. The artifacts, documents, and physical places discussed here reaffirm this message.

The influences of external developments and events (such as modernity, the Industrial Revolution, and other factors) on the decisions, movements, and future generations are also important themes discussed throughout this book. The pressure to sell land by those occupying Sarah Robins's parcel (on what became known as Keith Hill) was a direct result of New England becoming more densely occupied and moving toward the Industrial Era. The new industrial order reshaped what had remained a rural landscape. The numerous mill villages dotting the Blackstone River Valley were not as large as the burgeoning industrial cities of Lowell or Lawrence, Massachusetts, yet they nevertheless reflected a new uniformity on a landscape whose order was extended to a dizzying array of material goods such as cloth, shoes, cutlery, and ceramics. The artifacts from this site reflect the changing consumption patterns of its occupants over time as industry provided greater access to a wider range of material goods. By the 1850s bourgeoning cities like Worcester offered more opportunities for people like John Hector, whose decision to relocate left his niece with the responsibility of preserving the last piece of Moses Printer's parcel.

Perhaps most importantly, this book connects the pasts we explore with the present, the histories that have futures: a critical component in any study of Native people and places. Our chapters engage contemporary and political issues, in particular, through the connections made between the objects and documents we investigated, the individuals connected to them, their decisions over the centuries, and the landscapes that they navigated. The Nipmuc

Nation's experience with the federal acknowledgment process, repatriation of ancestors through NAGPRA, and a defined status as a state-recognized (versus federally recognized) tribe are all tied to how Nipmuc history has been interpreted, told, and retold over time.

This book serves as a model for exploring similar places and asking similar questions. How have other indigenous cultural landscapes changed and been perceived over time? What events, decisions, and actions by those associated with these places—individual or collective—resulted in their preservation (or loss)? What was the role of tribal women in these events, decisions, and actions? And do the interpretations of these places and people affect the contemporary descendants on the landscape today and perhaps have important ramifications for their futures?

## Transformations of Nipmuc Spaces

The individuals explored in this book were instrumental in the transformations of Nipmuc spaces at Magunkaquog, the Burnee/Boston Homestead, and 80 Brigham Hill Road. The transition of Magunkaquog into a seventeenth-century praying town was one component of the legacy of Christianizing Indian people in southern New England born from that movement. This transformation became foundational to Nipmuc religious practices over the centuries up to today. Sarah Walker's decision to sell her family's parcel in Grafton resulted in the loss of that 1727 allotment to Nipmuc residents at Hassanamesit, leaving the Printer parcel across town on Brigham Hill as the last piece of Nipmuc land. Sarah Arnold Cisco's decision to stay at the homestead after her uncle sold his parcel enabled this remnant piece of Moses Printer's allotment to become a tribal center and reservation in the decades between 1860 and 1900. The Cisco family used this cultural landscape as a bounded, politically charged place to achieve certain goals (first as individuals, then as tribal leaders), the most important of which was the preservation of the homestead and land.

Regardless of the BIA's definition of the Nipmuc Tribe or this place, the Hassanamisco Reservation remains important to a people who have used it for tribal gatherings and educational programs to teach both Nipmuc youth and the public about Nipmuc history and culture. It is both the beginning point of modern Nipmuc tribal culture and a physical reality to pass on to the future, in addition to being an embodiment of the tribe's past. There is no doubt (in most people's minds) that today this publicly recognized reservation makes a statement about the continued presence of Nipmuc people over time, because of the struggles that Sarah Arnold Cisco began as steward of this land.

Our work on the sites discussed throughout this book is part of the changing understandings of these places and of the people associated with them. We are working to reappropriate and redefine not only how the past of Nipmuc people is understood but also how the discipline of historical archaeology engages with Native people today and in the future. We are part of an ongoing transformation involving scholars actively and consciously refashioning, reshaping, and redefining how the past is interpreted and, most importantly, successfully working to preserve the braided knowledge about these cultural landscapes that we have gained through working collaboratively.

Isaac Nehemiah, Sarah Robins and her descendants, and the Printer descendants felt the burden of being Indian as their homeland transformed from a land occupied by indigenous people to one dominated by colonial settlers, as their stories reveal. They passed this burden along to those who came after them and made them understand that, when one generation fades, the next one assumes the responsibilities of maintaining Nipmuc heritage and passing it to future generations, always connecting the past to the future. The communication of these responsibilities may exist in many forms: a letter to a cousin, a document recalling the short life of Isaac Nehemiah, artifacts from a homestead foundation, a plea to hold onto the land from a nursing home, the restoration of a homestead, the decision to write down our stories in this book, or a simple conversation where one person says to the other, "This is yours now," as a tribal elder once said to Rae Gould.

The struggles for power that still exist between Native and non-Native people of southern New England (and elsewhere) are often played out on the physical landscape. Struggles focused on control over land and autonomy, capital, and political authority that have defined this country's making for the past 400 years continue today and did not end with the claim that Indians vanished from the New England landscape long ago. And these struggles to define our identities—that both Native and non-Native people engage in on a daily basis—are directly related to who gains (and maintains) control over the future by manipulating perceptions of the past and present.

The conscious decisions that Moses Printer's descendants made to preserve the Nipmuc tribal land base, following the loss of Sarah Boston's parcel, became a defining moment in the history of the Nipmuc Tribe. Had Sarah Arnold Cisco (or later generations) decided to abandon the struggle to keep this land and homestead in Grafton, the tribe would probably not exist as it does today. This book is one way that we can remember the sacrifices that individuals like Isaac Nehemiah, Sarah Walker, Sarah Arnold Cisco, and Zara Ciscoe-Brough made to protect, preserve, and maintain Nipmuc spaces, when they could. While Nipmuc people today continue to identify with their ancestry, their heritage and the sense of history and permanence that is afforded by *place* is what binds them together in the twenty-first century and, without a doubt, into the future.

## Notes

1. Atalay 2012.
2. Historical documentation of this role is discussed in Brooks 2008. A more modern example, beyond those in this book, is the role of Mohegan tribal women in the twentieth century (see Federal Acknowledgement petition [May 14, 1994], at https://www.bia.gov/as-ia/ofa/038-mohegn-ct).
3. Grafton Land Trust, Inc., Hassanamesit Woods, http://www.graftonland.org/openspaces.properties.details.php (accessed May 28, 2019).
4. Thomas 2000.
5. Weiner 1986, 1992.
6. Weiner 1992.
7. Nipmuc Nation Tribal Archives, Document H1788.
8. Earle 1861.F

# Bibliography


Acts and Resolves. 1869–1922. *The Acts and Resolves, Public and Private, of the Province of the Massachusetts Bay*. 9 vols. Boston: Wright and Potter.

Adams, William Hampton. 2003. "Dating Historical Sites: The Importance of Understanding Time Lag in the Acquisition, Curation, Use, and Disposal of Artifacts." *Historical Archaeology* 37(2):38–64.

Allard, Amélie. 2015. "Foodways, Animal Husbandry and Nipmuc Identity: Faunal Analysis from Sarah Boston's Farmstead, Grafton, MA, 1790–1840." *International Journal of Historical Archaeology* 19(1):208–231.

Atalay, Sonya. 2006. "Indigenous Archaeology as Decolonizing Practice." *American Indian Quarterly* 30(3/4):280–310.

———. 2012. *Community-Based Archaeology: Research with, by, and for Indigenous and Local Communities*. Berkeley: University of California Press.

Austin, John Osbourne. 1887. *Genealogical Dictionary of Rhode Island*. Albany, NY: J. Musell's Sons.

Bagley, J. 2013. "Cultural Continuity in a Nipmuc Landscape." MA thesis. University of Massachusetts, Boston.

Bagley, J. M., S. A. Mrozowski, H. Law Pezzarossi, and J. Steinberg. 2015. "Continuity of Lithic Practice at the Eighteenth- through Nineteenth-Century Nipmuc Homestead of Sarah Boston, Grafton, Massachusetts." *Northeast Historical Archaeology* 43(1):121–142.

Baron, Donna Keith, J. Edward Hood, and Holly V. Izard. 1996. "They Were Here All Along: The Native American Presence in Lower-Central New England in the Eighteenth and Nineteenth Centuries." *William and Mary Quarterly* 53(3):561–586.

Barry, William. 1847. *A History of Framingham, Massachusetts Including the Plantation, from 1640 to the Present Time*. Boston: James Munroe and Company.

Bender, Barbara. 1993. "Introduction: Landscape—Meaning and Action." In *Landscape: Politics and Perspectives*, edited by Barbara Bender, 1–18. Oxford: Berg Publishers.

Bendremer, Jeffrey C. 1993. "Late Woodland Settlement and Subsistence in Eastern Connecticut." Ph.D. diss. University of Connecticut.

Bergson, Henri. 1999 [1922]. *Duration and Simultaneity, with Reference to Einstein's Theory*. Manchester: Clinamen Press.

Biglow, William. 1830. *History of the Town of Natick, Mass., from the Days of the Apostolic Eliot, 1650, to the Present Time*. Boston: March, Capen, and Lyon.

Bowden, Henry W., and James P. Ronda, eds. 1980. *John Eliot's Indian Dialogues: A Study in Cultural Interactions*. Westport, CT: Greenwood Press.

Bowditch, Charles P. 1889. *An Account of the Trust Administered by the Trustees of the Charity of Edward Hopkins.* Cambridge, MA: Privately printed.

Boyle, Robert. 1772. *The Works of Robert Boyle.* Edited by Thomas Birch. London: Privately printed.

Bragdon, Kathleen. 1988. "Occupational Differences Reflected in Material Culture." In *Documentary Archaeology in the New World*, edited by Mary C. Beaudry, 83–91. Cambridge: Cambridge University Press.

———. 1996. *Native People of Southern New England, 1500–1650.* Norman: University of Oklahoma Press.

Brenner, Elise. 1980. "To Pray or to Be Prey: That Is the Question, Strategies for Cultural Autonomy of Massachusetts Praying Town Indians." *Ethnohistory* 27(2):135–152.

———. 1984. "Strategies for Autonomy: An Analysis of Ethnic Mobilization in Seventeenth Century Southern New England." Ph.D. diss. University of Massachusetts Amherst.

———. 1986. "Archaeological Investigations at a Massachusetts Praying Indian Town." *Bulletin of the Massachusetts Archaeological Society* 47(2):69–78.

Brigham, William. 1835. *An Address Delivered before the Inhabitants of Grafton, on the First Centennial Anniversary of That Town, April 29, 1835.* Boston: Light and Horton.

Brooks, Lisa. 2008. *The Common Pot: The Recovery of Native Space in the Northeast.* Minneapolis: University of Minnesota Press.

———. 2018. *Our Beloved Kin: A New History of King Philip's War.* New Haven, CT: Yale University Press.

Buckley, B., and S. W. Nixon. 2001. *An Historical Assessment of Anadromous Fish in the Blackstone River: Final Report to the Narragansett Bay Estuary Program Blackstone River Valley National Heritage Corridor Commission, and Trout Unlimited.* Narragansett, RI: University of Rhode Island Graduate School of Oceanography.

Cady, John Hutchins. 1957. *The Civic and Architectural Development of Providence.* Providence, RI: Akerman Standard Press.

Calloway, Colin G., ed. 1994. *The World Turned Upside Down: Indian Voices from Early America.* Boston, MA: Bedford Books.

———. 1997. *After King Philip's War: Presence and Persistence in Indian New England.* Lebanon, NH: University Press of New England.

Carlson, Catherine C. 1986. *Archival and Archaeological Research Report on the Configuration of the Seven Original 17th Century Praying Indian Towns of the Massachusetts Bay Colony.* Amherst: UMass Archaeological Services, University of Massachusetts.

Cave, Alfred A. 1996. *The Pequot War.* Amherst: University of Massachusetts Press.

Chilton, Elizabeth S. 2002. "'Towns They Have None': Diverse Subsistence and Settlement Strategies in Native New England." In *Northeast Subsistence-Settlement Change A.D. 700–1300*, edited by John P. Hart and Christina B. Rieth, 289–300. Albany: New York State Museum.

Cipolla, Craig N., and James Quinn. 2016. "Field School Archaeology the Mohegan Way: Reflections on Twenty Years of Community-Based Research and Teaching." *Journal of Community Archaeology & Heritage* 3(2):118–134.

Cogley, Richard W. 1999. *John Eliot's Mission to the Indians before King Philip's War.* Cambridge, MA: Harvard University Press.

Collection of the Charity of Edward Hopkins (CCEH). 1668–1958. Documents Relating to the Charity of Edward Hopkins. Harvard University Archives, Cambridge, MA.

Colwell-Chanthaphonh, Chip, and T. J. Ferguson, eds. 2008. *Collaboration in Archaeological Practice: Engaging Descendant Communities*. Walnut Creek, CA: AltaMira Press.

Copplestone, J. Tremayne. 1998. *John Eliot and the Indians, 1604–1690*. Boston, MA: Privately printed.

Cronon, William. 1983. *Changes in the Land: Indians, Colonists, and the Ecology of New England*. New York: Hill and Wang.

Daniels of Massachusetts Bay Colony—Generation IV Major Joseph Daniels (1724–1779). http://freepages.genealogy.rootsweb.ancestry.com/~danielsofmassachusettsbaycolony/gen4.html, accessed December 8, 2017.

Deetz, James. 1977. *In Small Things Forgotten: The Archaeology of Early American Life*. New York: Knopf Doubleday Publishing Group.

———. 1990. "Landscapes as Cultural Statements." In *Earth Patterns: Essays in Landscape Archaeology*, edited by W. M. Kelso and R. Most, 1–4. Charlottesville: University Press of Virginia.

Delle, James A., Stephen A. Mrozowski, and Robert Paynter, eds. 2000. *Lines That Divide: Historical Archaeologists of Race, Class, and Gender*. Knoxville: University of Tennessee Press.

Deloria, Vine, Jr. 1969. *Custer Died for Your Sins: An Indian Manifest*. Norman: University of Oklahoma Press.

———. 1970. *We Talk, You Listen: New Tribes, New Turf*. New York: Macmillan.

———. 1992. *God Is Red: A Native View of Religion*. 2nd ed. Golden, CO: North American Press.

———. 1999. "Indians, Archaeologists, and the Future." In *Spirit and Reason: The Vine Deloria, Jr., Reader*, edited by Barbara Deloria, Kristen Foehner, and Sam Scinta, 72–77. Golden, CO: Fulcrum Publishing.

DeLucia, Christine M. 2018. *Memory Lands: King Philip's War and the Place of Violence in the Northeast*. New Haven, CT: Yale University Press.

Diamant, Judith, Rolf Diamant, Nadine Gerdts, and Rosemary Wells. 1987. *Working Water: A Guide to the Historic Landscape of the Blackstone River Valley*. Providence, RI: Rhode Island Parks Association.

Dincauze, Dena. 1968. *Cremation Cemeteries in Eastern Massachusetts*. Cambridge, MA: Peabody Museum Press, Harvard University.

———. 1976. *The Neville Site: 8,000 Years at Amoskeag, Manchester, New Hampshire*. Cambridge, MA: Peabody Museum Press, Harvard University.

Doughton, Thomas L. 1997. "Unseen Neighbors: Native Americans of Central Massachusetts, a People Who Had Vanished." In *After King Philip's War: Presence and Persistence in Indian New England*, edited by Colin Calloway, 207–230. Lebanon, NH: University Press of New England.

Drake, James D. 2000. *King Philip's War: Civil War in New England, 1675–1676*. Amherst: University of Massachusetts Press.

Earle, John Milton. 1652–1863. John Milton Earle Papers. Worcester, MA: American Antiquarian Society.

———. 1861. *Report to the Governor and Council, concerning the Indians of the Commonwealth, under the Act of April 6, 1859*. Boston, MA: William White, Printer to the Commonwealth.

Eliot, John. 1671. *A Brief Narrative of the Progress of the Gospel amongst the Indians in New*

*England*. London: J. Allen. Reprinted in *Old South Leaflets* 1:21 (n.d.):1–11. Boston: Old South Meeting House.

———. 1834. "A Late and Further Manifestation of the Progress of the Gospel amongst the Indians in New-England." *Massachusetts Historical Society Collections*, 3rd series, 4:261–287.

———. 1846. "The Christian Commonwealth: Or the Civil Polity of the Rising Kingdom of Jesus Christ." *Massachusetts Historical Society Collections*, 3rd series, 9:127–164.

———. 1865 [1660]. *A Further Account of the Progress of the Gospel amongst the Indians in New England*. Reprint, New York: Joseph Sabin.

———. 1882a. "Letter to Mr. Steele, 1652." *New England Historical and Genealogical Register* 36:294–297.

———. 1882b. "Letter to Mr. Winslow, 1651." *New England Historical and Genealogical Register* 36:291–294.

Eliot, John, and Thomas Mayhew. 1834. "Tears of Repentance; or, A Further Narrative of the Progress of the Gospel amongst the Indians in New England, 1653." *Massachusetts Historical Society Collections*, 3rd series, 4:197–260.

Estes, D. F. 1894. *The History of Holden Massachusetts 1684–1894*. Worcester, MA: Press of CF Lawrence and Co.

Fairbanks, Charles H. 1971. *The Florida Seminole People*. 1st ed. Phoenix, AZ: Indian Tribal Series.

———. 1984. "The Plantation Archaeology of the Southeastern Coast." *Historical Archaeology* 18(1):1–14.

Ferguson, Leland. 2004. *Uncommon Ground: Archaeology and Early African America, 1650–1800*. Washington, DC: Smithsonian Books.

Fernow, B. 1881. "Documents Relating to the History and Settlements of the Towns along the Hudson and Mohawk Rivers (with the Exception of Albany), from 1630 to 1684. And Also Illustrating the Relations of the Settlers with the Indians." In *Documents Relating to the Colonial History of the State of New York, Vol. 13*, 513–530. Albany, NY: Weed, Parsons, and Company.

Fitzhugh, William W. 1985. "Commentary on Part II." In *Cultures in Contact: The Impact of European Contacts on Native American Cultural Institutions, A.D. 1000–1800*, edited by William W. Fitzhugh, 99–106. Washington, DC: Smithsonian Institution Press.

Fogel, Robert William, and Stanley L. Engerman. 1974. *Time on the Cross: The Economics of American Negro Slavery*. 2 vols. Boston, MA: Little Brown and Company.

Forbes, Harriet Merrifield. 1889. *The Hundredth Town: Glimpses of Life in Westborough, 1717–1817*. Boston, MA: Rockwell and Churchill.

Ford, John W. 1970 [1896]. *Some Correspondence between the Governors and Treasurers of the New England Company in London and the Commissioners of the United Colonies in America, the Missionaries of the Company and Others between the Years 1657 and 1712 to Which Are Added the Journals of the Rev. Experience Mayhew in 1713 and 1714*. Reprint, New York: Burt Franklin.

Garman, James C., and Holly Herbster. 1996. *Results of a Site Examination Survey of the Magunco III Archaeological Site (ASH-HA-5), Apple Ridge III, Ashland, Massachusetts*. Pawtucket, RI: Public Archaeology Laboratory.

Garroutte, Eva Marie. 2003. *Real Indians: Identity and Survival of Native America*. Los Angeles: University of California Press.

Gary, Jack. 2005. *Phase 1 Archaeological Intensive Survey of Hassanamesitt Woods, Grafton, Massachusetts.* Cultural Resources Management Study No. 14. Boston, MA: Center for Cultural and Environmental History, University of Massachusetts, Boston.

Gookin, Daniel. 1836 [1677]. "An Historical Account of the Doings and Sufferings of the Christian Indians of New England, in the Years 1675, 1676, 1677." In *Transactions and Collections of the American Antiquarian Society,* 425–534. Vol. 2. Cambridge: Cambridge University Press.

———. 1970 [1792]. *Historical Collections of the Indians in New England.* Reprint, Boston, MA: Towtaid Press.

Gould, Donna Rae. 2005. "Wabbaquasset: An Ethnohistorical Analysis and Methodology for Locating a 17th-Century Praying Village." MA thesis. University of Connecticut, Storrs.

———. 2010. "Contested Places: The History and Meaning of Hassanamisco." Ph.D. diss. University of Connecticut, Storrs.

———. 2013. "Cultural Practice and Authenticity: The Search for Real Indians in New England in the 'Historical' Period." In *The Death of "Prehistory,"* edited by Peter Schmidt and Stephen A. Mrozowski, 241–266. Oxford: Oxford University Press.

———. 2017. "NAGPRA, CUI and Institutional Will." In *The Routledge Companion to Cultural Property,* edited by Jane Anderson and Haidy Geismar, 134–151. London: Routledge Press.

Greenwood, Janette Thomas. 2010. *First Fruits of Freedom: The Migration of Former Slaves and Their Search for Equality in Worcester, Massachusetts, 1862–1900.* Chapel Hill: University of North Carolina Press.

Groth, Paul. 1997. "Frameworks for Cultural Landscape Study." In *Understanding Ordinary Landscapes,* edited by Paul Groth and Todd W. Bressi, 1–21. New Haven, CT: Yale University Press.

Handsman, Russell, and Ann McMullen. 1987. "An Introduction to Woodsplint Basketry and Its Interpretation." In *A Key into the Language of Woodsplint Baskets,* edited by Ann McMullen and Russell Handsman, 17–35. Washington, CT: American Indian Archaeological Institute.

Herbster, Holly. 2005. "A Documentary Archaeology of Magunkaquog." MA thesis. University of Massachusetts, Boston.

Historical Records Survey (HRS). 1942. *History of the Town of Ashland.* Prepared by the Historical Records Survey, Division of Community Service Programs, Work Projects Administration. Framingham, MA: Lakeview Press.

Hoffman, Curtiss R. 1989. "Figure and Ground: The Late Woodland Village Problem as Seen from the Uplands." *Bulletin of the Massachusetts Archaeological Society* 50(1):24–48.

———. 1990. *People of the Fresh Water Lake: A Prehistory of Westborough, Massachusetts.* New York: Peter Lang.

Hume, Noel. 1969. *A Guide to Artifacts in Colonial America.* 1st ed. New York: Knopf.

Jackson, John Brinckerhoff. 1984. *Discovering the Vernacular Landscape.* New Haven, CT: Yale University Press.

Johnson, Eric S., and James W. Bradley. 1987. "The Bark Wigwams Site: An Early Seventeenth Century Component in Central Massachusetts." *Man in the Northeast* 33:1–26.

Johnson, Troy. 1994. "The Occupation of Alcatraz: Roots of American Indian Activism." *Wicazo Sa Review* 10(2):63–79.

Jones, Brian. 1997. "The Late Paleoindian Hidden Creek Site in Southeastern Connecticut." *Archaeology of Eastern North America* 25:45–80.

———. 1999. "The Middle Archaic Period in Connecticut: The View from Mashantucket." *Bulletin of the Archaeological Society of Connecticut* 62:101–123.

———. 2004. "Paleoindian Population Dynamics in New England: Possible Typological Consequences." In *Hunters and Gatherers in Theory and Archaeology*, edited by George M. Crothers, 48–67. Occasional Paper No. 31. Carbondale: Center for Archaeological Investigations, Southern Illinois University.

Jones, Brian, and Daniel T. Forrest. 2003. "Life in a Postglacial Landscape: Settlement-Subsistence Change during the Pleistocene-Holocene Transition in Southern New England." In *Geoarchaeology of Landscapes in the Glaciated Northeast*, edited by David L. Cremeens and John P. Hart, 75–89. New York State Museum Bulletin 497. Albany: New York State Education Department.

Kawashima, Yasu. 1969. "Legal Origins of the Indian Reservation in Colonial Massachusetts." *American Journal of Legal History* 13(1):42–56.

Kehoe, Alice B., and Peter R. Schmidt. 2017. "Introduction: Expanding Our Knowledge by Listening." *SAA Archaeological Record* (September):15–19.

Kellaway, William. 1961. *The New England Company 1649–1776: Missionary Society to the American Indians*. New York: Barnes and Noble.

Kelley, John W. 1999. "Burial Practices of the Praying Indians of Natick, Ponkapoag, and Marlboro." MA thesis. University of Massachusetts, Boston.

Larned, Ellen D. 1976 [1874]. *History of Windham County, Connecticut*. Vol. 1. Reprint, Chester, CT: Pequot Press.

Lauber, Almon Wheeler. 1913. *Indian Slavery in Colonial Times within the Present Limits of the United States*. New York: Columbia University.

Lavin, Lucianne. 2013. *Connecticut's Indigenous Peoples: What Archaeology, History, and Oral Traditions Teach Us about Their Communities and Cultures*. New Haven, CT: Yale University Press.

Law, Heather B. 2008. "Daily Negotiations and the Creation of an Alternative Discourse: The Legacy of a Colonial Nipmuc Farmstead." MA thesis. University of Massachusetts, Boston.

———. 2014. "Traces of Residence: Indigenous Mobility and Materiality in 19th C. New England." Ph.D. diss. University of California, Berkeley.

Law, Heather, Stephen Mrozowski, and Guido Pezzarossi. 2008. *Archaeological Intensive Excavation, Hassanamesit Woods Property, the Sarah Boston Farmstead, Grafton, Massachusetts. Part 2*. Cultural Resource Management Study No. 26. Boston, MA: Andrew Fiske Memorial Center for Archaeological Research, University of Massachusetts, Boston.

Law Pezzarossi, Heather. 2014a. "Assembling Indigeneity: Rethinking Innovation, Tradition and Indigenous Materiality in a 19th-Century Native Toolkit." *Journal of Social Archaeology* 14(3):340–360.

———. 2014b. "Native Basketry and the Dynamics of Social Landscapes in Southern New England." In *Things in Motion: Object Histories, Biographies and Itineraries*, edited by Rosemary Joyce and Susan Gillespie, 179–200. Santa Fe, NM: School of Advanced Research Press.

———. 2019. "Brewed Time: Considering Anachronisms in the Study of Indigenous Persistence in New England." In *Indigenous Persistence in the Colonized Americas*, edited by Heather Law Pezzarossi and Russell Sheptak. Albuquerque: University of New Mexico Press.

Leone, Mark, and Jocelyn E. Knauf, eds. 2015. *Historical Archaeologies of Capitalism*. 2nd ed. New York: Springer Books.

Lepore, Jill. 1998. *The Name of War: King Philip's War and the Origins of American Identity*. New York: Vintage Books.

Lester, Joan. 1987. "'We Didn't Make Fancy Baskets Until We Were Discovered': Fancy-Basket Making in Maine." In *A Key into the Language of Woodsplint Baskets*, edited by Ann McMullen and Russell G. Handsman, 38–59. Washington, CT: American Indian Archaeological Institute.

Leveillee, Alan. 1999. "Transitional Archaic Ideology as Reflected in Secondary Burials at the Millbury III Cremation Complex." *Archaeology of Eastern North America* 27:157–183.

Lewis, Peirce F. 1979. "Axioms for Reading the Landscape: Some Guides to the American Scene." In *The Interpretation of Ordinary Landscapes*, edited by D. W. Meinig, 11–32. New York: Oxford University Press.

Luedtke, Barbara E. 1999a. "Gunflints in the Northeast." *Northeast Anthropology* 57:27–43.

———. 1999b. "What Makes a Good Gunflint." *Archaeology of Eastern North America* 27:71–79.

MacCulloch, Susan. 1965. "A Convergence of Cultures in the Sixteenth Century Indian Missions of Massachusetts." MA thesis. University of Massachusetts Amherst.

Malkki, Lisa H. 1997. "National Geographic: The Rooting of Peoples and the Territorialization of National Identity among Scholars and Refugees." In *Culture, Power, Place: Explorations in Critical Anthropology*, edited by Akhil Gupta and James Ferguson, 52–74. Durham, NC: Duke University Press.

Mandell, Daniel R. 1991. "'To Live More Like My Christian English Neighbors': Natick Indians in the Eighteenth Century." *William and Mary Quarterly: A Magazine of Early American History and Culture* 48(4):552–579.

———. 1996. *Behind the Frontier: Indians in Eighteenth-Century Eastern Massachusetts*. Lincoln: University of Nebraska Press.

———. 1999. "The Saga of Sara Muckamaug." In *Sex, Love and Race: Crossing Boundaries in North American History*, edited by Martha Hodes, 72–90. New York: New York University Press.

———. 2010. *King Philip's War: Colonial Expansion, Native Resistance, and the End of Indian Sovereignty*. Baltimore, MD: Johns Hopkins University Press.

Massachusetts Anti-Slavery and Anti-Segregation Petitions. 1853. *Passed Resolves, Resolves 1853, c.47, SC1/ series 228*. Massachusetts Archives, Boston.

Massachusetts Archives (MA). n.d. Materials Relating to Indians in Massachusetts. Microfilm volumes 30–33. Boston, MA.

Massachusetts Archives Collection (MAC). 1603–1705. *Indians Vol. XXX*. Massachusetts State Library, Boston.

———. 1643–1775. Petitions. Volume 105, page 32a. Massachusetts State Library, Boston.

———. 1701–1750. Indians Vol. XXXI. Massachusetts State Library, Boston.

———. 1750–1757. *Indians Vol. XXXII*. Boston: Massachusetts State Library.

Massachusetts, Office of the Secretary of State. 1904. *Massachusetts Soldiers and Sailors of the Revolutionary War: A Compilation from the Archives, Prepared and Published by the Secretary of the Commonwealth in Accordance with Chapter 100, Resolves of 1891*. Vol. 12. Boston, MA: Wright and Potter Printing Co., State Printers.

Mather, Cotton. 1967 [1702]. *Magnalia Christi Americana: or, the Ecclesiastical History of New-England, from Its First Planting in the Year 1620, unto the Year of Our Lord 1698*. Reprint, New York: Russell and Russell.

McBride, Kevin. 1984. "The Archaeology of the Lower Connecticut River Valley." Ph.D. diss. University of Connecticut, Storrs.

———. 1989. *Prehistory of Eastern Connecticut: Phase I, II & III Archaeological Surveys, Relocation of Route 6/I-84 Project*. 2 vols. Storrs, CT: PAST, Inc.

———. 1992. "Prehistoric and Historic Patterns of Wetland Use in Eastern Connecticut." *Man in the Northeast* 43:10–23.

McBride, Kevin, and Mary G. Soulsby. 1986. "The Native Americans." In *Heritage and Horizons: Woodstock Remembers 300 Years*. Woodstock, CT: Woodstock Tercentenary Committee.

McCarthy, B. Eugene, and Thomas L. Doughton, eds. 2007. *From Bondage to Belonging: The Worcester Slave Narratives*. Amherst: University of Massachusetts Press.

McCord, David. 1957. "Notes on the Charity of Edward Hopkins." In *Publications of the Colonial Society of Massachusetts, Vol. 43, Transactions 1956–1963*, 291–304. Boston: Published by the Colonial Society of Massachusetts.

McGuire, Randall H., and Robert Paynter, eds. 1991. *The Archaeology of Inequality*. Oxford: Basil Blackwell.

McLouglin, William. 1986. *Rhode Island: A History*. New York: W. W. Norton and Co.

McMullen, Ann. 1987. "Looking for People in Woodsplint Basketry Decoration." In *A Key into the Language of Woodsplint Baskets*, edited by Ann McMullen and Russell G. Handsman, 120–123. Washington, CT: American Indian Archaeological Institute.

Meinig, D. W. 1979a. "The Beholding Eye: Ten Versions of the Same Scene." In *The Interpretation of Ordinary Landscapes: Geographical Essays*, edited by D. W. Meinig, 33–48. New York: Oxford University Press.

———. 1979b. "Introduction." In *The Interpretation of Ordinary Landscapes: Geographical Essays*, edited by D. W. Meinig, 1–7. New York: Oxford University Press.

Mihesuah, Devon A. 1996. "Commonalty of Difference: American Indian Women and History." *American Indian Quarterly* 20(1):15–27.

Mohler, P. J. 2000. "Soil Phosphate Analysis: The Evaluation of a New Testing Method." MA thesis. University of Massachusetts Boston.

Mrozowski, Stephen A. 2009. "Christian Indian Communities in New England after King Philips War." In *Archaeology in America: An Encyclopedia*, edited by Francis P. McManomon, 143–147. Westport, CT: Greenwood.

———. 2013. "The Tyranny of Prehistory and the Search for a Deeper History." In *The Death of Prehistory*, edited by Peter R. Schmidt and Stephen A. Mrozowski, 220–240. Oxford: Oxford University Press.

Mrozowski, Stephen A., Holly Herbster, D. Brown, and K. L. Priddy. 2009. "Magunkaquog Materiality, Federal Recognition, and the Search for a Deeper History." *International Journal of Historical Archaeology* 13(4):430–463.

Mrozowski, Stephen, and Heather Law Pezzarossi. 2015. *The Archaeology of Hassanamesit Woods: The Sarah Burnee/Sarah Boston Farmstead*. Cultural Resource Management Study No. 69. Boston: Andrew Fiske Memorial Center for Archaeological Research, University of Massachusetts Boston.

Mrozowski, Stephen A., Grace H. Ziesing, and Mary C. Beaudry. 1996. *Living on the Boott: Historical Archaeology at the Boott Mills Boardinghouses, Lowell, Massachusetts*. Amherst: University of Massachusetts Press.

Murphy, John P. 2002. "Crystal Quartz from Magunco." MA thesis, University of Massachusetts Boston.

Nipmuc Nation Tribal Archive, Nipmuc Nation Tribal Office, Grafton, MA.

Oberg, Michael Leroy. 1999. *Dominion and Civility: English Imperialism and Native America, 1585–1685*. Ithaca, NY: Cornell University Press.

O'Brien, Jean M. 1997. *Dispossession by Degrees: Indian Land and Identity in Natick, Massachusetts, 1650–1790*. Cambridge: Cambridge University Press.

———. 2010. *Firsting and Lasting: Writing Indians Out of Existence in New England*. Minneapolis: University of Minnesota Press.

Original Indian Record Book (OIRB). Transcribed from the original by Austin Bacon in 1858. Morse Institute Library, Natick, Massachusetts.

Orser, Charles E., Jr. 1996. *An Historical Archaeology of the Modern World*. New York: Plenum Press.

———. 2007. The Archaeology of Race and Racialization in Historic America. Gainesville: University Press of Florida.

Parker, Patricia L. and Thomas F. King. 1990 Guidelines for Evaluating and Documenting Traditional Cultural Properties. National Register Bulletin 38. U.S. Department of Interior, National Park Service (revised 1992, 1998).

Pezzarossi, Guido. 2014. "Camouflaging Consumption and Colonial Mimicry: The Materiality of an Eighteenth and Nineteenth-Century Nipmuc Household." *International Journal of Historical Archaeology* 18(1):146–174.

Pezzarossi, Guido, J. Ryan Kennedy, and Heather B. Law. 2010. "'Hoe Cakes and Pickerel': Cooking Traditions and Community at a Nineteenth Century Nipmuc Farmstead." Annual Meetings for the Society for American Archaeology, St. Louis, MO.

Phillips, Ruth. 1998. *Trading Identities: The Souvenir in Native North American Art from the Northeast, 1700–1900*. Seattle and Montreal: University of Washington Press and McGill-Queen's University Press.

Piechota, Dennis. 2015. "Micromorphology at the Sarah Burnee/Sarah Boston Home Site." In *The Archaeology of Hassanamesit Woods: The Sarah Burnee/Sarah Boston Farmstead*, 115–128. Cultural Resource Management Study No. 69. Boston: Andrew Fiske Memorial Center for Archaeological Research, University of Massachusetts Boston.

*Proceedings of the Worcester Society of Antiquity*. 1891. Vol. 9. Worcester, MA.: Worcester Historical Society.

Prude, Jonathan. 1999. *The Coming of Industrial Order: Town and Factory Life in Rural Massachusetts, 1810–1860*. Amherst: University of Massachusetts Press.

Pulsipher, Jenny Hale. 1996. "Massacre at Hurtleberry Hill: Christian Indians and English Authority in Metacom's War." *William and Mary Quarterly* 53(3):459–486.

Quintal, George, Jr. 2005. *Patriots of Color: "A Peculiar Beauty and Merit," African American and Native Americans at Battle Road & Bunker Hill*. Washington, DC: U.S. Government Printing Office.

Rapoport, Amos. 1990. *The Meaning of the Built Environment: A Nonverbal Communication Approach*. 2nd ed. Tucson: University of Arizona Press.

Rhode Island Historic Preservation Commission. 1989. *Historical and Architectural Resources of the East Side, Providence: A Preliminary Report.* Providence: Rhode Island State Historical Preservation Office.

Rice, Franklin P. 1906. *Vital Records of Grafton, Massachusetts, to the End of the Year 1849.* Boston, MA: Stanhope Press.

Rockman, Diana Diz, and Nan A. Rothschild. 1984. "City Tavern, Country Tavern: An Analysis of Four Colonial Sites." *Historical Archaeology* 18(2):112–121.

Rowlandson, Mary. 2007 [1682]. *Narrative of the Captivity and Restoration.* N.p.: Book Jungle.

Rubertone, Patricia. 1986. "Historical Landscapes: Archaeology of Place and Space." *Man in the Northeast* 31:123–138.

Samford, Patricia. 2014. "Colonial and Post-Colonial Ceramics." Presentation. Maryland Archaeological Conservation Laboratory, Jefferson Patterson Park and Museum Maryland Historical Trust/Maryland Dept. of Planning. http://www.jefpat.org/Documents/Colonial-PostColonialCeramics.pdf.

Sassaman, Kenneth E. 2006. "Dating and Explaining Soapstone Vessels: A Comment on Truncer." *American Antiquity* 71(1):141–156.

———. 2010. *The Eastern Archaic, Historicized.* Walnut Creek, CA: AltaMira Press.

———. 2016. "A Constellation of Practice in the Experience of Sea-Level Rise." In *Knowledge in Motion: Constellations of Learning across Time and Place*, edited by A. P. Roddick and A. B. Stahl, 271–298. Tucson: University of Arizona Press.

Sassaman, Kenneth E., and S. O. Brookes. 2017. "Situating the Claiborne Soapstone Vessel Cache in the History of Poverty Point." *American Antiquity* 82(4):781–797.

Schmidt, Peter, and Stephen A. Mrozowski, eds. 2013. *The Death of Prehistory.* Oxford: Oxford University Press.

Schultz, Eric B., and Michael J. Tougias. 2000. *King Philip's War: The History and Legacy of America's Forgotten Conflict.* Woodstock, VT: Countryman Press.

Sewall, Samuel. 1973. *The Diary of Samuel Sewall, 1674–1729.* (1878). Edited by M. H. Thomas. Reprint, New York: Farrar, Strauss, and Giroux.

Shepard, Thomas. 1834a. "The Clear Sun-shine of the Gospel Breaking Forth upon the Indians in New-England." *Massachusetts Historical Society Collections*, 3rd series, (4):25–67.

———. 1834b. *The Day Breaking, If Not the Sun-Rising of the Gospell with the Indians in New-England.* In *Massachusetts Historical Society Collections*, 3rd series, (4):1–23.

Shurtleff, Nathaniel B., ed. 1853–1854. *Records of the Governor and Company of the Massachusetts Bay in New England, 1629–1686 (RMB).* 5 vols. Boston: William White.

Silliman, Stephen. 2005. "Culture Contact or Colonialism?: Challenges in the Archaeology of Native North America." *American Antiquity* 70(1):55–74.

———. 2009. "Change and Continuity, Practice and Memory: Native American Persistence in Colonial New England." *American Antiquity* 74(2):211–230.

Silliman, Stephen, ed. 2008. *Collaborating at the Trowel's Edge: Teaching and Learning in Indigenous Archaeology.* Tucson: University of Arizona Press.

Simon, Brona G. 1990a. "Native American Culture Change and Persistence in Contact Period New England: Analysis of Mortuary Data from a Praying Indian Burial Ground in Massachusetts." Paper presented at the 55th Annual Meeting of the Society for American Archaeology, Las Vegas, Nevada.

———. 1990b. "Proposal for the Archaeological Data Recovery of Seven Burials at the Chapman Street Praying Indian Burial Ground in Canton, MA." Presented at the Massachusetts Historical Commission, Boston.

Simpson, Alan. 1957. "A Candle in the Corner: How Harvard College Got the Hopkins Legacy." In *Publications of the Colonial Society of Massachusetts*, vol. 43, *Transactions 1956–1963*, 304–324. Boston, MA: Published by the Colonial Society of Massachusetts.

Snow, Dean. 1980. *The Archaeology of New England*. New York: Academic Press.

Snow, Dean, and Kim M. Lanphear. 1988. "European Contact and Indian Depopulation in the Northeast: The Timing of the First Epidemics." *Ethnohistory* 35(1):15–33.

South, Stanley. 1977. *Method and Theory in Historical Archaeology*. New York: Academic Press.

Starna, William A. 1992. "'Public Ethnohistory' and Native-American Communities: History or Administrative Genocide?" *Radical History Review* 53:126–139.

Steinitz, Michael, Claire Dempsey, Myron Stachiw, and Charlotte Worsham. 1985. *Historic and Archaeological Resources of Central Massachusetts: A Framework for Preservation Decisions*. Boston: Massachusetts Historical Commission.

Stock, Leo Francis, ed. 1924. *Proceedings and Debates of the British Parliaments Respecting North America*. Washington, DC: Carnegie Institution.

Sweetser, Sarah S. and John A. to Samuel B. Woodward, Worcester District Registry of Deeds, Book 1670, 406–407. Worcester, MA.

Tantaquidgeon, Gladys, and Jayne G Fawcett. 1987. "Symbolic Motifs on Painted Baskets of the Mohegan-Pequot." In *A Key into the Language of Woodsplint Baskets*, edited by Ann McMullen and Russell G. Handsman, 94–101. Washington, CT: American Indian Archaeological Institute.

Temple, Josiah H. 1887a. *History of Framingham*. Framingham, MA: Town of Framingham.

———. 1887b. *The History of North Brookfield*. North Brookfield, MA: Town of North Brookfield.

Thomas, David Hurst. 2000. *Skull Wars: Kennewick Man, Archaeology, and the Battle for Native American Identity*. New York: Basic Books.

Tilley, Christopher. 1994. *A Phenomenology of Landscape: Places, Paths and Monuments*. Oxford: Berg.

Tinker, George E. 2003. *Missionary Conquest: The Gospel and Native American Cultural Genocide*. Minneapolis, MN: Augsburg Fortress.

Tooker, William Wallace. 1901. *The Significance of John Eliot's Natick and the Name Merrimac, with Historical and Ethnological Notes*. New York: Francis P. Harper.

Trigger, Bruce. 2006. *A History of Archaeological Thought*. Cambridge: Cambridge University Press.

Trumbull, J. Hammond. 1852. *The Public Records of the Colony of Connecticut from 1665 to 1678*. Hartford, CT: F. A. Brown.

———. 1881. *Indian Names of Places, Etc., in and on the Borders of Connecticut: with Interpretations of Some of Them*. Hartford, CT: Case, Lockwood and Brainard Co.

Truncer, James. 2004. "Steatite Vessel Age and Occurrence in Temperate Eastern North America." *American Antiquity* 69(3):487–513.

Tuhiwai Smith, Linda. 1999. *Decolonizing Methodologies: Research and Indigenous Peoples*. London: Zed Books.

Turnbaugh, Sarah Peabody, and William A Turnbaugh. 1987. "Weaving the Woods: Tradition and Response in Southern New England Splint Basketry." In *A Key into the Language of Woodsplint Baskets*, edited by Ann McMullen and Russell G. Handsman, 77–94. Washington, CT: American Indian Archaeological Institute.

Ulrich, Laurel Thatcher. 2001. *The Age of Homespun: Objects and Stories in the Creation of an American Myth*. New York: Vintage Books, Random House.

Upton, Dell. 1983. "The Power of Things: Recent Studies in American Vernacular Architecture." *American Quarterly* 35(3):262–279.

Valosin, Christine. 2016. "The Saratoga Battles in Fifty Artifacts." In *The Saratoga Campaign: Uncovering an Embattled Landscape,* edited by William A Griswold and Donald W. Linebaugh, 195–227. Hanover, NH: University Press of New England.

Van Lonkhuyzen, Harold W. 1990. "A Reappraisal of the Praying Indians: Acculturation, Conversion, and Identity at Natick, Massachusetts, 1646–1730." *New England Quarterly* 63:396–428.

Weiner, Annette. 1986. "Inalienable Wealth." *American Ethnologist* 12(2):178–183.

———. 1992. *Inalienable Possessions: The Paradox of Keeping While Giving*. Berkeley: University of California Press.

Weis, Frederick L. 1959. "The New England Company of 1649 and Its Missionary Enterprises." In *Publications of the Colonial Society of Massachusetts*, vol. 38, *Transactions 1947–1951*, 134–218. Boston: Colonial Society of Massachusetts.

Whipple, Charles M., Jr., and Barbara R. Carroll. 2003.

"Yeoman and Princes: Benjamin, David, & Joseph, Sons of Captain John Whipple" (December 18, 2018), http://www.whipple.org/charles/yeomenandprinces/.

Whitfield, H. 1834a. "The Light Appearing More and More toward the Perfect Day, or a Further Discovery of the Present State of the Gospel amongst the Indians in New England." *Massachusetts Historical Society Collections*, 3rd series, (4):101–147.

———. 1834b. "Strength Out of Weaknesse; or a Glorious Manifestation of the Further Progresse of the Gospel among the Indians in New England." *Massachusetts Historical Society Collections*, 3rd series, (4):149–196.

Wilkinson, Israel. 1869. *Memoirs of the Wilkinson family in America: Comprising Genealogical and Biographical Sketches of Lawrence Wilkinson of Providence, RI, Edward Wilkinson of New Milford, Conn., John Wilkinson of Attleborough, Mass., Daniel Wilkinson of Columbia Co., N.Y.* Jacksonville, IL: Davis and Penniman, Printers.

Williams, Lorraine E. 1972. "Ft. Shantok and Ft. Corchaug: A Comparative Study of Seventeenth-Century Culture Contact in the Long Island Sound Area." Ph.D. diss. New York University.

Winship, George Parker. 1967 [1920]. *The New England Company of 1649 and John Eliot: The Ledger for the Years 1650–1660 and the Record Book of Meetings between 1656 and 1686 of the Corporation for the Propagation of the Gospel in New England*. Reprint, New York: Burt Franklin.

Winslow, Ola Elizabeth. 1968. *John Eliot "Apostle to the Indians."* Boston, MA: Houghton Mifflin Company.

Wolf, Eric. 1959. *Sons of the Shaking Earth*. Chicago, IL: University of Chicago Press.

*Worcester Directory: Containing a General Directory of the Citizens, a Business Directory and the City and County Register*. 1852 and 1856. Worcester, MA: H. J. Howland.

Yamin, Rebecca, and Karen Beschere Metheny, eds. 1996. *Landscape Archaeology: Reading and Interpreting the American Historical Landscape.* Knoxville: University of Tennessee Press.

Yentsch, Anne E. 1988. "Legends, Houses, Families, and Myths: Relationships between Material Culture and American Ideology." In *Documentary Archaeology in the New World*, edited by Mary C. Beaudry, 5–19. New York: Cambridge University Press.

# About the Authors

**D. RAE GOULD** is a member of the Nipmuc Nation of Massachusetts and associate director of Native American and Indigenous Studies at Brown University. She has worked on projects related to federal acknowledgment, the Native American Graves Protection and Repatriation Act (NAGPRA), and historic preservation. She has taught anthropology and Native Studies courses at Connecticut College, University of Connecticut, American University, Catholic University of America, and University of Massachusetts Amherst. Her publications include contributions to volumes on federal acknowledgment, NAGPRA, indigenous archaeology, international cultural heritage issues, and Native American culture and history. She received her Ph.D. from the University of Connecticut.

**HOLLY HERBSTER** has an MA from the University of Massachusetts Boston and is senior archaeologist at the Public Archaeology Laboratory, Inc., a nonprofit cultural resource management company based in Rhode Island. Over the past twenty-five years she has directed more than 100 archaeological projects in New England with a focus on Massachusetts and has coordinated extensively with the Native American groups whose homelands include these areas. She has also been an adjunct instructor at the University of Massachusetts Boston teaching undergraduate courses in introductory archaeology and a public archaeology graduate course. She has worked closely with and for the Wampanoag Tribe of Gay Head/Aquinnah for more than twenty years on collaborative archaeological projects on and off tribal lands on Martha's Vineyard. She co-authored a chapter detailing these close interactions in *Cross Cultural Collaboration: Native Peoples and Archaeology in the Northeastern United States*, edited by Jordan Kerber. She is currently working with the Aquinnah tribal historic preservation officer (THPO) to develop an interactive Geographic Information System (GIS) of historic and archaeological information about the tribe's ancestral and present-day homelands in Aquinnah.

**HEATHER LAW PEZZAROSSI** has a Ph.D. from the University of California, Berkeley (2014) and an MA from University of Massachusetts, Boston (2008). She is currently a visiting scholar at Syracuse University. She has published articles in the *Journal of Social Archaeology* and in four edited volumes: *Rethinking Colonialism*; *Object Stories: Artifacts and Archaeologists*; *The Menial Art of Cooking*; and *Things in Motion*. She is a member of the Society for Historical Archaeology and the Society for American Archaeology and has also presented conference papers at the annual meeting of the Society for Ethnohistory and the American Anthropological Association. She has extensive field experience in New England and has helped to foster a long-term collaborative relationship with the Nipmuc Nation through her dissertation project at Hassanamesit Woods in Grafton, Massachusetts.

**STEPHEN A. MROZOWSKI** is professor of Anthropology at the University of Massachusetts Boston, where he also serves as director of the Andrew Fiske Memorial Center for Archaeological Research. He has carried out archaeological and ethnographic fieldwork in eastern North America, Alaska, New Mexico, northern Britain, Iceland, and Barbados. His publications include more than eighty scholarly essays. He is co-editor of *The Death of Prehistory* and *Contemporary Archaeology in Theory: The New Pragmatism*. He is also co-editor of *Lines That Divide: Historical Archaeologies of Race, Class, and Gender* and *The Archaeology of Sylvester Manor*, a special publication of the *Journal of Northeast Historical Archaeology*. He is the author of *The Archaeology of Class in Urban America* and co-author of *Living on the Boott: Historical Archaeology of the Boott Cotton Mills in Lowell Massachusetts*. He received his Ph.D. from Brown University.

# Index

Page numbers in *italics* refer to illustrations.

Printed in the United States
By Bookmasters